Women's Artistic Gymnastics

This book lifts the lid on the high pressured, complex world of women's artistic gymnastics. By adopting a socio-cultural lens incorporating historical, sociological and psychological perspectives, it takes the reader through the story and workings of women's artistic gymnastics.

Beginning with its early history as a 'feminine appropriate' sport, the book follows the sport through its transition to a modern sports form. Including global cases and innovative narrative methods, it explores the way gymnasts have experienced its intense challenges, the complexities of the coach-athlete relationship, and how others involved in the sport, such as parents and medical personnel, have contributed to the reproduction of a highly demanding and potentially abusive sporting culture.

With the focus on a unique women's sport, the book is an important read for researchers and students studying sport sociology, sport coaching, and physical education, but it is also a valuable resource for anyone interested in the development of sporting talent.

Roslyn Kerr is Associate Professor in Sociology of Sport and Dean of the Faculty of Environment, Society and Design at Lincoln University in New Zealand.

Natalie Barker-Ruchti is Associate Professor in the Division of Sport Science, School of Health Sciences, Örebro University, Sweden.

Carly Stewart is Head of Department of Sport and Event Management at Bournemouth University, UK.

Gretchen Kerr is Professor in the Faculty of Kinesiology and Physical Education at the University of Toronto, Canada.

Women, Sport and Physical Activity

Edited by Elizabeth Pike, University of Hertfordshire, UK

The *Women, Sport and Physical Activity* series showcases work by leading international researchers and emerging scholars that offers new perspectives on the involvement of women in sport and physical activity. The series is interdisciplinary in scope, drawing on sociology, cultural studies, history, politics, gender studies, leisure studies, psychology, exercise science and coaching studies, and consists of two main strands: thematic volumes addressing key global issues in the study of women, sport and physical activity; and sport-specific volumes, each of which offers an overview of women's participation and leadership in a particular sport.

Available in this series:

Women's Artistic Gymnastics
Socio-cultural Perspectives
Edited by Roslyn Kerr, Natalie Barker-Ruchti, Carly Stewart and Gretchen Kerr

For more information about this series, please visit: https://www.routledge.com/sport/series/WSPA.

Women's Artistic Gymnastics

Socio-cultural Perspectives

Edited by
Roslyn Kerr, Natalie Barker-Ruchti,
Carly Stewart and Gretchen Kerr

LONDON AND NEW YORK

First published 2020
by Routledge
2 Park Square, Milton Park, Abingdon, Oxon OX14 4RN

and by Routledge
52 Vanderbilt Avenue, New York, NY 10017

Routledge is an imprint of the Taylor & Francis Group, an informa business

© 2020 selection and editorial matter, Roslyn Kerr, Natalie Barker-Ruchti, Carly Stewart and Gretchen Kerr; individual chapters, the contributors

The right of Roslyn Kerr, Natalie Barker-Ruchti, Carly Stewart and Gretchen Kerr to be identified as the authors of the editorial material, and of the authors for their individual chapters, has been asserted in accordance with sections 77 and 78 of the Copyright, Designs and Patents Act 1988.

All rights reserved. No part of this book may be reprinted or reproduced or utilised in any form or by any electronic, mechanical, or other means, now known or hereafter invented, including photocopying and recording, or in any information storage or retrieval system, without permission in writing from the publishers.

Trademark notice: Product or corporate names may be trademarks or registered trademarks, and are used only for identification and explanation without intent to infringe.

British Library Cataloguing in Publication Data
A catalogue record for this book is available from the British Library

Library of Congress Cataloging-in-Publication Data
A catalog record has been requested for this book

ISBN: 978-0-367-44001-5 (hbk)
ISBN: 978-1-003-00700-5 (ebk)

Typeset in Goudy
by Taylor & Francis Books

Contents

List of illustrations   viii
List of contributors   ix
Preface   xi
ELIZABETH PIKE

Introduction   1
ROSLYN KERR, NATALIE BARKER-RUCHTI, CARLY STEWART AND
GRETCHEN KERR

PART I
The history, politics, commercialisation, and diversification of women's artistic gymnastics   7

Jenny's story Part I: Frank   7
JAMES POPE

1 Acrobatisation and establishment of pixie-style women's artistic gymnastics   11
GEORGIA CERVIN

2 Perfectionisation of women's artistic gymnastics   24
GEORGIA CERVIN

3 The commercialisation of women's artistic gymnastics since the 1980s   35
GEORGIA CERVIN, ELIZABETH BOOTH AND DIANA-LUIZA SIMION

4 Diversification of women's artistic gymnastics since the fall of Communism   51
NATALIE BARKER-RUCHTI, ELIZABETH BOOTH, FRANCESCA CAVALLERIO, GEORGIA CERVIN, DIANA-LUIZA SIMION, MYRIAN NUNOMURA AND FROUKJE SMITS

PART II
The gymnast experience 65

Jenny's story Part II: An unexpected event 65
JAMES POPE

5 Living with stories of gymnastics in higher education 69
CARLY STEWART AND MICHELE CARBINATTO

6 Media narratives of gymnasts' abusive experiences: Keep smiling and point your toes 81
ASHLEY STIRLING, ALEXIA TAM, AALAYA MILNE AND GRETCHEN KERR

7 Trampoline gymnasts' body narratives of the leotard: A seamless fit? 99
RHIANNON LORD AND CARLY STEWART

PART III
Coach-athlete relationships 117

Jenny's story Part III: Worries and pressures 117
JAMES POPE

8 Power in coach-athlete relationships: The case of women's artistic gymnastics 121
SOPHIA JOWETT AND SVENJA WACHSMUTH

9 When the coach-athlete relationship influences vulnerability to sexual abuse of women's artistic gymnasts 143
GRETCHEN KERR, ASHLEY STIRLING AND ERIN WILLSON

10 Critical reflections on (adult) coach-(child) athlete 'no touch' discourses in women's artistic gymnasts: Out of touch 158
MELANIE LANG AND JOANNE MCVEIGH

PART IV
The multiple actors involved in creating an elite gymnast 173

Jenny's story Part IV: Enough's enough 173
JAMES POPE

11 The sorting of gymnasts: An Actor-Network Theory approach to examining talent identification and development in women's artistic gymnastics 177
ROSLYN KERR

12 Using a multilevel model to critically examine the grooming
process of emotional abusive practices in women's
artistic gymnastics 190
FROUKJE SMITS, FRANK JACOBS AND ANNELIES KNOPPERS

13 A figurational approach to women's artistic gymnastics 203
CLAUDIA PINHEIRO AND NUNO PIMENTA

14 Navigating sports medical practice in women's artistic
gymnastics: A socio-cultural analysis 216
ASTRID SCHUBRING AND NATALIE BARKER-RUCHTI

Conclusion 231
ROSLYN KERR, NATALIE BARKER-RUCHTI, CARLY STEWART AND
GRETCHEN KERR

Index 235

Illustrations

Figures

1.1	Vera Caslavska at the Olympic Games in Mexico, 1968	15
1.2	Romanian gymnasts warming up at the Olympic Games in Moscow, 1980. The different body types to those exemplified by Caslavska (Figure 1.1) can be clearly seen	19
2.1	Romanian gymnast Christina Elena Grigoras during her floor exercise at the Olympic Games in Moscow, 1980	25
8.1	The dyadic power–social influence model	132
12.1	Dutch WAG multilevel model (drawn by author)	192
12.2	Discourses and discursive practices in Dutch WAG multilevel model (drawn by author)	194

Tables

4.1	Conditions and events that have shaped the six countries' WAG development prior to and since 1989	55
5.1	Sample of gymnasts	72
8.1	Major power theories (taken from Simpson et al., 2015 with permission)	130

Contributors

Natalie Barker-Ruchti is Associate Professor in the Division of Sport Science, School of Health Sciences, Örebro University, Sweden.

Elizabeth Booth is Senior Lecturer in Tourism Management at the University of Greenwich, London, UK. She is also Editor and Author of the blog *Rewriting Russian Gymnastics*.

Michele Carbinatto is Lecturer in Sport Pedagogy and Gymnastics at the University of Sao Paulo, Brazil.

Francesca Cavallerio is Senior Lecturer in Sport and Exercise Psychology in the School of Psychology and Sport Sciences, at Anglia Ruskin University, UK.

Georgia Cervin is Honorary Research Fellow in History at the University of Western Australia.

Frank Jacobs is Senior Researcher at the Faculty of Health, Nutrition and Sport at The Hague University of Applied Sciences, The Netherlands.

Sophia Jowett is Professor of Psychology in the School of Sport, Exercise and Health Sciences at Loughborough University, UK.

Gretchen Kerr is Professor in the Faculty of Kinesiology and Physical Education at the University of Toronto, Canada.

Roslyn Kerr is Associate Professor in Sociology of Sport and Dean of the Faculty of Environment, Society and Design at Lincoln University in New Zealand.

Annelies Knoppers is Professor (emerita) in Sociology and Management of Sport at the Utrecht School of Governance, Utrecht University in the Netherlands.

Melanie Lang is Senior Lecturer of Child Protection in Sport, in the Department of Social Sciences at Edge Hill University, UK.

Rhiannon Lord is Lecturer in Sociology of Sport in the Division of Sport and Exercise Sciences at Abertay University, UK.

Joanne McVeigh is Senior Lecturer in Physical Education and School Sport in the Department of Sport and Physical Activity at Edge Hill University, UK.

Aalaya Milne is a Masters student in the Faculty of Kinesiology and Physical Education at the University of Toronto, Canada.

Myrian Nunomura is Professor in Sports Pedagogy and Artistic Gymnastics at the School of Physical Education and Sport of Ribeirao Preto, University of Sao Paulo, Brazil.

Elizabeth Pike is Professor and Head of Sport, Health and Exercise at the University of Hertfordshire, UK.

Nuno Pimenta is Assistant Professor in Sociology of Sport and Coordinator of the Sports Training Bachelor, at the Polytechnic Institute of Maia (IPMAIA) in Portugal.

Claudia Pinheiro is an Assistant Professor in Sociology of Sport at the University Institute of Maia (ISMAI) in Portugal and a collaborative researcher in the Research Center in Sports Sciences, Health Sciences and Human Development (CIDESD).

James Pope is Principal Academic in English and Communication at Bournemouth University, UK.

Astrid Schubring is Associate Professor in Sport Science at the Department of Food and Nutrition, and Sport Science at the University of Gothenburg, Sweden.

Diana-Luiza Simion is Senior Lecturer in Communication Studies at the Faculty of Communication and Public Relations, at the National University of Political Science and Public Administration in Bucharest, Romania.

Froukje Smits is Senior Researcher of Sport in Society at the Utrecht University of Applied Sciences, The Netherlands.

Carly Stewart is Head of Department of Sport and Event Management at Bournemouth University, UK.

Ashley Stirling is Associate Professor in Sport Psychology and Vice Dean of Academic Affairs in the Faculty of Kinesiology & Physical Education at the University of Toronto, Canada.

Alexia Tam is a doctoral student in the Faculty of Kinesiology and Physical Education at the University of Toronto, Canada.

Svenja Wachsmuth is a post-doctoral researcher in the Institute of Sports Science at the University of Tübingen, Germany.

Erin Willson is a doctoral student in the Faculty of Kinesiology and Physical Education at the University of Toronto, Canada.

Preface

Elizabeth Pike

The world of women's sport and physical activity is complex and often fast changing. While the opportunities for participation in sports have increased among females in many countries in recent years, these trends mask a range of issues that continue to confront women and girls in sporting arenas.

It is important to acknowledge that sport has moved a long way from traditional views that sport was the exclusive domain of men. For example, while Pierre de Coubertin, the man credited with being the founder of the modern Olympic Games, is often quoted as claiming that women's involvement would be impractical, uninteresting, and improper, in recent Olympiads women have made up almost half of the participants at the Games. However, it is also the case that women lag a long way behind men in leadership roles; at the Olympics, as in other major sporting events, the proportion of female coaches is rarely more than one in ten of the total number; there continues to be shocking evidence of abusive regimes in many sports; and we are still relatively early in fully understanding the intersectionality of gender with factors such as race, age, disability, or the experiences of trans and intersex athletes.

This book provides detailed attention to a range of issues that continue to be experienced by women and girls in sport by focusing on the world of women's artistic gymnastics (WAG). This includes exploring the complex social contexts which frame, enable, and constrain sporting opportunities for females; the social worlds within which female athletes compete, all too often requiring the sacrifice of wellbeing for sporting achievement; alongside the possibilities for hope with stories of humane and empowering policies and practice which demonstrate progress in many areas of WAG, and in women's sport and physical activity more generally.

The analysis of WAG is given breadth and depth by the way the authors draw on multiple methods and theoretical approaches to ensure a comprehensive and nuanced understanding of this sport and the experiences of its participants. Woven through the book is Jenny's story: a fictional but realistic narrative of the life of one participant in WAG. Jenny's story invites us to ask serious questions about women's sport and physical activity, and challenges anyone who cares about sporting worlds to contribute to debates about the future of sport.

I am delighted that this is the first book to be published in the *Women, Sport, and Physical Activity* series. It will challenge anyone who is complacent about progress in women's sport and physical activity; provide guidance for students, researchers, practitioners, and policy-makers engaged with the future direction of WAG and sport more widely; and deliver insightful and thought-provoking reading for anyone concerned with women's sport.

Introduction

Roslyn Kerr, Natalie Barker-Ruchti, Carly Stewart and Gretchen Kerr

Women's artistic gymnastics (WAG) has long been one of the most popular Olympic sports. For the 2020 Tokyo games, ticket prices for the finals are some of the highest priced of any sport (Tokyo Organising Committee, 2018). The appeal of the sport is claimed to be due to its unique combination of spectacular acrobatics and artistic grace. At the 1952 Olympic Games, the four apparatus were confirmed as vault, uneven bars, balance beam, and floor; each require a different type of mastery and allow individual gymnasts to showcase varied abilities. At the same time, particularly historically, the sport has also been considered an icon of feminine appropriateness (Barker-Ruchti, 2009; Cervin, 2015).

For many sports, the relationship between sport and gender is defined by masculinity. Sport, in being originally designed for boys and men, showcases traits generally deemed masculine, such as strength and aggression (Messner, 1992). Indeed, some traditional male sports, such as football (Caudwell, 2011; Skelton, 2000) or rugby union (Pringle & Markula, 2005), have been critiqued for their reinforcement of hegemonic masculinity (Connell, 1995) and poor treatment of women. Such sports focus on the men's game as of far more importance, and women have struggled to gain pay equity and support to participate (Caudwell, 2011; Travers, 2008).

For gymnastics, the story is very different. Although it has historical links to men's military training, it is the women's form that has gained greater popularity and attention (Chisholm, 1999). Particularly due to the performances of Olga Korbut and Nadia Comaneci in the 1970s, and followed by stars such as Svetlana Khorkina in the 1990s and the current champion Simone Biles, WAG gained immense worldwide attention and eclipsed men's gymnastics as the preferred form of the sport. The emphasis on flexibility, dance and expression was seen as feminine appropriate (Barker-Ruchti & Tinning, 2010; Chisholm, 1999). Nonetheless, the relationship between WAG and femininity is far from simple.

The aim of this book is to explore WAG's many complexities: the sport's unique history, the individual experiences of gymnasts, the complicated coach-athlete relationship and the wider actors that affect the practice of gymnastics. As a sport dominated by female athletes, it is unusual but, at the same time, gymnasts and coaches have struggled with the same male–female power imbalances experienced by many other women in sport. WAG therefore presents a fascinating and fruitful case for study.

As detailed in the first section of the book, originally gymnasts were mature adult women with sexually developed bodies and over time the body types that dominated the sport became younger and less mature. As a result, child-like bodies became the norm, arguably owing to their biomechanical advantages in performing acrobatics. Thus, an ironic situation developed, where on the one hand gymnastics celebrated women and femininity in a way most sports did not, while on the other hand the sexually immature bodies on display lacked markers of female femininity such as breasts and hips.

The second section of the book explores the lives and voices of gymnasts, as they battle with the intense demands of the sport that have often included abuse, and the difficulty of living with their own body–self relationships, associated identities, and stories. The amazing skills that gymnasts perform are the result of countless hours of training per week over many years, and many gymnasts derive pleasure and satisfaction from the abilities of their bodies. At the same time, gymnasts are also constantly subjected to the demands and gaze of others, such as coaches, judges, and spectators, and are required to wear the most revealing of garments as they both train and compete.

Exacerbating this contradictory scenario is the norm of men coaching prepubescent girls, with the coach-athlete relationship being the focus of the book's third section. From the 1970s onwards, it became a common sight on the competition floor to see an older male coach looking after a team of very young girls. Therefore, what could have been an opportunity for a sport to showcase women as powerful athletes in their own right instead became an example of male domination. Yet regardless of the sex of the coaches, the coach-athlete relationship offers its own set of complexities. As this section points out, the same closeness that is needed for a successful coach-athlete relationship also leaves athletes vulnerable to abuse, particularly due to the power imbalance that exists within the relationship. It is further complicated in the case of gymnastics because of the need for coaches to touch athletes in order to assist them with learning new skills. Whereas in other sports it may be possible to ban touching in order to protect athletes, the situation is more problematic in gymnastics.

Yet while coaches are acknowledged as one of the major figures in a gymnast's life, they are not the only figures who affect the way gymnastics occurs. The final section of the book considers how parents, sports scientists, doctors, judges, and technology all contribute to the making of the gymnast. This section uses a variety of theoretical approaches to highlight the networked or figurational nature of the various actors that work together to create gymnastics. It demonstrates how at times these actors end up converging to disempower the athlete, but also shows how, for some medical personnel, they struggle to reconcile the demands of the sport with their medical ethic.

The four sections of the book were conceptualised after a 2016 conference, in which a 'research tree' approach was utilised to thematically identify the most important areas of research in WAG. Efforts have been made to focus not only on issues of particular importance to gymnastics, but to wider sport as well. For example, macro global processes such as globalisation and scientification are referred to alongside an acknowledgement of the significance of studying the micro interactions between gymnasts, coaches, and others involved in the sport. To study these disparate areas, the book draws on research from several disciplines, primarily sociology, history, and psychology.

Overall, the book highlights how many in the sport are subject to immense pressures, which have led to significant issues in terms of athlete welfare. The book emphasises how, as shown in a large number of reported cases of abuse and maltreatment, the culture of WAG is dominated by surveillance and control, by coaches and a range of other actors. Through many of these influencers, the belief in needing to be both thin and young in order to win has dominated, with many gymnasts developing eating disorders or other health problems as a result of an inadequate diet. In some regimes, not even water was permitted to be drunk during 4–5-hour-long training sessions. Most recently, the conviction of Larry Nassar, the US gymnastics team doctor, for sexually abusing female gymnasts, is the most prominent example of the extreme control that gymnasts have been under.

At the same time, the Nassar case suggests that perhaps the tide is turning, that gymnasts are able to embody female athlete empowerment at last. The testimonies of over 250 gymnasts bring hope that gymnasts may finally have a voice. There is also evidence to suggest that the accepted representations of gymnasts may be expanding beyond tiny white girls. The domination of youth appears to be reversing, with the average age of the World Championships now around 20 years old (Barker-Ruchti et al., 2017), and the field now filled with many gymnasts in their 20s or higher, led by Oksana Chusovitina, who will contest her eighth Olympic Games in 2020 at the age of 45. The last two Olympic Games have been won by African American gymnasts, who, while recognised as receiving some racially driven-criticism (Eagleman, 2015), indicate that success is possible for gymnasts outside of the traditional white stereotype (Chisholm, 1999).

In this book, we bring together a range of disciplinary and theoretical perspectives in order to explore the many complexities of WAG. The book is timely, since recent events, such as the Nassar case, the increased age of gymnasts, and the heightened profile as a result of the star status of Simone Biles, have highlighted many contradictions in the sport. However, often the sport can be difficult to understand for those less familiar with its unique ways of working. Therefore, to provide an entry way into the world of elite gymnastics, we draw on the power of storytelling.

Each of the four sections of the book opens with a section of a fictional story detailing the career of a gymnast called Jenny. At the outset, Jenny is a child, inspired by some historic gymnastics figures, and the story follows her career under the care of a demanding coach until she reaches adolescence. Jenny's four-part story is informed by a creative fiction tradition. Such an approach, while informed by empirical evidence, need not be based on real events or real people other than suggesting these things may have occurred. Recognising that good stories have certain capacities to move and affect people and things in the world, we worked with professional fiction writer James Pope in order to do this as effectively as we could have. The process was one of dialogue and reflexivity that involved bringing together gymnastics stories from research with our own experiences and self-awareness to co-create a story which brings to life the embodied struggles of the fictional character, Jenny. Framed by narrative devices, we hope to have animated a plausible plotline, characters, scenarios, behaviours, and emotion that speak to all sections of this book. This said, we encourage readers to think with and about the story, to respond but not finalise any interpretations that might be made. If the story is heard and retold through a multitude of interpretations, it is doing the work we would like it to do. That is, to create new stories and leverage opportunity for change.

References

Barker-Ruchti, N. (2009). Ballerinas and pixies: A genealogy of the changing female gymnastics body. *The International Journal of the History of Sport*, 26(1), 45–62.

Barker-Ruchti, N., & Tinning, R. (2010). Foucault in leotards: Corporeal discipline in women's artistic gymnastics. *Sociology of Sport Journal*, 27(3), 229–250.

Barker-Ruchti, N., Kerr, R., Schubring, A., Cervin, G., & Nunomura, M. (2017). 'Gymnasts are like wine, they get better with age': Becoming and developing adult women's artistic gymnasts. *Quest*, 69(3), 348–365.

Caudwell, J. (2011). Reviewing UK football cultures: Continuing with gender analyses. *Soccer & Society*, 12(3), 323–329.

Cervin, G. (2015). Gymnasts are not merely circus phenomena: Influences on the development of women's artistic gymnastics during the 1970s. *The International Journal of the History of Sport*, 32(16), 1929–1946.

Chisholm, A. (1999). Defending the nation: National bodies, US borders, and the 1996 US Olympic women's gymnastics team. *Journal of Sport and Social Issues*, 23(2), 126–139.

Connell, R. W. (1995). *Masculinities*. Berkeley: University of California Press.

Eagleman, A. N. (2015). Constructing gender differences: Newspaper portrayals of male and female gymnasts at the 2012 Olympic Games. *Sport in Society*, 18(2), 234–247.

Messner, M. (1992). *Power at play: Sports and the problem of masculinity*. Boston, MA: Beacon Press.

Pringle, R., & Markula, P. (2005). No pain is sane after all: A Foucauldian analysis of masculinities and men's rugby experiences of fear, pain, and pleasure. *Sociology of Sport Journal*, 22(4), 472–497.

Skelton, C. (2000). 'A passion for football': Dominant masculinities and primary schooling. *Sport, Education and Society*, 5(1), 5–18.

Tokyo Organising Committee of the Olympic and Paralympic Games. (2018). Tokyo 2020 announces outline of Olympic Games ticket prices. Retrieved from: https://tokyo2020.org/en/news/notice/20180720-03.html.

Travers, A. (2008). The sport nexus and gender injustice. *Studies in Social Justice*, 2(1), 79–101.

Part I

The history, politics, commercialisation, and diversification of women's artistic gymnastics

Jenny's story Part I: Frank

James Pope

When you watch real champions, you see this amazing skill, amazing strength and control and balance, and you just think of the beauty, you never think of what made that beauty, the massive effort that goes into the 'effortless' elegance. You wouldn't, would you? Unless you're a gymnast yourself or you know someone who is.

I used to watch the TV and my mum's old videos: her hero was Nadia Comaneci, but I really loved Svetlana Khorkina. The 2000 Olympics when she won gold on the bar. Wow! Tall and slim, not really the stereotype. I was only six or so, and had just started really, but I was captivated and I still feel that thrill of how she impressed me. I still get goosebumps if I watch YouTube videos of her. I still love to watch it. I made a scrapbook with WAG photos, and news stories, and I wrote all my own notes on the pages. I've still got that scrapbook, and I see how absorbed I was. I got hooked quickly.

But now when I think back, it's as if there was a different person there, not really me, although of course it was me, is me. I've left it behind, on purpose left it behind … but it's all still just there, somehow, in the wings of my memory.

So … well, my mum had been a gymnast in her childhood and teens. I've seen some old videos, and she was pretty good, to be fair, but maybe not really good enough to go far. I know she competed at regional level. She did know her stuff, and she knew people, and I definitely wouldn't have got anywhere if she hadn't been in the sport before me, to guide me.

Mum didn't push me into it at all. She just said, 'You don't have to do gymnastics. And even if you do, you can choose artistic or rhythmic.' I know she had to give up in the end because she had an injury. She did artistic and injured her back and had to stop, so I think maybe she wasn't so keen on me doing artistic. It was up to me though. She said, 'You could do swimming, maybe?' She did want me to do something, but that wasn't pressure: she just didn't want me kind of doing nothing. Anyway, I chose artistic, probably because I knew Mum had done that.

I remember the very first session. I was just excited, not nervous, because at that point I had no idea what was really going to happen. It just felt like going to brownies or something, but a lot more glamorous. Mum had bought me a leotard and shoes. It felt exciting! My first coach, I'll call him Pete, was so lovely and friendly, and the whole thing seemed so welcoming. It wasn't too hard to begin with. I mean, we did practise, and we did learn things, but it was just super fun for the first couple of years: I met other girls and we used to chatter and laugh and the coaches would sometime get a bit irritated. But it was lovely. And I fell in love with it. *And*, I was good. I didn't really know I was then, but I suppose I must have been, because when I was eight Mum said I was going to have a new coach. 'You've been noticed,' she said. That phrase stuck with me. I didn't know what it even meant, but it seemed important!

So I swapped to be with Frank. And I think I sort of swooned when I met him properly and he shook my hand. I'd seen him before of course, because he worked with other girls at the gym. But when Mum actually introduced me, I went a bit melty inside. Frank was old, or that's how he seemed to me – much older than Mum. But he seemed so big and strong and like a grandad in some way. I remember seeing his big brown forearms, and the black hairs on his arms. It's odd what you remember, but his arms were so big! So, I wasn't frightened of him at all. You do hear some people who say they were frightened of their coach, but I wasn't scared of Frank. I was definitely excited. He had a reputation too – he'd worked in Russia in the past, and that made him like a star. Mum said he was brilliant.

I do remember being a bit nervous to meet Frank again – but the first few sessions were fun, and I loved it immediately. A new level. The buzz when you began to be able to do things you'd never done before. It felt like flying! I was so into it, I couldn't get enough. I would go home and make up routines and spin and leap around in the garden, pretending I was in the Olympics. Being with Frank seemed to turn me up a notch, or something. Something happened inside me and I was 100% into it. And, also, I always wanted him to like me, that was the thing, so I always tried my best. I wanted him to be pleased with me, and when he was pleased I felt amazing and Mum loved it too.

The first time Frank got angry, I cried, and I remember that made him even more angry. I can't really remember what I did, or didn't do, but he yelled at me and made me do the exercise again, and then I started crying even more, and then I remember he came over and comforted me, so I calmed down. I told Mum about it and she said, 'Well, Frank *is* the best, Jenny. He had a good reason to shout, I'm sure. He wants you to do your best, that's all it is.'

And in a way, she was right. He did want me to do my best, and so did I, and so did Mum. It's not like I was resisting it. I just remember the sudden shock of his voice, so loud, out of the blue, and then it felt confusing maybe, when he was comforting me.

Anyway, it's a bit hard to remember everything. I was just doing it, not really thinking about it.

So, we carried on, and I got better. Frank did shout a lot, but we always ended up friends, and I know I always wanted to go back. I never refused. Dad used to ask how it had gone, and I would tell him I'd learned this or that routine and he'd be pleased. Mum was a bit like Frank, I guess, now I think back – she wanted me to improve all the time. I was entering local competitions almost right away, even before I started with Frank. It quite quickly became my whole life. I trained five days a week, before school and after school. And if there was a competition coming up I would get pulled out of classes, because I think the gymnastic club had a link with our school, so they didn't make a fuss. And I suppose the school quite liked having someone competing in events – probably it looked good for the school's image. Maybe, I don't know. I didn't mind missing school, of course! Who would? I thought I was getting kind of free holidays when all the other kids had to slog away.

Really and truly, it *was* cool. I was a little bit of a star at school, when I was at juniors anyway. There was one other girl at our school who did gymnastics, and she did artistic too. She wasn't really a friend as such, but what happened was, we spent a lot of time together by being at the club so much. We aren't friends now. We lost contact. She stopped gymnastics when she went to secondary school. I remember she told me she'd had enough of being 'tortured', as she put it.

I didn't see it, certainly not then. I guess I do now ... 'Torture' ... bit strong! But when you had to do oversplits, Frank would make you hold the position, push your legs down until it hurt and then if you looked like you were going to ease up he'd shout, and you'd be so startled for a moment that you'd stretch even harder, and then it would hurt so much! My God, the pain sometimes. It was necessary though – you would get bad injuries in full performance if you didn't do all the right exercise, but those oversplits were sometimes brutal. But if I ever moaned to Mum she'd say, 'OK, Jenny, you stop. Maybe take up netball ...' And right away, I'd be like 'NOOOOO! I don't want to do netball!' It seemed so dull compared to what I did. I already had heroes, and I kind of felt important by doing it. Mum knew that anyway, that's why she said it. I was going to be like Khorkina. So, I was determined, even when Frank made me want to quit ...

Chapter 1

Acrobatisation and establishment of pixie-style women's artistic gymnastics

Georgia Cervin

Introduction

At its first Olympic Games in 1952, women's artistic gymnastics (WAG) was one of the few sports available for women to compete in. It was a graceful, elegant sport, associated with femininity. Its athletes were women in their twenties, performing routines based on balletic training. But 20 years later, pre-pubescent girls somersaulting through the air on all apparatus came to represent the sport. This chapter explores the phenomena of this 'acrobatisation' and the key figures and moments behind it. Beginning with an introduction to gymnastics and its nineteenth-century roots, it explores the global spread of the sport, from European men to European (and colonial) women. It then surveys the first 20 years of the sport as it was established in the Olympic movement, and the key actors that came to dominate it.

Locating the late 1960s and early 1970s as a time of change, the process of acrobatisation is then discussed, with particular reference to the role of the media in advertising and popularising this new style of WAG. In doing so, the difference in gymnast cohorts is discussed through the themes of femininity and style, maturity, and behaviour including political engagement. This chapter shows that the European, patriarchal thinking that established the sport in the nineteenth century still had a large effect on its development over a century later, and that it was only through fissures in the system – several actors and events over a number of years – that the new, acrobatic style of WAG was finally able to emerge by the 1970s.

Roots of sportive gymnastics

Gymnastics earned its name from the classical training of ancient Greek warriors and athletes[1] (Pfister, 2013), which was adopted when Johann Friedrich GutsMuths and Friedrich Ludwig Jahn created the modern sport. The two Germans devised of several of the key apparatus of gymnastics: the parallel bars, rings, balance beam, and high bar at the turn of the eighteenth century. Modern readers will realise that such apparatus is only used in WAG in a modified manner. Indeed, when GutsMuth and Jahn created their system for the training of bodies, they did so thinking only of European men (Pfister, 2013). Jahn's *Turnen* was not a competitive sport, nor was it centred around the individual: it was about building the 'nation's strength' and accordingly imbued with German nationalism (Pfister, 2013). The founder of the Swedish tradition of physical education, Pehr Ling drew on GutsMuth and Jahn's work to devise 'educational gymnastics', which had greater emphasis on training and drill and the authoritarian manner in which it was practised (Barker-Ruchti, 2011). When the *Sokol* movement in Czechoslovakia grew from the German *Turnen*, it was adapted to promote Czechoslovakian nationalism. In the wake of the Napoleonic wars, national revolutions spread throughout Europe, ushering in new political ideas and the need to formulate systematic physical training regimes to defend the nation. It is no surprise then that gymnastics, as a form of military training and promotion of nationalism, arose in this context and became practised throughout Europe. This was also a time when the nations promoting military strength would soon cast their eyes outward in search of creating an empire. Such political aspirations were premised on ideas of European supremacy, rationalised by emerging disciplines like physical anthropology, anthropometry, and phrenology (the study of skull measurements and intelligence).

These ideas played important roles in the creation of modern gymnastics and the ideals it espoused. Soon, the advocacy of these ideals through physical activity leant itself to promoting the supremacy of European women as well as men in imperial contexts. Adapted to be suitably feminine, women's gymnastics was further differentiated from its masculine gymnastic roots with the new name: calisthenics (Chisholm, 2007). Calisthenics were part of a discourse that 'sought to propagate a modern mode of disciplinary power that aimed to train and (re)form female bodies and behaviours in accordance with conceptions of (genuine) true womanhood' (Chisholm, 2007, p. 433). That is, just as gymnastics was originally conceived to instil and promote traditional masculine qualities of military prowess, women's gymnastics was designed to promote femininity: the ultimate example of which being motherhood.

As early gymnastics was being modified into something more appropriate for women, it was also spreading rapidly from Europe through immigrant communities and physical education institutions. In this early globalisation, the nationalist component of the sport was adopted and adapted in each country. Thus, when the first Olympic Games were held in 1896, gymnastics was both popular and important enough in promoting national prestige that it was invited to participate. But it would take the better part of the next 50 years until women's gymnastics would reach the same permanent status in the Olympic sporting line-up.

Early Olympic gymnastics

While men's gymnastics became a core feature of the Olympic roster at the Games' inception, women's gymnastics was not a consideration. The Fédération Internationale de Gymnastique (FIG) had formed in 1881 to reflect the growing interest in the sport, but it would not be until 1928 that a women's version of the sport appeared at the Games (Cervin, Nicolas, Dufraisse, Bohuon, & Quin, 2017). It was only in 1933 that a committee for women's gymnastics was formed (Berliox, 1985). But it would be a further two decades before WAG became a standardised sport.

Although the women's performances at the 1928 Amsterdam Games certainly opened the door for the development of women's gymnastics as a sport, they were, at the same time, something of an outlier. The competition was a team event only – no doubt influenced by aversion to competitiveness in women (Cahn, 1995; Vertinsky, 1994) – and involved only vault, and the vague 'apparatus' which evidently included rope climbing and team drill (Van Rossem, 1928). Not only was the competition format and apparatus not familiar as WAG, the inclusion of women's gymnastics in the Games was also exceptional: it would not appear again until 1936, then again in 1948.[2] However, each of these occasions represented one step closer to the modern format. In 1936, gymnasts performed both compulsory and voluntary routines, and competed on vault, parallel bars, and balance beam. But they also performed two group exercises, and the competition was only a team event (Evans, Gjerde, Heijmans, & Mallon, 2016a). In 1948, it was again a team-only event, the gymnasts competed on rings instead of bars, and the group exercises persisted. However, we can see women's vault was renamed 'side horse' by this time, pointing to the evolution in how the apparatus was used for women (Evans, Gjerde, Heijmans, & Mallon, 2016b).

Further details about the contents of the 'group exercises' of these Games are not known. But it is possible these included handheld apparatus, influenced by Ling's Swedish Gymnastics. Certainly, by the 1952 and 1956 Olympics 'portable' apparatus remained in the program before it split off into 'modern gymnastics': what we now call 'Rhythmic Gymnastics'. Indeed, the development of Rhythmic Gymnastics in the late 1960s and 1970s is tied to shifting ideas of femininity as women's artistic gymnastics evolved. But for now, we can conclude that WAG came into being at the 1952 Olympics. These were the first Games where 'artistic' was included in the name of the sport, and the first Games where gymnasts competed on the standard four apparatus: vault, bars, beam, and floor (Cervin, 2017). Despite minor changes to the programme over the next 60 years, the basic competition format and apparatus have remained the same.

The first 20 years of Olympic WAG

The first Olympic Games in which WAG was contested were also the first Games in which the Soviet Union competed. That event in 1952 began half a century of Soviet domination of the sport. Until its collapse 40 years later, the Soviet Union won the team gold medal at every Olympics in which it competed, and only lost the all-around gold three times: to Czechoslovak Vera Caslavska in 1964 and 1968, and to Romanian Nadia Comaneci in 1976.[3] Thus, in a sport where participants are judged to a commonly understood ideal, the constant winners came to define what that ideal was.

In 1952, that ideal remained rooted in historic understandings of femininity. As Ann Chisholm (2005) has explained, women's gymnastics was linked to ideals about womanhood and housework, and most of all, that women's labour should not be seen as strenuous for women's weak bodies. Thus, athletes performed light, graceful movements with minimal acrobatics or risk. Demonstrating strings of poses, the gymnasts exhibited flexibility and passivity, moving softly between each position. Many of these gymnasts were former ballerinas. Hence, WAG came to have a dance component founded in ballet. The Soviet Union drew on its strong balletic tradition to inform the artistic component of WAG and link it to feminine ideals.

As a result of these features, the gymnasts during WAG's first 20 years were older than what is familiar to modern readers. As former ballerinas, the gymnasts were old enough to have already had a career in ballet. So, on average, they were women in their mid to late twenties. Furthermore, as the sport was so strongly linked to feminine ideals including motherhood, the women competing in WAG demonstrated those ideals through their bodies. Gymnasts like Larissa Latynina, Olympic all-around champion 1956 and 1960, had breasts and hips. Latynina further exhibited the feminine ideal, becoming a mother in the middle of her successful international career (Evans, Gjerde, Heijmans, & Mallon, 2016c). Their leotards emphasised shapely hips as well as modesty through their low-cut leg line. Meanwhile, the popular wide V-necks accentuated long, graceful necks and drew attention to the bust. Gymnasts' hairstyles contributed to their feminine impressions too. Unlike the practical ponytails that have dominated the sport over the last three decades, in its early years, WAG athletes wore the most fashionable hairdos of the day. Take for example Vera Caslavska's beehive coiffure sported at the 1968 Mexico Olympics (Figure 1.1).

The comportment of gymnasts like Caslavska also reflected their maturity. These gymnasts were politically engaged and active in their civic duties. As a student, Caslavska signed a petition protesting Soviet involvement in Czechoslovakia. The 'Two Thousand Words' petition called for progress towards democracy in Czechoslovakia (Langer, 2016). Two months before the Games, the Soviet Union's Red Army invaded the country. Caslavska went into hiding in the Jesiniky Mountains, but continued her preparations

Figure 1.1 Vera Caslavska at the Olympic Games in Mexico, 1968
Bildlegende: Kunstturnerin Vera Caslavska an den Olympischen Sommerspielen in Mexiko, 1968
Source: RiBiDi © StAAG/RBA8_OlympischeSpiele_Mexiko1968_Turnen_SW_1.

for the Games. 'A tree that had fallen became my beam. I ran up to vault on a forest path. I turned the forest into a gym' (Telegraph, 2016).[4] Swinging from branches was evidently adequate preparation for Caslavska, who went on to win gold in the all-around, vault, bars, and floor, as well as silver for balance beam and the team event. During the medal ceremonies first for balance beam, then for floor (for which she tied with a Soviet victor), Caslavska bowed her head down while the Soviet anthem played, turning her face to the right, away from the rising Soviet flag. She explained her protest to a media a year later: 'It is understandable that every Czechoslovak citizen is deeply disturbed. I am a Czechoslovak citizen. We all tried harder to win in Mexico because it would turn the eyes of the world on our unfortunate country' (Cady, 1969).

Caslavska represents not just the old style of gymnastics, and the mature bodies that performed it. She also represents the mature minds of gymnasts in the sport's first 20 years. Being older (26 at the 1968 Olympics), Caslavska had a more acute understanding of social and political issues. Moreover, she saw herself being in a unique position to advocate for her compatriots. As a successful and celebrated gymnast, not just at home but also abroad, she was able to draw attention to her country, and she used that attention to focus on the issues her people were facing.

While Caslavska might be an extreme example of the civic-mindedness of early gymnasts, her successor as Olympic victor provides another example. In 1972, Soviet Ludmilla Tourischeva was crowned the new queen of gymnastics, taking the all-around at the Munich Olympics as well as an assortment of other medals. Tourischeva was seen as very self-controlled and composed, a reliable team-mate and someone to trust (Mertin, 2009). While she was overshadowed in the West by the celebrity of Olga Korbut, at home her respectability earned her more fame than any of her teammates (Kerr, 2003). Not only did Tourischeva captain the gymnastics team, she was also elected to the Central Committee of the All Union Lenin Young Communist League, Komsomol, which was effectively the youth communist party (Mertin, 2009). This political engagement, as well as academic and sporting success, created an image for Tourischeva as the ideal Soviet woman. Like Caslavska, Tourischeva was perceived as leveraging her gymnastic success to defend the honour and fame of Soviet socialist society in other countries (Mertin, 2009).

Tourischeva also bridged the gap between the old and new styles of gymnastics. At 20 in 1972, she was younger than previous victors but still an adult. It was, however, her second Olympics, having debuted at the 1968 Olympics as a 16-year-old. In 1972, her body was mature, but she wore her hair in two pigtails. In addition to her age and style, Tourischeva also performed a new kind of gymnastics, characterised by greater complexity and height. Tourischeva trained under the famed coach Vladislav Rastorotsky, who was renowned for the original gymnastic elements his gymnasts performed.[5] Rastorotsky, like many of his peers, drew on the Russian circus tradition to inform his work. Indeed, soon the Russian Gymnastics Federation would invite circus experts to work with their coaches and gymnasts on acrobatics (Barker-Ruchti, 2011). Held in the same regard as the *Ballet Russe*, the circus had become a national institution in the Soviet era, renowned for acrobatics and contortion (Birch, 1988). And like the Russian ballet, the importance of the circus in Soviet cultural heritage saw its features transferred to WAG, linked with female performance and spectacle.

The link with performance is important. Men's artistic gymnastics (MAG) athletes were already performing acrobatic feats in their gymnastics. But muscularity and risk were sanctioned masculine traits: when seen in women it did not communicate femininity, the ideal in WAG. Perhaps the reason men were already performing acrobatics was also due to the longer life span of the sport for men. After 60 years of Olympic competition, MAG was acrobatic. After only 20 years, WAG was becoming acrobatic.

The scope of gymnastics elements would be limited if it had not been for the quest to go higher, faster, and stronger through the use of increasingly difficult, and acrobatic, elements. In its original Greek, *acro* meant summit. Chisholm (2002, p. 418) argued that acrobatics 'refers to bodies that leave the earth, that master gravity and centrifugal force, and that seemingly defy natural laws'. If WAG is a competition of mastery of the elements, then that mastery of timing and space is best demonstrated by doing more than one's competitors. After 20 years of flexibility and grace, WAG gymnasts of the late 1960s and early 1970s began to turn their attention to acrobatics. After all, what is more impressive than a perfect cartwheel? A perfect cartwheel with no hands. What is more impressive than a simple somersault? Performing that somersault on the balance beam. In this manner, gymnasts and coaches began to push the sport in a new direction.

Acrobatisation

The trend towards acrobatics is most commonly associated with Olga Korbut. But while Korbut was a solid endorsement for this trend, she was certainly not its creator. Rather, a number of gymnasts before her presented increasingly difficult and acrobatic routines. The reaction to these routines had to be negotiated in the gymnastics community as it reluctantly adjusted to new ideals. Korbut's fame meant to some extent that the gymnastics community had to accept at least some form of acrobatisation, but this was an on-going discussion throughout the 1970s.

First, Larissa Petrick won the Soviet national championships at just 15 years of age in 1964, at a time when her contemporaries were well into their twenties (Kerr, 2003). If a biologically immature 15-year-old could demonstrate the feminine ideal, then it points to underlying changes in how that ideal was perceived. Two years later, 16-year-old Natalia Kuchinskaya won the gold on bars and balance beam at the world championships (Kerr, 2003), again suggesting that youth and dynamicity might be a new feminine ideal.

When a 17-year-old Tourischeva performed a routine so full of difficulty at the 1969 world championships she lost points for it, the judges advised Rastorotsky to change her routine. But Rastorotsky refused, seeing this style as the future direction of gymnastics (Kerr, 2003). Indeed, one year later, Tourischeva would become the world champion. If there were any doubt as to the influence of the circus on the nascent acrobatisation of WAG, Tourischeva put it to rest when she performed her floor routine at the 1972 Olympic Games to a tune from the film *Circus* by Isaak Dunaevsky.

While Soviet gymnasts were bringing an acrobatic influence to WAG, it was actually the Americans who began the trend towards youth that appeared concurrently with acrobatisation. In the context of amateurism, where receiving money, awards, or employment because of sporting prowess was prohibited, all but the wealthiest of people were prevented from elite sport. Few had the economic capital, nor the time available to facilitate the full-time commitment necessary for Olympic success. Soviet and other Eastern bloc gymnasts practised what was known as 'state amateurism', where their facilities, coaching, and living costs were met by the state, as they retained a nominal student status or employment. The closed nature of the state meant it impossible for the International Olympic Committee (IOC) to prove the 'professional' status of such athletes. This was not the case for athletes in the West, whose sponsorship contracts and employment status were readily visible to authorities. In this context, women in Western countries, with their domestic and familial duties and no outside funding or assistance, faced significant barriers to practising their sport full time. Hence, the child gymnast emerged, with few responsibilities but to train, while their needs were taken care of by family support (Cervin, 2015). So, for example, the average of American gymnasts was beneath 20 as early as 1956.

Then came Olga Korbut and her eponymous skills. At the 1972 Olympic Games, Korbut performed somersaults on the balance beam and bars, and contorted hyper-arched positions. Her coach, Renald Knysh, considered gymnastics to be 'acrobatics on the apparatus' (Kerr, 2003) and that is certainly apparent in the style that Korbut performed. The 17-year-old Korbut still had a child's slight body, and she wore her thin hair in pigtails. She smiled, laughed, and cried throughout the competition. Through both her gymnastics and her comportment, she gave the impression of a child in a playground unlike the composed women gymnasts who had been the talk of the Games at each Olympiad before her.

Even before Korbut entered the scene, the FIG was anxious about the acrobatic development of WAG. In 1971, it issued a warning to countries using young gymnasts and emphasising acrobatics that: 'Nobody should be so irresponsible as to think only of producing "competitive animals," hastily trained, frequently damaged and incapable of continued progress after a

Figure 1.2 Romanian gymnasts warming up at the Olympic Games in Moscow, 1980. The different body types to those exemplified by Caslavska (Figure 1.1) can be clearly seen
Bildlegende: Rumänische Kunstturnerinnen beim Einturnen an den Olympischen Sommerspielen in Moskau, 21.07.1980
Source: Dölf Preisig © StAAG/RBA13-RC1679-3_41.

certain level has been reached' (Cervin, 2015, p. 1931). But the necessary traits belying acrobatisation were problematic for the FIG's conceptions of femininity and artistry. Barker-Ruchti (2011, p. 179) suggested that 'Feminine qualities require gymnasts to perform gracefully and effortlessly; the acrobatics on the other hand, demand muscle power, fitness and courage, which are perceived masculine characteristics'.

After Korbut's success, the FIG attempted to ban her skills in an effort to prevent further emulation of her acrobatic antics. Threatening to leave the sport if it did so, Korbut's fame was the saving grace for acrobatics. But much of the FIG's opposition to acrobatisation was not actually aimed at the acrobatics themselves, but rather the perceived turn away from femininity. This was seen both in the risk of acrobatic elements, as well as the muscled young bodies performing it. The FIG instilled a minimum age rule and began to refine artistry from the 1968 definition as 'harmonious flexibility and feminine grace,' to musicality, rhythm, and originality (Cervin, 2015). Moreover, acrobatisation was occurring in an era of increased codification. That is, where for its first 20 years WAG was judged on subjective ideas of performance ideals, in the 1970s the International Olympic Committee was placing a greater demand on sporting federations to impose more objective measures of determining a winner. In trying to better establish gymnastic ideals, the FIG was better able to codify acrobatics as its ideal is related to measurements of angles, lines, and height rather than subjective ideas about 'artistry' (Cervin, 2017).

Further, throughout the 1970s the FIG was responsible for a number of technological developments that propelled acrobatisation forwards. The two bars of the uneven bars were separated further apart, the vaulting horse and springboard raised, and springs added under the floor. Safety matting was thickened, while padding was also added to the balance beam (Cervin, 2017). The increased safety standards aided gymnasts in their quest to perform greater acrobatics, and if there was any confusion about the new direction of gymnastics, the Women's Technical Committee – responsible for creating the Code of Points rulebook – demanded from 1970 onwards that a number of acrobatic skills be compulsory (Cervin, 2017).

Media analysis

While a number of factors explain the sport's transition from poise to power, these factors collided with a new era of media coverage that shone the spotlight on WAG. In 1968, Caslavska achieved her successes four years before the Games were widely televised. She was voted runner up to Jackie Kennedy in a poll of world's most popular women that same year (Telegraph, 2016). But photographs and newspaper articles ceased soon after the Games, the Czechoslovakian regime ostracising her in the wake of her medal ceremony protest, barring her from travel or involvement in gymnastics (Langer, 2016). Further, audiences' attachment to her was not based on performances they had seen, with the exception of those in attendance at the competition. The extent to which her looks underscored her popularity is apparent in how they were emphasised in her obituaries around the world.

Four years later, Olga Korbut's performances were broadcast into living rooms around the world. She appealed to audiences for a number of reasons. First, this was when the world was introduced to the emerging acrobatic style of gymnastics; it was awe-inspiring to see such risk and spectacle being performed so effortlessly by someone who appeared to be a child. Second, Korbut inspired emotion in audiences. Her smiling, flirting performances engaged viewers; she appeared to be having fun. This was a conscious effort by both Korbut and her coach, who had decided that she must smile in order to mask the difficulties of her performance (Varney, 2004). Then when she missed her mount on the uneven bars on her first two attempts, audiences shared her grief as the camera zoomed in on the tears that had wiped away her smile. Such emotion was particularly striking in a Soviet, who were known for their stern composure.

Korbut played an ideal character in a new format of sports broadcasting. The use of close-ups invited viewers to share in emotions, and invest in a story arc. Barker-Ruchti (2009, p. 56) observed that the use of close-ups and slow-motion replays 'intensified the erotic theatricalization of the athletic body'. Meanwhile, Kerr (2003) argued that Korbut's progress through the competition created a narrative for viewers to follow. In the team competition, she was the exceptionally talented underdog to Tourischeva; in the all-around competition, she crumbled, making several serious mistakes; but in the apparatus finals, Korbut was able to regroup and triumph, winning the beam and floor. Kerr (2003) suggested that such a format was similar to that of a soap opera. Indeed, four years later, sports commentators would begin to describe the competition that way as new rival characters were introduced in the era of perfectionisation.

Conclusion

Conceived as a sport promoting strength and nationalism, these ideas had to be negotiated in order to make space for women's participation in gymnastics. Over the first half of the twentieth century, feminine ideals were applied to gymnastics, and the sport of WAG emerged. Its athletes demonstrated softness, passivity, ease of movement, and grace. They performed in womanly bodies, with leotards and hairstyles that emphasised their looks. But the nationalist aspect of gymnastics remained: it was the driving force behind the will to win, and it inspired political engagement from its most successful participants.

After two decades, however, gymnasts and coaches began to chase success in new ways. Younger athletes found success. Gymnasts performed increasingly acrobatic and risky routines. And while the gymnastics authorities pushed back against these developments, they nonetheless persisted through the performances of different gymnasts over a number of years. Catalysed by increased safety standards and the IOC's push for greater objectivity in scoring, the FIG too contributed to this trend as much as any coach or gymnast. Moreover, the media facilitated acrobatisation, advertising it to viewers around the world who would come to associate it with Olga Korbut. By the early 1970s, the acrobatic style of WAG was all but cemented. As the decade progressed, attention would begin to turn to the absolute mastery of this new style of gymnastics: from acrobatisation to perfectionisation.

Notes

1 *Gymnos* in Greek, referring to the nakedness in which athletes practised.
2 There 1932 Olympic Games did not include women's gymnastics; between 1936 and 1948 there were no further Olympic Games due to the Second World War.
3 When Mary Lou Retton won the all-around gold at the 1984 Olympics, the Soviet Union was not present, having boycotted those Games.
4 This story is corroborated by a number of media outlets, but the first appearance of it the author could find was from 1990 in the *Los Angeles Times* (Harvey, 1990). Caslavska was ostracised by the Czech regime after her 1968 protest, so there is

only very limited media coverage of her until the Velvet Revolution that dismantled the Communist regime in 1989.
5 Fans of gymnastics will be interested to know that two of the most essential skills in modern gymnastics, the Yurchenko vault and the Shaposhnikova and its varieties on the uneven bars, were created by gymnasts under the guidance of Rastorotsky.

References

Barker-Ruchti, N. (2009). Ballerinas and pixies: A genealogy of the changing female gymnastics body. *International Journal of the History of Sport*, 26(1), 45–62.
Barker-Ruchti, N. (2011). *Women's artistic gymnastics: An (auto-)ethnographic journey.* Basel: Gesowip.
Berlioux, M. (1985, April). Olympic encyclopedia: Gymnastics and archery. Retrieved from www.library.la84.org.
Birch, M. (1988). *Inside the Soviet Circus*. Film. Soviet Union: National Geographic.
Cady, S. (1969, 1 February). A citizen of Prague speaks her mind. *New York Times*. Retrieved from www.proquest.com.
Cahn, S. (1995). *Coming on strong: Gender and sexuality in twentieth century women's sport*. Cambridge: Harvard University Press.
Cervin, G. (2015). Gymnasts are not merely circus phenomena: Influences on the development of women's artistic gymnastics during the 1970s. *The International Journal of the History of Sport*, 32(16), 1929–1946.
Cervin, G. (2017). *A balance of power: Women's artistic gymnastics during the Cold War and its aftermath.* PhD diss. Crawley: University of Western Australia.
Cervin, G., Nicolas, C., Dufraisse, S., Bohuon, A., & Quin, G. (2017). Gymnastics' centre of gravity: The Fédération Internationale de Gymnastique, its governance and the Cold War, 1956–1976. *Sport in History*, doi:10.1080/17460263.2017.1363081.
Chisholm, A. (2002). Acrobats, contortionists, and cute children: The promise and perversity of US women's gymnastics. *Signs*, 27(2), 415–450.
Chisholm, A. (2005). Incarnations and practices of feminine rectitude: Nineteenth-century gymnastics for US women. *Journal of Social History*, 38(3), 737–763.
Chisholm, A. (2007). The disciplinary dimensions of nineteenth-century gymnastics for US women. *The International Journal of the History of Sport*, 24(4), 432–479.
Evans, H., Gjerde, A., Heijmans, J., & Mallon, B. (2016a). Gymnastics at the 1936 summer games: Women's team all-around. *Sports-reference*. Retrieved from www.sports-reference.com.
Evans, H., Gjerde, A., Heijmans, J., & Mallon, B. (2016b). Gymnastics at the 1948 London summer games: Women's team all-around. *Sports-reference*. Retrieved from www.sports-reference.com.
Evans, H., Gjerde, A., Heijmans, J., & Mallon, B. (2016c). Larysa Latynina. *Sports-reference*. Retrieved from www.sports-reference.com.
Harvey, R. (1990, 5 April). Blossoming in the Prague Spring: Gymnastics: Vera Caslavska won Olympic medals in 1964 and '68, then disappeared because she had signed a paper critical of government. Democracy has given her new stature. *Los Angeles Times*. Retrieved from www.articles.latimes.com.
Kerr, R. (2003). *The evolution of women's artistic gymnastics since 1952*. MPhil thesis. Sydney: University of Sydney.

Langer, E. (2016, 31 August). Vera Caslavska, Olympic gymnast and national heroine to Czechs, dies at 74. *Washington Post*. Retrieved from www.washingtonpost.com.

Mertin, E. (2009). Presenting heroes: Athletes as role models for the New Soviet Person. *The International Journal of the History of Sport*, 26(4), 469–483.

Pfister, G. (2013). *Gymnastics, a transatlantic movement: From Europe to America*. London: Routledge.

Telegraph. (2016, 1 September). Vera Caslavska, Czech gymnast and dissident – obituary. Retrieved from www.telegraph.co.uk.

Van Rossem, G. (1928). *The Ninth Olympiad: Amsterdam 1928: official report*. Amsterdam: J.H. De Bussy Ltd, pp. 644–673. Retrieved from www.library.la84.org.

Varney, W. (2004). A labour of patriotism: Female Soviet gymnasts' physical and ideological work, 1952–1991. *Genders Online*. Retrieved from www.colorado.edu.

Vertinsky, P. (1994). *The eternally wounded women: Women, doctors, and exercise in the late nineteenth century*. Champaign: University of Illinois Press.

Chapter 2

Perfectionisation of women's artistic gymnastics

Georgia Cervin

Introduction

One might consider 'perfectionisation' an odd choice of word. Indeed, it does not exist as a word in English: the more usual choice might be 'mastery'. However, gymnastics until 1976 was about mastery: having total control over the elements performed, and doing so to an excellent standard – being a master of women's artistic gymnastics (WAG). But in 1976, mastery ceased to be the driving force behind gymnastic success. Instead, 'perfection' became the ultimate goal, characterised by consistency, confidence, and flawlessness. This chapter describes the process by which 'perfect' became the dominant discourse in WAG, hence 'perfectionisation'.

This chapter explores the factors behind Nadia Comaneci's 'perfect 10s', and their implications on the sport. From the problems of judging to conscious manipulation of scores, this chapter shows that Comaneci's scores were a symptom of Cold War rivalries and the way WAG was contested. Nonetheless, this chapter argues that those 10s were a turning point for the sport. They re-iterated WAG's acrobatic direction, and added the component of perfection to WAG's artistic ideals. The body in which Comaneci achieved her 10s also reconciled the problems acrobatisation posed for femininity, as demonstrated through media discourse. The way it did this though caused a new emphasis in WAG on child athletes. Further, the means by which such child athletes were coached in order to attain perfection created a new, problematic norm for the sport.

From pixies to perfect

The acrobatic style of WAG that prevailed in the early 1970s took hold over the remainder of the decade. Acrobatics were now clearly required to become a WAG champion, and regardless of the Fédération Internationale de Gymnastique (FIG)'s position on them, they captured the public imagination, transforming WAG into one of the Olympic Games' most popular spectator sports. Wendy Varney (2004, p. 59) suggested that following on from Korbut's impression on the public and the gymnastics world, there was an assumption that 'for Korbut's feats to be duplicated, so would her body type'. Thus began a trend towards smaller, lighter, younger female gymnasts.

At the 1976 Games, the gymnastics world knew to expect greatness from Romania. But the rest of the world was caught by surprise when a team of children in white leotards with matching white ribbons in their hair dominated a competition of much more experienced athletes. Like Knysh had with Korbut, Romanian coach Bela Károlyi knew the importance of publicity in achieving maximum impact for his athletes. When the announcer called the Romanian team into the Montreal Olympic Arena, he had to do so three times before the team would appear. Károlyi had crafted suspense, and drawn attention to the team, which he perceived as a vital step to dislodging the dominance of the Soviet Union (Károlyi & Richardson, 1994). The athletes worked with military precision, marching in in silence, performing their routines one after another with no apparent communication between them, and doing so with effortless consistency. At that competition, Comaneci would achieve the first perfect 10 in history – a feat previously considered impossible, to the extent that the scoreboards had only been programmed to display a single figure before the decimal point. She would

Figure 2.1 Romanian gymnast Christina Elena Grigoras during her floor exercise at the Olympic Games in Moscow, 1980
Bildlegende: Die rumänische Kunstturnerin Christina Elena Grigoraş bei ihrer Bodenübung an den Olympischen Sommerspielen in Moskau, 21.07.1980
Source: Dölf Preisig © StAAG/RBA13-RC1679-2_40.

go on to receive six further perfect scores, demonstrating not only perfection, but consistent perfection.

In this context, the soap-opera coverage of gymnastics took off. Comaneci was the young, hopeful underdog. Korbut was portrayed as the aging supporting actress. The camera flicked between each woman, searching for reactions to one another's performances, creating a story of competitive animosity between them, and leaving audiences wanted to know who would triumph (Deford, 1976; Kerr, 2003). This format would persevere: by the 1980s, it was a story of Cold War contest between the old order and the new; East versus West. By the 1990s and 2000s, this format came to represent the emerging world order, in glittering leotards and sleek ponytails.

The mechanisms operating behind Comaneci's perfect 10s illuminated the way gymnastics has been contested for a long time. Ironically, concerns over judging would, 30 years later, cause the abandonment of the perfect 10 in favour of an open-ended scoring system (Kerr & Obel, 2015; Cervin, 2017). Gymnasts have always been judged against the commonly understood ideal standard of each element, as well as an overall impression of the performance. A 1974 report from the FIG observed: 'We rely on the more or less subjective assessment of experienced judges who more or less consciously compare the performances with some stereotyped perfect performance that is presumably accepted and known by all concerned' (Cervin, 2015, p. 9).

This means that there is inescapably some element of bias; whether based in different understandings of the ideal, pre-conceived expectations of how a gymnast will perform, or a conservative approach to scoring based on the assumption that a superior performance may come later in the competition and room must be left in the scoring range for later athletes to score higher. Thus, there is also a comparative element to judging, not only comparing a gymnast's performance to the ideal, but also to other gymnasts, or what the judges *anticipate* other gymnasts to perform. It was this last point that was consciously manipulated to create the conditions for Comaneci to score her perfect 10s.

With score fixing an established practice in gymnastics, it was particularly prevalent amongst Eastern bloc countries: the Soviet Union and its satellites. Romania was not invited to this club (Cervin, 2015). In fact, the Soviet Union was determined to keep hold of its gymnastics dominance and concurrent claim to ideological supremacy in the Cold War. Within the gymnastics world, Comaneci was already known, and already seen as a threat to Soviet domination before the 1976 Games. Thus, when the competition began, there were many scores in the high 9.0s. Judges that were unaware of the plan nonetheless participated in order to keep their scores aligned with their peers. Gymnasts and coaches did not complain – receiving high scores suited them (Cervin, 2015).

The abundance of scores in the high 9.0s reduced the range between Comaneci and her competitors. If the next best athletes were already scoring 9.9s, then Comaneci's scores were limited by the ceiling of the scoring system at 10.0. There was no room for Comaneci to make a mistake: if she did, the competition would easily outscore her (Cervin, 2015). Thus, while Comaneci may have been the most outstanding gymnast at the 1976 Games, and her victories certainly merited, her scores, on the other hand, were orchestrated.

A year later, Romania would complain to the FIG that only the mean score of the judging panel was ever displayed: from 1977 onwards, it became mandatory that each judge display their score in an effort towards greater transparency (Cervin, 2015). While Comaneci's scores were a great story for attracting attention to gymnastics, it was vital that the FIG continued on its path of increasing objectivity if it were to remain a credible sport and included in the Olympic movement. Indeed, by the 1980s, the 'abundance' of perfect 10s being awarded was a significant concern to the FIG, who saw it not as a reflection of many perfect performances, but rather a symptom of subjective judging. Yuri Titov, president of the FIG in the 1980s, announced that such scoring put the continued existence of gymnastics in the Olympic Games in vital danger (Titov, 1986). Comaneci's 10s, and the judging behind them, had changed gymnastics competitions forever.

Thus, despite the obsession with perfection that would surround her and her achievements for the rest of her life, Comaneci was never perfect. Nonetheless, Comaneci's achievements inspired great interest in the sport, and an obsession with perfection, rather than the previous ideal of mastery. Chisholm (2002, p. 438) pointed out that the numerical assessment of women's attractiveness on a team point scale emerged from Comaneci's achievements, as did the 1979 film *10* which inspired this 'cult of the 10'.

Moreover, Comaneci's perfect 10s implied a stylistic shift in WAG. Until her achievements, mastery had been the aim of gymnastics, with a 10.0 demonstrating absolute control over and excellence of the performance. 10.0s were never awarded. Kerr (2006) suggested that until 1976, two aesthetics had underscored this idea of mastery. The first was an emotive element, expressed through dance on beam and floor, fluidity of movement, and rhetoric about feminine grace. The second was a spectacular element, demonstrated on the vault and bars and in the new heights of acrobatic gymnastics. Comaneci's victories showed that consistency and precision were becoming ascendant: 'beauty through perfection was created' (Kerr, 2006, p. 94). Comaneci demonstrated that this aesthetic was now as important as the others.

But had technical perfection replaced artistry, or was perfection in itself a new form of beauty? The lack of expression shown by these athletes (both facially as well as through bodily movements) only reinforced the FIG's concerns about the limitations of young athletes. Indeed, critics complained that such gymnastics was 'soul-less' (Kerr, 2003). However, technical mastery and expression are not mutually exclusive. Consider the beauty of a world-class ballet, with leaps and turns performed with such precision that it must be considered technical mastery, but a critical feature of ballet performance is the expression that accompanies such mastery. Or further, consider the expression of joy we see from contemporary athletes, whose acrobatic feats are far greater than could have been foreseen in the 1970s: Simone Biles, tumbling, spinning, flying, and grinning with enjoyment as she does so. Perhaps the criticism of artistic expression is misplaced in aversion to Comaneci, her 10s, and acrobatics: perhaps the lack of expression comes instead from the new coaching methods that produced it. Such coaching included de-emphasising dance training, and a strict, authoritarian approach to coaching that may have induced fear.

Age

As discussed in the previous chapter, the FIG was concerned about the decreasing age even before the 1970s, instituting its first minimum age rule at the beginning of the decade. But even so, age continued to be a problem. In particular, it was left to the national federations to enforce the age rule, and as a result, a year before the Montreal Olympics, the FIG complained that the 14-year-old gymnasts competing at the 1975 test-event were too young, and their performances suffered for it (Cervin, 2015). After Comaneci's successes in 1976, the FIG would acknowledge the 'astonishing' performances that such young athletes could produce, yet remained determined to bring the age back up (Cervin, 2015). By the following Olympiad in 1980, the International Olympic Committee (IOC) would begin to add to the pressure on the FIG to exclude child athletes, but the trend was already firmly in place by then (Cervin, 2015).

Notwithstanding external pressures from the IOC, and public relation pressures that would arise in the 1990s after exposure of the conditions in which young gymnasts were trained, in the 1970s the FIG's opposition to young athletes was entwined with its stance on acrobatisation. Cervin (2015, p. 1934) argued that:

> Disapproval of younger gymnasts went hand in hand with the resistance to masculine traits inherent in acrobatization: risky, dynamic movements, adopted from MAG [men's artistic gymnastics] which threatened to displace WAG's older balletic ideals. The FIG's resistance to younger gymnasts, therefore, can be interpreted as resistance to acrobatization, which was in turn a failure to adjust to new (masculine) notions of artistry.

But equally, displays of youthfulness were vital to the acceptability of women's acrobatics in WAG in the public eye. Concerns over the compatibility of acrobatics and femininity were allayed in the new, youthful packaging of the sport. Less than a year after Korbut's victories in 1972, women gymnasts came to be cast as 'pixies' (Amdur, 1973). Reportage of fairies, sprites, and otherworldly creatures with the power of flight soon became the norm in media portrayals of female gymnasts. Ann Chisholm (2002, p. 415) explained that the dualities represented in such language appealed to wide audiences as 'women gymnasts ... maintain a precarious balance not only between the superhuman and the merely human but also between the superhuman and the infrahuman (freakish)'.

Another reading is that such language minimised the gymnasts' achievement by casting them as 'other'. For example, *Sports Illustrated* writer Frank Deford (1976) described the 1976 Olympic WAG competition as 'parade of little sugar plums', a reference to *The Nutcracker* ballet of Russia, and the femininity and youth it portrays.[1] Deford further proclaimed that the gymnasts appeared as 'bouncy dolls ... they don't seem to be real people'. Indeed, when describing acrobatics and the strength required of performing them, journalists contrasted these masculine traits with feminine frailty (Carlisle Duncan, 1986). Comaneci, in particular, was invariably depicted as 'a deceptively frail-looking sprite ... an infinitely solemn wisp of a girl ... 86lbs; dark circles above her cheeks; a Kean-eyed elf' (Time Magazine, 1976); 'a grim-faced sprite' (Lorge, 1980); and 'a fragile-looking child' (Verschoth, 1976). Such media coverage trivialised her achievements by portraying weakness and fragility (Carlisle Duncan, 1986). Those characteristics, along with an idealisation of youth, have had strong associations with femininity since the eighteenth century, and thus contribute to reconciling acrobatisation with femininity.

Further, the mythical element of such reportage has ties to fantasy and childhood. The diminutive size of the athletes, whether they were actually that young in age or not, actively contributed to prevalence of the descriptors above. Their acrobatics did not conflict with their femininity, because they embodied it not as women but as frail girls performing unreal feats of flight. In this context, acrobatisation was acceptable to audiences. It did not challenge femininity. And indeed, it reinforced the idea within the sport that youthful-appearing bodies are best suited to the acrobatic style of WAG.

There was also a sexual element at play. While the gymnasts' 'cuteness' offset their acrobatic transgressions of femininity, it also invited viewers to assume a carer or parental role (Chisholm, 2002). Ryan (1995, p. 68) observed that American gymnasts were portrayed as 'daddy's girls', which is a trope with perverse connotations. Indeed, the childishness, defencelessness, and docility of these new, young gymnasts appealed to perverse notions of domesticated femininity: incestuous sexuality and, sometimes, paedophilia (Chisholm, 2002). Media reportage confirms the sexualisation of athletes: Weber and Barker-Ruchti (2012) observed photographic sexualisation of athletes in the editing of images to centre and focus on the athletes' genitals and bottoms. They also argued that the movements gymnasts were encouraged to use to demonstrate femininity enticed sexual desire. Playful body language, smiling, and looking down all suggest feminine flirtation. Meanwhile Frigga Haug (1999, p. 183) noted that the way media have written about female gymnasts, as 'treats', and 'whetting the appetite' have purposefully sexualised gymnasts. Haug supposes that herein might lie some of the popularity of women's gymnastics as a spectator sport.

After Comaneci re-iterated the power of the new style of WAG in 1976 and the bodies that performed it, the age of international gymnasts around the world continued on its rapid decline. By 1980, the American gymnastics team included two 14-year-olds and two 13-year-olds (Cervin, 2015). Despite American teams having always been of a younger age, this was a significant jump downwards, no doubt inspired by 14-year-old Comaneci's success. The Soviet Union too used increasingly younger gymnasts: at the 1980 Olympics, five gymnasts out of their team of six were younger than 20 (Evans, Gjerde, Heijmans, & Mallon, 2016a). When China entered the Olympic movement in 1984, its team include two 16-year-olds and one 15-year-old (Evans, Gjerde, Heijmans, & Mallon, 2016b).

By 1994, the FIG, concerned with its public image as much as it was with its gymnasts, increased the minimum age from 15 to 16 for senior competitions, and from 12 to 13 for junior international competitions. However, these changes would not come into effect until 1997, and in this time, the public perception of gymnastics worsened (Cervin, 2017). As gymnastics continued to grow in popularity between the 1970s and 1990s, the increasing use of child gymnasts saw the sport come under intense scrutiny, particularly in American media. The *New York Times* observed: 'At best, women's gymnastics, which are really teen-age gymnastics, is darling and cute, a recital in agility and flexibility. At worst, it's a subtle form of child abuse' (Anderson, 1992). Three years later, Joan Ryan (1995) would publish an exposé on WAG, in which she argued that the cost of perfection was breaking American girls. The convergence of child gymnasts and the coaching methods they endured – inspired by the Károlyi method and the drive for perfection at any cost – were the cause of these critiques.

Coaching

The decrease in age and increase in acrobatics were intimately entangled with new coaching techniques that emerged in the 1970s. Barker-Ruchti (2011) established that the 1970s saw an influx of male coaches transferring their skills to WAG. This migration from the men's to the women's discipline was particularly prominent in the Eastern bloc, which operated on a system of rewards. WAG was attractive to formerly MAG coaches because those rewards could be won on an accelerated timeline in WAG. Barker-Ruchti (2011, p. 147) argued that 'scientific and practical coaching young girls with morphologies similar to those of male gymnasts could learn acrobatic gymnastics elements. They could be molded and manipulated to learn risky gymnastics skills and practice long hours'. That is, pre-pubescent girls (and extremely lean women, like Korbut) resembled the male athletes that male coaches were accustomed to working with. There was also a belief that these linear bodies were more aerodynamic, and their lightness would help them reach greater heights (Kerr, 2006). The confluence of acrobatics achieving victories and a greater number of male coaches working in WAG reinforced the new realities of practising WAG.

Further, the docility of youth also emerged ascendant in this period of gymnastics. Younger athletes had less fear of the dangers of the elements they were performing, as they were not yet mature enough to be aware of the risk to themselves. They were also less likely to 'push back' against their coaches. Barker-Ruchti (2011, p. 189) suggested that 'the gymnast begins to obey whatever [she] is ordered to do; [her] obedience is prompt and blind; an appearance of docility, the least delay would be a crime'. Being in the gym from a young age, the athletes were conditioned to work to prescribed expectations on the apparatus, moulded, disciplined, and punished by their coaches. Such was the docility and conditioning of Comaneci and her teammates that their competition at the 1976 Games involved nearly no talking amongst the gymnasts and very little between coaches and gymnasts (Károlyi, 1994). The passivity of women and children made young girls particularly pliable for these conditions (Barker-Ruchti, 2011).

While we have seen that acrobatics increased exponentially as the role of male coaches in WAG expanded, the change in the nature of training should also be emphasised. Kerr (2006) found that Comaneci's coaches, Bela and Marta Károlyi, prompted enormous change in the conception of gymnastics training, taking very young girls and working them unusually hard. Like the Soviet sports schools, the Károlyis put talented children into a full-time gymnastics training program, where their food intake was carefully monitored, medical needs taken care of, and academic tuition provided. But gymnastics training remained the priority, the Károlyis training their gymnasts up to six hours per day (Kerr, 2006; Comaneci, 2004). Their training was typified by an immense number of repetitions of each skill (Kerr, 2006). Martha Károlyi was firmly of the belief that only perfectly executed repetitions were worth practising (Comaneci, 2004). Comaneci was one of the first athletes to sport a bandage during the competition, an ankle brace showing the toll that her training regime had taken on her body when she was just 14 (Barker-Ruchti, 2009). Thus, a high training volume and expectations of perfection came to dominate this new style of training, and went hand in hand with the obsession with perfection in competition performance.

The resulting 'perfect' performances were described as 'machine like' (Kerr, 2003). The performances of the team were uniform in style, while their bodies and hairstyles were equally consistent. Perfect gymnastics operated like a smooth machine: athlete robots. Indeed, media commentary and analysis from gymnastics insiders emphasised the artificial, non-human nature of these performance.[2] The Károlyis would later export this premise to their work in the United States, while it was soon emulated and normalised around the world. These athletes were under immense pressure to perform: not only from their coaches and the state investment in their careers, but also in the Cold War context.

The Cold War gave new meaning to WAG. Where gymnastics had always had a nationalist component, the tensions of the Cold War raised the stakes. It was no longer a matter of proving national supremacy through sport, but a bigger contest of ideological, technological, and cultural supremacy. WAG provided one of the largest spaces for women in sport in this context, and the imperative to win at any cost came to define WAG training. Communist states invested heavily in physical education and sport, resulting in the sports schools described above, along with a system of incentives and rewards for gymnastic success on the world stage (Riordan, 1977; Barker-Ruchti, 2011; Cervin, 2017). Western nations did not employ such comprehensive measures to achieve success, but would soon begin to emulate Eastern bloc gymnastics programs in the decades to come (Cervin, 2017). Coaches from Australia and the UK were sent to the Soviet Union to learn from the coaches there, not only the technical elements of gymnastics, but the whole system that supported their gymnastics success (Cervin, 2017). In this context, winning was the only acceptable outcome, and the costs – financial and human – were secondary. The most striking example is the case of Elena Mukhina, the 1979 world champion who would become paralyzed during training a year later. She claimed that under this system of training the gymnast did not matter: only the glory of the state (Cervin, 2017).

Adrienne Blue (1987) argued that the acrobatisation and the drive for younger, lighter gymnasts was a reaction against feminism. Indeed, despite the literal new heights that gymnasts were able to reach and master from the 1970s onwards, the conditions by which they achieved this were certainly not aligned with the liberal, empowered aims of second-wave feminism.

Conclusion

Comaneci's symbolic perfect 10s changed gymnastics forever. They cemented the acrobatic trend begun a decade earlier, and added a new component to them. Whereas spectacle and expression had been the dominant forms of artistry before, perfection, rather than mastery, became the ultimate goal for generations of gymnasts and coaches to follow. Comaneci became the ideal, to which all others were compared to, and to which they all strove to emulate. Thus, not only did acrobatics and perfection become priorities, so did the young body and rigorous coaching through which Comaneci achieved her successes. Child athletes became the new ideal. They reconciled the problems between acrobatics and femininity, and they were fearless, docile, and pliable pupils. Around the world, coaches and athletes began adhering to strict training regimes, characterised by early specialisation, authoritarian coaching styles, and rehearsed, mechanical, repetition. Although prompted by the win-at-all-costs drive of the Cold War, these developments would take root over the coming decades, resulting in intense criticism of gymnastics practices by the 1990s, and continuing to today.

Notes

1 The main characters of this ballet are children, and toys and magic are invoked to sustain the plot.
2 References to machines and robots are too numerous to name here, but can easily be found amongst newspapers like the *New York Times*, magazines like *Sports Illustrated*, and various books and articles.

References

Amdur, N. (1973, 8 March). A Soviet pixie invades the United States. *New York Times*. Retrieved from www.proquest.com.

Anderson, D. (1992, 31 July). Just let those kids be kids. *New York Times*. Retrieved from www.proquest.com.

Barker-Ruchti, N. (2009). Ballerinas and pixies: A genealogy of the changing female gymnastics body. *The International Journal of the History of Sport*, 26(1), 45–62.

Barker-Ruchti, N. (2011). *Women's artistic gymnastics: An (auto-)ethnographic journey*. Basel: Gesowip.

Blue, A. (1987). *Grace under pressure: The emergence of women in sport*. London: Sidgwick & Jackson.

Carlisle Duncan, M. (1986). A hermeneutic of spectator sport: The 1976 and 1984 Olympic Games. *Quest*, 38(1), 50–77.

Cervin, G. (2015). Gymnasts are not merely circus phenomena: Influences on the development of women's artistic gymnastics during the 1970s. *The International Journal of the History of Sport*, 32(16), 1929–1946.

Cervin, G. (2017). *A balance of power: Women's artistic gymnastics during the Cold War and its aftermath*. PhD diss. Crawley: University of Western Australia.

Chisholm, A. (2002). Acrobats, contortionists, and cute children: The promise and perversity of U.S. women's gymnastics. *Signs*, 27(2), 415–450.

Comaneci, N. (2004). *Letters to a young gymnast*. New York: Basic Books.

Deford, F. (1976, 2 August). Nadia awed ya. *Sports Illustrated*. Retrieved from www.si.com.

Evans, H., Gjerde, A., Heijmans, J., & Mallon, B. (2016a). Soviet Union at the 1980 Moskva summer games. *Sports-reference*. Retrieved from www.sports-reference.com.

Evans, H., Gjerde, A., Heijmans, J., & Mallon, B. (2016b). China gymnastics at the 1984 summer games. *Sports-reference*. Retrieved from www.sports-reference.com.

Haug, F. (1999). *Female sexualisation: A collective work of memory*. London: Verso.

Károlyi, B., & Richardson, N. (1994). *Feel no fear*. New York: Hyperion.

Kerr, R. (2003). *The evolution of women's artistic gymnastics since 1952.* MPhil thesis. Sydney: University of Sydney.

Kerr, R. (2006). The impact of Nadia Comaneci on the sport of women's artistic gymnastics. *Sporting Traditions*, 23(1), 87–102.

Kerr, R., & Obel, C. (2015). The disappearance of the perfect 10: Evaluating rule changes in women's artistic gymnastics. *The International Journal of the History of Sport*, 32(2), 318–331.

Lorge, B. (1980, 26 July). Comaneci finally wins two golds as judging controversies continue. *Washington Post*. Retrieved from www.washingtonpost.com.

Riordan, J. (1977). *Sport in Soviet society: Development of sport and physical education in Russia and the USSR.* Cambridge: Cambridge University Press.

Ryan, J. (1995). *Little girls in pretty boxes: The making and breaking of elite gymnasts and figure skaters.* New York: Doubleday.

Time Magazine. (1976, 2 August). Olympics, the games: Up in the air. Retrieved from www.time.com.

Titov, Y. (1986, December). Report of the president, Yuri Titov. *FIG Bulletin*, 131, 60.

Weber, J., & Barker-Ruchti, N. (2012). Bending, flirting, floating, flying: A critical analysis of female figures in 1970s gymnastics photographs. *Sociology of Sport*, 29(1), 22–41.

Varney, W. (2004). A labour of patriotism: Female Soviet gymnasts' physical and ideological work, 1952–1991. *Genders Online*. Retrieved from www.colorado.edu.

Verschoth, A. (1976, 12 April). A great leap backward. *Sports Illustrated*. Retrieved from www.si.com.

Chapter 3

The commercialisation of women's artistic gymnastics since the 1980s

Georgia Cervin, Elizabeth Booth and
Diana-Luiza Simion

Introduction

In the 1980s, the economics of international sport underwent massive change. With the great stalwarts of amateurism, Avery Brundage in particular, now absent from the International Olympic Committee (IOC) leadership, the organisation led the charge for a new, commercialised sporting era. Despite the conservatism of the Fédération Internationale de Gymnastique (FIG), changes to Olympic sport signalled a new era for gymnastics. Meanwhile, growing economic instability in the Eastern bloc affected gymnastics in the Soviet Union and Romania, in terms of reduced rewards for success, declining funding, and increasingly open and lucrative pathways westwards. This chapter explores the economic shifts of the 1980s and 1990s, and their impact on women's artistic gymnastics (WAG) to today. It begins with an exploration of Olympic policy in terms of a departure from amateurism and a move towards commercialisation and professionalisation, before situating gymnastics within this changing tide. It then looks at how these and broader economic shifts in America, the Soviet Union, and Romania affected WAG in those nations. From here, this chapter explores the emerging Eastern bloc diaspora of coaches, and examines the impact of these migrants on their destination countries and the WAG worldwide.

Economic history

Economist John Wilson (2016, p. 3) observed that 'sport relies on the skill set of players in order to produce entertainment', while Olympian and sports scholar Bruce Kidd (2013, p. 381) described athletes as 'sweat-suited philanthropists, ensuring the careers of hundreds of well-paid coaches, sports scientists and sports administrators'. As sport became increasingly professional throughout the twentieth century, it offered such opportunities for the generation of income: be it for administrators and coaches, organisations like the IOC, or the athletes themselves.

Professionalisation also created prospects for players to migrate between countries (Wilson, 2016), and studies have shown that this migration is not limited to athletes, but also includes coaches (Kerr & Cervin, 2017). Financial incentives have clearly affected the development of sports, but they may also have an impact on individual athletes. Baruch, Wheeler and Zhao (2004) found that financial rewards based on athletic performance were particularly appealing to athletes in individual sports, and women were more likely to be motivated by a monetary reward system. Thus tracing the history of gymnastics from amateur to professional, at both a private level and an organisational level, reveals how shifts in gymnastic success mirror shifts in sports economics of the later twentieth and early twenty-first centuries.

Olympic commercialisation and professionalisation

Starting at an organisational level, above the FIG, the IOC guided the economic shifts of late twentieth-century gymnastics. In 1981, new IOC President Juan Antonio Samaranch outlined his agenda for a new Olympic order in the forthcoming decade. 'The Olympic movement must forget the word 'amateur' and open its doors to the world's best athletes. The Olympics Games are now the major sports event in the world, and we must allow the best athletes to take part' (*Canberra Times*, 1981, p. 15). A major departure from the amateurism that had defined the Olympic movement to that point, Samaranch's philosophy was that the best athletes should not be prevented from competing, and, moreover, that the Olympic Games could be a lucrative rather than costly event if they would professionalise.

At the request of the tennis, ice hockey, and football associations, the IOC Executive Committee voted in 1985 to allow professional players to compete at the Olympic Games, so long as they were younger than 23 (Thomas Junior, 1985). Pressure from these international federations, combined with Samaranch's sympathy for professionalisation, saw this experimental rule created as a trial towards professionalising the Games more widely. However, outside the Olympic Executive, there was less support for the move. National Olympic Committees also resisted the move towards professionalisation, with particular resistance coming from Eastern bloc countries whose state-supported athletes were at an advantage against Western athletes who did not have funding and support from government (Thomas Junior, 1985). Under the amateur rules, any private sponsorship rendered a gymnast ineligible for being professional, so nations that provided state support to athletes held an advantage in this economic climate. The resistance towards professionalisation was not limited to Eastern bloc National Olympic Committees, but also included each international sports federation as they retained the right to decide on athlete eligibility (*Canberra Times*, 1986).

FIG commercialisation and professionalisation

Like most international federations, the FIG was unenamoured with Samaranch's changes. In a 1986 Bulletin, it declared that as far as it was concerned, the amateur rules remained in place (Titov, 1986). And in keeping with Eastern bloc resistance to professionalisation, the leader of the FIG at the time was a Soviet, Yuri Titov. However, the explanation he gave for the FIG's unwillingness to professionalise was related to the traditional stature of the sport, rather than any political motives or concerns over athlete safety. 'Professionalism in gymnastics would rapidly lead us on a downward path,' suggested Titov, with coaches quickly 'replaced by "publicity agents" or, worse, by "impresarios …"' (Titov, 1986, p. 93).

The FIG's lack of progressive economic policy took a toll on the organisation's coffers, and by the early 1990s, it was running its flagship event, the World Championships, at a loss (Titov, 1992). As a result, it undertook a new economic policy towards the end of Titov's tenure as FIG president. In 1996, the FIG partnered with International Sport and Leisure (ISL) – a Swiss sports marketing company founded by Horst Dassler of Adidas. ISL had partnered with the IOC early in its professionalising process, acquiring broadcasting rights to the Games and maximising profits for the IOC. By 1995, the IOC had dropped ISL in favour of an in-house communications and marketing team. However, thanks to its initial opposition to professionalisation, the FIG was only at the beginning of its journey into sports marketing at this time. ISL purchased US $2 million worth of broadcasting rights for the world championships, and a further US $2 million of sponsorship money for the FIG. They also assisted the FIG in gaining US $4.6 million from the IOC, in addition to another Olympic grant to pay for the costs associated with hosting the 1997 world championships (Cervin, 2017). ISL's involvement saw the FIG's finances recover well, but also spurred on new thinking about income and spectatorship.

When Bruno Grandi took over as FIG president in 1997, he brought a new focus on packaging gymnastics competitions for television (Cervin, 2017). In competition with the rise of new aerial sports – BMX, skateboarding, and snowboarding – the FIG began to develop policies to attract viewers. It attempted to decrease length of competitions, avoid ties, and become more relevant in the three years between Olympics. The 1996 Olympic Games were the last in which audiences had to watch gymnasts repeat the same 'compulsory' routines, and it was also at this time that discussions of the post-10 Code of Points seriously took hold. Although the implementation of the 'new' Code stalled until the new millennium, its roots were planted in the context of economic concerns and attractiveness to the IOC. Meanwhile, the FIG began offering prize money at world championships, throwing its weight behind the already shifting economic outcomes available for gymnasts.

American gymnastics, professionalisation, and career lucrativeness

Indeed, despite the FIG's slow adoption of professional sport, opportunities to generate income for individual gymnasts had begun a decade earlier in the USA. Regardless of the FIG's position, the IOC's relaxation of the rules around professionalism in sport prompted new perspectives on investment from private companies. So when American Mary Lou Retton won the 1984 Olympic all-around gold medal in Los Angeles, she was swamped with sponsorship opportunities. And unlike successful athletes from other sports who had gone before her, she was able to accept these offers in this new economic sporting context. Retton became the first in a series of American gymnasts since then to appear on the box of cereal Wheaties, and, with her voluminous hair, became a spokesperson for global hair product behemoth Vidal Sassoon. She was soon given her own television show, and became an ambassador for the fast-food chain McDonalds (Cervin, 2017). Retton was one of the first Western gymnasts to enjoy such perks of professionalism resulting from her gymnastic success, setting a trend for those who followed her.

In Australia, for example, the national training centre took on sponsorship from Milo and the Australian Broadcasting Association.[1] In the USA, while many elite gymnasts did not professionalise, in order to maintain their amateur status to be eligible for collegiate gymnastics and the accompanying tuition waivers, many of the top gymnasts chose to accept money, and business partnerships and commercial engagements on the back of their gymnastic success. For example, following Retton's lead, Kristie Phillips also pursued a career in entertainment as an actress, as did Kathy Johnson, Julianne McNamara, Betty Okino, Dominique Dawes, Tasha Schwikert, Shawn Johnson, Nastia Liukin, Gabby Douglas, McKayla Maroney, and Laurie Hernandez. Others pursued different careers in entertainment: in singing, stunts, and the post-Olympic gymnastics and ice-skating tours. Many of those who did not pursue show business nonetheless signed sponsorship deals with various companies: Jordyn Weiber, Aly Raisman, and Simone Biles being more recent examples. The 1996 'Magnificent Seven' Olympic team, followed by Carly Patterson then Nastia Liukin, would appear on Wheaties boxes too. By 1993, the US Olympic Committee was awarding medal bonuses of up to $15,000 (Kirshenbaum, 1993). Most Olympians since then have published their own books and created leotard lines with gymnastic apparel manufacturer GK Elite Sportswear. Nastia Liukin, Shawn Johnson, and Alicia Sacramone became 'spokesmodels' for Covergirl. Many have opened their own gymnastics clubs, while more recent champions have appeared on television shows like *Dancing with the Stars*.

Russian gymnastics, professionalisation, and perestroika

Before and upon accession to the Olympic movement in 1951, the Soviet Union faced significant global criticism and cynicism for its 'professional' sports structure, with Olympic athletes supported by the state in order to train full time (Riordan, 1993). From the 1960s onwards, the Soviet Union created a system of financial incentives for both athletes and coaches. This was not simply in terms of funding governance, coach training, a thorough talent identification programme, or facilities, but, rather, it offered cultural and economic capital as rewards for gymnastic success. Domestic and international success in gymnastics saw gymnasts and coaches among the most respected in society. Some like Tourischeva were even afforded positions within the Communist Party. Medal successes provided many gymnasts with job opportunities at a high level. However, those who did not wish to pursue life as a coach, judge, or high-ranking official often drifted away from the expected path. Most athletes and coaches were immediately rewarded for their success with comfortable lifestyles: good salaries, cars, and the nicest apartments in sought-after suburbs (Barker-Ruchti, 2009; Riordan, 1980). Coaches were on salaries that increased based on national and international rankings, supplemented by bonus payments for medals. However, under *glasnost* (open-ness) and *perestroika* (restructuring) of the 1980s, support for such a hierarchical system decreased, while it concurrently became apparent to coaches that their livelihoods could perhaps be more lucrative abroad.

Perestroika was a well-publicised, organised approach to new socio-economic organisation in the 1980s Soviet Union. In terms of sport, however, it is clear that there was relatively little restructuring. In fact, the sports system went into free-fall after the disintegration of the Soviet Union, as funds were either reduced or withdrawn completely. Vladimir Zaglada (2010), former Director of the Dynamo Club in Moscow, and before that a national coach for the Soviet Union WAG team, referred to the years from 1991 to 2000 as his country's 'dark decade', describing a state of extreme instability and lack of personal and general security that presided over the whole of Russian society at the time, and affected his life as a gymnastics coach on a daily basis. At the national level, funds were not available to pay the national coaches for the first six months of 1993 (Arkayev, cited in Vaitsekhovskaya, 1993). Efforts led by world and Olympic champion Dmitri Bilozerchev to establish a commercial touring display team of national team gymnasts failed. This led to the exclusion of him and his gymnasts from the national team, as rival and head coach Leonid Arkayev fought – and, eventually, succeeded – to maintain control of the national team on similar terms to those operational during the Soviet era.

In the early 1990s, parts of the national training centre at Round Lake, just outside of Moscow, were repurposed as a casino and hotel, with the associated crime causing problems of security for the gymnasts and coaches (Vaitsekhovskaya, 1993). As time passed, the physical structure of the national training centre began to fall to wrack and ruin, and the team's training relied more and more on the leadership of Arkayev, who had three jobs as president of the Russian Gymnastics Federation, head coach of the men's gymnastics team, and head coach of the women's gymnastics team.

The successes of Russian gymnasts in the 1990s and early 2000s were the last remnants of a system that had been in decline since the loss of funding since the 1980s. Svetlana Boguinskaia (Belarus), Oksana Chusovitina (Uzbekistan), Svetlana Khorkina (Russia), and Lilia Podkopayeva (Ukraine) all trained and competed under both the Soviet and post-Soviet systems. This legacy survived until the early 2000s, with a decline in both Russia's rankings, and the fellow states of the Soviet Union. The breakup of the Soviet Union in the 1990s only exacerbated the problems in sport caused by *perestroika*, and, moreover, divided the talent pool into separate countries. These factors contributed to a decline in Russia's rankings by the late 1990s and the 2000s, while a number of former Soviet states remained in the top handful of international rankings, despite suffering the same problems.

By 2006, the national training centre stood derelict and following a dismal showing at the 2004 Olympics, Arkayev's time was up. Sponsorship from the state bank VTB, responding to a call from President Putin to help Russia re-establish itself as a leading world sporting power (Jokisipila, 2011), enabled the refurbishment of the centre to its current state as one of the world's leading training facilities for gymnastics. Andrei Rodionenko, former head coach of the Soviet national team and director of the Canadian gymnastics programme, was invited by the Ministry of Sports of the Russian Federation to return home and begin the work of physically rebuilding the training centre and re-establishing training norms for the gymnasts and coaches.

But the rationale for sport in Russia no longer remains exclusively the domain of social empowerment and diplomacy. A win-at-all-costs mentality has imbued sport on many levels, leading to a programme of state-funded doping which has tainted the past decade or more of Russian sport. Gymnastics, as a 'clean' sport, has remained relatively unaffected by these problems. Yet, as the implications of the scandal filter through, an emerging softening in the narrative is evident. Success is no longer measured in numbers of medals, but gymnasts are urged by the national coaches to remain competitive, and perform to the best of their ability. It remains to be seen if this is a lasting change in the Russian approach to sporting motivation and hence professionalism.

The Soviet era saw girls selected at an early age for the elite pathway. Gymnastics is now, however, a participation sport based on the child's desire to join a class, for which their parents or guardians must pay. Once they reach the national team, which can be as young as 12, gymnasts are paid a weekly wage at a rate roughly equivalent to the national average income (Kalugina, personal correspondence with the author, 5 May 2013). In gymnastics, the athletes can also receive food, clothing, and equipment. As many of them come from poor families, this can be an important source of support for the whole family.

However, at elite level the rewards system of the Soviet era remains. At the London Olympics in 2012, medallists were given Audi sedans worth many thousands of dollars. Financial rewards varied from sport to sport, and could be as much as $500,000 for a gold medal. While these echo the incentives of the Soviet model, widespread government sponsorship is now absent. Most club coaches are paid at a below-subsistence level, and only once their gymnasts reach the national teams do the rewards increase. Work in the regions is supported inconsistently, and depends on the filtering through of good practice from the top level, rather than systematic training programmes. In practice, many local clubs continue to close down through lack of financial support at the regional level.

In 2020, as globalised sport sees top athletes all over the world eligible for corporate sponsorship or state funding, Russian sport has come full circle and remains a state-sponsored activity. Yet, the scale and scope of funding for artistic gymnastics, a minority sport of limited appeal in the Russian Federation, has been cut back significantly since the Soviet era. Today, artistic gymnastics in Russia is a poor second to rhythmic gymnastics and the scale and profitability of the sport is modest. The opportunity for Russian gymnasts to earn the 'big bucks' associated with Olympic gold in countries such as the USA is rather limited. Sport is commodified for the state as a means of attracting economic multiplier impacts associated with the staging of mega-events; for the individual gymnast, or the coach working in a club, the only way of making a living through sport is to qualify for the national team. Gymnastics is still in the process of being rebuilt from the ground up.

Romanian gymnastics, professionalisation, and economic decline

While sponsorships and endorsements were the results of increased professionalisation in the USA from the 1980s onwards, gymnastics in Romania did not have a similar trajectory. For one, its starting point was different: due to Comăneci's series of Perfect 10s at the 1976 Olympic Games and the 'Golden Era' of the Romanian dominance in WAG, gymnasts already enjoyed high popularity and, thus, a privileged social status. The Deva training centre, where the 'Goddess of Montreal' and all the other 'Romanian golden girls' trained, was just the tip of the iceberg for what the Romanian WAG system meant: a solid centralised system for which local clubs worked as resourceful pipelines and the authoritarian training practices as the *sine qua non* condition for performance.

Usually coming from poor families, it was not only the prospect of glory and seeing the world outside the (closed) borders that attracted the little girls and their parents, but also the socio-economic safety of having accommodation, education, and training equipment costs covered. This, in turn, was perceived as a great opportunity for an upward social mobility push and, to some extent, made all the restrictive training practices acceptable – a fair price to pay for a better future.

Despite the shifts in government after the fall of communism, and the shifts in global sports economics, the Romanian gymnastics system changed little since Comăneci's victories, remaining financially dependent on governmental funding. If this worked as a competitive advantage for a while, attesting to the common Western accusation that Eastern bloc sport, and its ample state funding, effectively meant that athletes from these countries were professionals, the same state-dependency became a liability after the 1990s. Still, the rhetoric of sacrifice, devotion, and hard work, against all financial constraints, continued to be part of the perceived magic of Comăneci's Perfect 10 and served as a sort of Cinderella model of success. It made the nation even more proud of its performances, standing as a proof that money cannot compete against 'talent' and 'tradition'.

Caught in leveraging the symbolic heritage of Comăneci's Perfect 10, Romanian WAG was in the grips of nostalgia, failing to ride the professionalisation and commercialisation wave. With no clear policies to attract and encourage private funding and private club-structures that could have balanced the lack of consistent and strategic public investments, the system continued its downfall.

While Nadia was mastering the celebrity endorsement game both in and outside Romania, Romanian gymnastics remained off big brands' sponsorship radar. Although the high decline in the number of practising gymnasts had been a significant drawback for the Romanian gymnastics since the early 2000s, it was only in 2013 that Romanian gymnastics took an important 2.5 million euro private sponsorship to support a three year-project aimed to increase the selection base and regain popularity among children (Romanian Gymnastics Federation, 2013). By that time, there were only 32 clubs affiliated to the Romanian Gymnastics Federation, and a mere 453 WAG gymnasts registered across all age categories nationwide (Romanian Ministry for Education, Research, Youth, and Sports, 2012). Nonetheless, this commercial partnership was a one-off and, like other small steps taken on this road, remained just a sporadic action, reflecting, once again, the general lack of strategy in the Romanian sport system.

Loved by the public, Romanian gymnasts failed to leverage the full commercial potential of their 'national heroines' status. However, starting with the 2000s, their media coverage made a gradual shift from the performance-focused worship discourse towards gymnastics' tabloidisation. This came with higher interest for any seeds of controversy, whether related to their private life or training practices, as well as with their presence in entertainment television formats (i.e. *Dancing with the Stars*, lifestyle talk-shows). This did not bring along important sponsorship deals. The major source of income and financial incentives remained the post-competition state rewards and the life pension system introduced in 2000 by the new sport law (i.e. according to the number and value of the medals won in major competitions; Romanian Olympic Committee, 2000).

Meanwhile, media visibility and public debate around former gymnasts forced to migrate or to cope with financial difficulties after their retirement have intensified. Combined with the scarcity of expert and training infrastructure, this led to a sharp decline in the attractiveness of WAG among both children and parents.

Looking back at the last 40 years, the turning point in Romania's rise and fall story rests in its incapacity to adapt to market logic and to surpass the trap of the Perfect 10 nostalgia. Eminent coach Adrian Stan reflected that 'gymnastics for business is what dictates the development rhythm of performance in gymnastics… [In Great Britain] I learned half of gymnastics that I could not have learned in Romania: that is, the gymnastics for business' (Șchiopu, 2016). His experience, hence, illuminates reasons for the downfall of an inflexible, elusory self-sufficient system.

The emigration of Eastern bloc coaches

In the 1980s, select coaches migrated to Western countries. Labelled 'defections' at this point, the most famous of these was the departure of the Károlyis from the Romanian gymnastics programme seeking a new life in the USA. When the Soviet Union and Romania began to disintegrate in the late 1980s and early 1990s, the slow trickle of emigration became nearly a diaspora.

The Soviet Union

Emigration of coaches away from the motherland has been significant since the fall of the Soviet Union, and has naturally affected the development of the sport in Russia since 1991. In an interview in 2013, head coach Valentina Rodionenko estimated that around 364 coaches had left Russia to work overseas. This 'brain drain' levelled out standards worldwide as expertise has been disseminated and Western states have gradually grabbed the initiative and developed their own scientific training methods. Migration has simultaneously weakened the Russian system to a certain extent, as a gap in the gymnastics' legacy developed and the coach population aged. Alexandrov (2012) speaks of efforts to alter the standards required for Master of Sport classification in order to encourage young gymnasts and coaches working in the regions to remain in the sport and reinforce coach retention, as a response to the thinning of coach ranks, and the difficult social and economic circumstances that surround Russian sport (Booth & Alexandrov, 2012).

The earliest émigrés included Boris Orlov, coach to 1981 World Champion Olga Bicherova, who remained in Holland from 1986 to his death in

2018. Andrei Rodionenko, head coach of the USSR WAG team, moved to Australia in 1990, then spent more than 10 years as head coach of the Canadian national gymnastics team, before returning to Russia in 2006 as head coach of the national team. Shortly after arriving in Australia, the Rodionenkos recruited their friends to gyms all over Australia and New Zealand (Kerr & Cervin, 2017). Gymnasts' careers have been overturned as a result of migrating coaches; when Elvira Saadi left Moscow in 1991 to go and work in Canada, where she still resides, she left behind her personal gymnast, USSR national team member Tatiana Groshkova, whose promising career was curtailed. Similar stories exist of several of the current national team members as the wave of emigration continues to this day.

In addition to the availability of work in the West, instability within the former Eastern bloc states influenced the extent and nature of coach and gymnast migration. Yevgenia Kuznetsova, 1998 European Beam Champion, competed as a gymnast for Bulgaria when she could no longer qualify for the Russian national team; 2004 Olympian Anna Pavlova joined the Azerbaijan national gymnastics team when it became clear she would no longer be selected for her national team.

There have been relatively few returners to Russia. Former head coach of the USSR WAG team Alexander Alexandrov returned to Russia from the USA in 2009, but left to work in Brazil in 2013 after a troubled period as head coach of the Russian WAG team. He now works as a consultant in the USA. Alexandrov, a legendary coach well known for his inspirational training methods, and who has a strong following of fans in Russia and overseas, led his home team to their first ever team gold medal in the World Championships in 2010, but was unable to find a harmonious way of working with head coaches Andrei and Valentina Rodionenko. Returning coaches, having learned new ways of working from their adopted homes, bring conflicting cultures and ethics to their working practices and it is evident that this can provoke significant internecine conflict. Kalugina (personal correspondence with the author, 5 May 2013) has pointed out that the vast majority of Russian émigrés overseas are men, whereas the many female coaches and choreographers who were often as important to the gymnasts' success were left behind in Russia. Indeed, in Australia and New Zealand, male Soviet coaches were the main targets for recruitment while their wives were seen as bonuses (Kerr & Cervin, 2017).

Romania

Meanwhile, the pull-factors for Romanian coaches' migration had existed since Comăneci's heyday, as the world was fascinated with the 'secrets' of the Romanian school of gymnastics. Nadia's *Perfect 10* became the foundation for the Romanian gymnastics 'brand' and facilitated the Romanian coaches' mass exodus after the fall of communism. Nevertheless, the first important breakage happened in the 1980s, when Géza Pozsár, and Béla and Márta Károlyi – Nadia's choreographer and coaches – famously defected to the USA while on a gymnastics tour there, having been granted asylum by the American government.

Once in the USA, Pozsár and the Károlyis leveraged the wave of enthusiasm and popularity brought by Romania's success at Montreal (1976) and Moscow (1980). The coaches behind the *Perfect 10* started moulding the USA into the top gymnastics power it is today. But the story of their emigration was rather exceptional, risky and, due to media control, kept far from public debate. Although the Romanian WAG community was, at that point, resourceful enough to fill this gap and keep the successful system going, they set a precedent and provided a scenario for other Romanian coaches to look up to.

Therefore, fascinated with the endless opportunities and financial resources that developed countries had to offer, when the borders opened after the fall of communism, it marked the beginning of a mass exodus of coaches. Leaving Romania became a trend and these migrations planted the seeds for the new WAG order of today.

Nonetheless, Romania continued its success in WAG throughout the 1990s and 2000s. Its dominance over the big economic powers, despite the financial inequalities in terms of both the infrastructure and the human resources, created a David versus Goliath story of triumph at home. Romanians took the pride not only in this symbolic win over the 'rich West', but also in godfathering the new success of the West through its coaches. Thus, former Romanian coaches achieving success abroad were perceived as another sign of Romanian WAG dominance.

The silent legacy of this transition was covered up by two overlapping aspects: the performance inertia of the Romanian old system and the long-term building process of new programmes in countries with no history of competitiveness in WAG (i.e. UK, Australia, Italy, Holland). But, by the late 2000s, the results of these shifts were clearly visible as the map of success in WAG was redrawn. At this point, the Romanian 'faultless' system was drained of its key resources. By 2012, there were only 146 active coaches for both men's artistic gymnastics and WAG structures nationwide (Romanian Ministry for Education, Research, Youth, and Sports, 2012), Romania ending up with more coaches abroad than at home.

Ironically, the diaspora of Romanian emigrant coaches was now called on to return home: to input their expertise into reviving the old system. The discourse surrounding Romanian coaches at home and abroad stopped being about expertise or knowledge transfer, but rather about the heroic sacrifice that the 'ones who stayed' had to cope with: improper training facilities, old infrastructure, lack of resources, decreasing interest from both parents and children for gymnastics, and poor incomes (i.e. 200–300 Euro/month).

The involvement of Romanian coaches in the rise and fall of WAG powers is not only about different economic and investment models, but also about (lack of) adaptation and progressive thinking. The American Dream of Béla and Márta Károlyi, Géza Pozsár, Mihai Brestyan, Nadia Comăneci, Daniela Silivaș, and Adrian Stan are as much about the individuals as they are about the systems behind them. Looking at the big picture, the Romanian downfall should have been less of a shock for nostalgic Romanians, as the warning signs were there and their effects foreseeable. However, after decades of taken-for-granted dominance, Romanians found themselves left with taking pride in the success of their coaches standing by athletes competing for other countries.

Impacts on Western nations

The immigration of Soviet and Romanian coaches to the USA, Australia, New Zealand, and other Western countries was the beginning of a new stage of transnational co-operation in WAG. Where previously technical knowledge was a closely guarded secret, from the 1990s the international nature of coaching teams and the old colleagues now working across nations led to a new phase of open-ness and collaboration in international WAG. The increased ease of crossing borders, too, led to an increase in coaching exchanges and learning forums. The result of such migration and co-operation was an immediate increase in the quality of gymnastics being performed. However, with such widespread improvements, quality was no longer the exceptional differentiator of performance. Moreover, cultural clashes arose for these coaches: many Westerners viewed the methods of immigrant coaches as too strict; and they struggled to focus on a team of gymnasts rather than one or two particularly talented athletes. Conversely, many immigrant coaches found they 'softened' their coaching style as a result of cultural learnings in their new homes (Kerr & Moore, 2015). Nonetheless, many Western coaches observed (and perhaps misunderstood) not only the techniques, but the coaching styles of emigrant coaches, which they now emanate. The reverberations of the clashes of these cultures are yet to settle as concern over athlete welfare now increases.

Commodification, USA gymnastics, and abuse

Moreover, we might reflect on what effect the commercialisation and concurrent commodification of the athletes has had on American gymnastics in particular, where monetary reward has been most keenly observed. In 2016, USAG, the governing body of American gymnastics, netted $12 million USD from events and participation nationwide. Its tax records for that same year showed a revenue of $34 million, with 69 staff costing $5.2 million (Woods & Evans, 2018). After USAG team doctor Larry Nassar was found guilty of abusing hundreds of gymnasts in his care, USAG suffered a withdrawal of sponsorship. AT&T withdrew its support, 'suspending our sponsorship of the organization until it is rebuilt and we know that the athletes are in a safe environment' (Higa, 2018). This followed on from Procter & Gamble, Hershey's, Under Armour, and Kellogg's all failing to renew, or revoking, their sponsorship (Higa, 2018). Gymnastics success might bring money for a gymnast or a governing body, but that money is acutely tied to public relations and the image that company is trying to be associated with. As of December 2018, USAG filed for bankruptcy in the wake of nearly 100 lawsuits from gymnasts seeking damages due to USAG's employment of Larry Nassar and the creation of a system in which he operated (McCann, 2018). USAG estimated that the damages of Nassar's abuse could amount to between $75 million and $150 million dollars, for an organisation with declared assets of only $6.5 million USD (McCann, 2018).

Many of those suits alleged that USAG prioritised medals – and the concomitant revenue they attracted – over the welfare of the athletes themselves. Aly Raisman explained: '[USAG's] biggest priority from the beginning and still today is their reputation, the medals they win and the money they make off of us' (Higa, 2018). The gymnasts said that as team doctor Nassar abused generations of gymnasts over 30 years through the official positions granted to him by the USAG. Indeed, a key part of the allegations has revolved around USAG's cosiness with law enforcement. When the *IndyStar* investigation uncovered the abuse, they found that the FBI failed to begin an investigation into Nassar after the head of USAG, Steve Penny, reported him in 2015. Meanwhile, the pair were discussing a possible retirement job for the FBI agent. Later, a friend of Penney's who was the top police investigator specialising in child abuse tried to dissuade the *IndyStar* from going public with its investigation, and would try to discredit the reporting (Woods & Evans, 2018). Despite a year's worth of apologies under multiple new USAG leaders, the athletes still locate the problems in the culture of the sport and the governing body's emphasis on winning at any costs. Gymnast Ashton Locklear reflected in 2018: 'Nothing has changed. The same culture in the sport exists. Athletes are still afraid to speak out. The same mind-set exists, and I know that personally' (Macur, 2018).

If the allure of commercial sponsorship and revenue growth was a factor in USAG's masking of abusive practices under its watch, it has also become a powerful tool for athletes. When USAG replaced its president for the second time in 2018, the new head, Mary Bono, tweeted in opposition to Nike's use of Colin Kaepernick in a new advertising campaign. Kaepernick, a star quarterback in the American National Football League, had divided opinions over his kneeling during the national anthem in protest of law enforcement's treatment of Black people in the USA. Simone Biles – a Black woman who has won most of the gold medals at world championships and Olympics since 2014, and who is also sponsored by Nike – tweeted a response to Bono, criticising her stance (Bogage & Boren, 2018). A teammate of Biles', Aly Raisman, who had already been outspoken in her opposition to USAG practices and their role in perpetuating Nassar's abuse, added her voice to the mix, pointing out that Bono had previously worked for the law firm that advised USAG during the Nassar case. Bono was forced to resign within days (ESPN, 2018). But while this incident reflects how success, sponsorship deals, and the platforms they bring can magnify a gymnast's voice, such opportunities have only been afforded to a select few in the sport worldwide. It remains to be seen when the bulk of athletes, who never win international medals and commercial contracts, will also be heard.

Conclusion

Gymnastics, as part of the Olympic movement, was bound to the amateur rules of the twentieth-century sport. Yet, the state-sponsored nature of Soviet and Romanian gymnastics throughout much of this period led to accusations of professionalisation early on. Indeed, from the 1950s to the 1980s, Soviet and Romanian gymnasts raised both their income and standard of living through international victories and the rewards they brought from the state in the form of cash, housing, and gifts. However, the rhetoric around professional sport changed in the 1980s. The Soviet Union and Romania were both reluctant to shift towards a commercial model of gymnastics, as was the FIG. While Romania failed to keep pace with investment in gymnastics, the almost complete withdrawal of state funding in Russia after the 1992 Olympics led to a significant weakening in the professional training and incentive structures that underpinned success in the sport. But the new economic context of international sport, profiting from competitions – both for organisations and individuals – would become crucial to sustaining international gymnastics. The FIG learned this in the 1990s, seeking assistance from the professional sports marketing company ISL. Meanwhile, American gymnastics has steadily climbed since its adoption of professionalisation and commercial partnerships in the 1980s. Athletes began to receive rewards, and build lucrative public entertainment careers off the back of their gymnastic success. The governing body, too, reaped the rewards of this success, attracting millions of dollars in advertising and sponsorship revenue. Certainly, such funding represents a vested interest in protecting the status quo, and, indeed, many gymnasts are now suggesting that USAG allowed Nassar to abuse them because it was more concerned about protecting its sponsors than protecting its athletes. But as Biles and Raisman have demonstrated, gymnasts too can attract hefty sponsorship deals and use the platforms afforded them to challenge the governing body. If we follow the money, victory in WAG has been shaped by the funding, incentives, and opportunities offered by athletic success.

Note

1 Milo is a powdered malt drink made by Nestlé in Australia.

References

Barker-Ruchti, N. (2009). Ballerinas and pixies: A genealogy of the changing female gymnastics body. *The International Journal of the History of Sport*, 26(1), 45–62.

Baruch, Y., Wheeler, K., & Zhao, X. (2004). Performance-related pay in Chinese professional sports. *International Journal of Human Resource Management*, 15(1), 245–259.

Bogage, J., & Boren, C. (2018, 13 October). Mouth drop: Simone Biles blasts USA Gymnastics head over anti-Nike tweet. *Washington Post*. Retrieved from www.washingtonpost.com.

Booth, E., & Alexandrova, A. (2012). Alexander Alexandrov in his own words. Interview with the coach. Retrieved from www.rewritingrussiangymnastics.blogspot.com.

Canberra Times. (1981, 30 January). Olympics: Amateurism obsolete. Retrieved from www.trove.nla.gov.au.

Canberra Times. (1986, 26 April). 'No haste' in allowing Olympic pros. Retrieved from www.trove.nla.gov.au.

Cervin, G. (2017). *A balance of power: Women's artistic gymnastics during the Cold War and it's a=aftermath*. PhD diss. Crawley: University of Western Australia.

ESPN. (2018, 17 October). Interim president Mary Bono resigns from USA Gymnastics. Retrieved from www.ESPN.com.

Higa, L. (2018, 23 January). USA Gymnastics still values medals more than girls. *New York Times*. Retrieved from www.nytimes.com.

Jokisipila, M. (2011). World champions bred by national champions: The role of state-owned corporate giants in Russian sports. *Russian Analytical Digest*, 95(6 April), 8–11.

Kerr, R., & Cervin, G. (2017). An ironic imbalance: Coaching opportunities and gender in women's artistic gymnastics in Australia and New Zealand. *International Journal of the History of Sport*. doi:10.1080/09523367.2017.1283307.

Kerr, R., & Moore, K. (2015). Hard work or child's play? Migrant coaches' reflections on coaching in New Zealand. *World Leisure Journal*, 57(3), 185–195.

Kidd, B. (2013). The philosophy of excellence: Olympic performances, class power and the Canadian state. *Cultures, Commerce, Media, Politics*, 16(4), 372–387.

Kirshenbaum, J. (1993, 31 May). Scorecard: Bonus-plus. *Sports Illustrated*. Retrieved from www.si.com.

Macur, J. (2018, 24 July). USA Gymnastics' talk of reform falls on skeptical ears at Senate hearing. *New York Times*. Retrieved from www.nytimes.com.

McCann, M. (2018, 6 December). How USA Gymnastics' bankruptcy petition impacts Larry Nassar survivors. *Sports Illustrated*. Retrieved from www.si.com.

Riordan, J. (1980). *Sport in Soviet society*. Cambridge: Cambridge University Press.

Riordan, J. (1993). The rise and fall of Soviet Olympic champions. *Olympika: The International Journal of Olympic Studies*, II, 25–44.

Romanian Gymnastics Federation. (2013, 25 March). OMV Petrom finanţează cu 2,5 milioane Euro gimnastica românească. Retrieved from http://www.romgym.ro.

Romanian Ministry for Education, Research, Youth, and Sports. (2012). *Sport annual 2012*. Retrieved from www.mts.ro.

Romanian Olympic Committee. (2000, 28 April). *Physical Education and Sports Law 69*. Retrieved from: www.cosr.ro.

Șchiopu, V. (2016, 25 May). Gimnastica românească e o operă de artă care riscă să fie distrusă. *PressOne*. Retrieved from: www.pressone.ro.

Thomas Junior, R. (1985, 1 March). Olympics to allow pros in 3 sports. *New York Times*. Retrieved from www.proquest.com.

Titov, Y. (1986). FIG Executive Committee: Summary of the minutes of the meetings held in Washington from 27th February to 3rd March 1986. *FIG Bulletin*, 130(September).

Titov, Y. (1992). Report submitted to the Congress. *FIG Bulletin*, 154(September).

Vaitsekhovskaya, E. (1993). Leonid Arkayev: General without an army. *Sports Express*, Retrieved from www.velena.ru. Translation by Lioubov Baladzhaeva.

Wilson, J. (2016). Sport economics and the sport industry. In R. Pomfret and J. K. Wilson (Eds), *Sport Through the lens of economic history*. Cheltenham: Edward Elgar Publishing.

Woods, D., & Evans, T. (2018, 9 December). After Nassar, is there still a place in Indianapolis for Olympic gymnastics organization? *Indianapolis Star*. Retrieved from www.indystar.com.

Zaglada, V. (2010). *One coach's journey from East to West: How the fall of the Iron Curtain changed the world of gymnastics*. Bloomington, IN: Authorhouse.

Chapter 4

Diversification of women's artistic gymnastics since the fall of Communism

Natalie Barker-Ruchti, Elizabeth Booth, Francesca Cavallerio, Georgia Cervin, Diana-Luiza Simion, Myrian Nunomura and Froukje Smits

Introduction

From 1952 until the fall of Communism in 1989, the most successful women's artistic gymnasts emerged from Communist sport regimes. Soviet gymnast Olga Korbut, Romanian Nadia Comaneci, and East German Maxi Gnauck were key champions during this time. The regimes, driven by the aim to demonstrate the superiority of the Communist way of life, were state-governed and state-funded. They entailed modern training facilities, full-time coaching and support personnel, tertiary-level sport and coaching education, sport science research, a network of sports (boarding) schools, financial assistance for athletes and generous rewards for competitive success (also for coaches), and a nationwide talent identification procedure (Green & Oakley, 2001; Houlihan, 1994; Riordan, 1993; 2007). In addition to resembling a regime, an additional feature that typified the Communist WAG system was what Kerr and colleagues (2017) have termed the 'pixie-style model of WAG'. This model emerged at the end of the 1960s, and, as represented by gymnasts such as Korbut and Comaneci, prescribed gymnasts' age as young, bodies as small in length, free of fat, and sexually undeveloped, and behaviour as obedient, darling-like, and cute (Barker-Ruchti, 2009; Kerr, 2006). The training of 'pixie gymnasts' constituted early identification and specialisation, long hours with numerous repetitions to learn skills, and coach authority. These characteristics, and particularly the growing risks for gymnasts that became associated with the increasing acrobatic form of WAG, concerned media and WAG stakeholders, especially during the 1970s (Barker-Ruchti, 2011). However, in the context of Cold War politics, the competitive success of the Communist gymnasts afforded the WAG system international role model status (Petracovschi & Terret, 2013; Riordan, 1995) and convinced the international community that they needed to develop their WAG systems along pixie WAG policies, systems, and practices (Cervin, 2017). This copying was not limited to WAG, but represented what a number of scholars have called a 'global sporting flow from East to West' (Green & Collins, 2008; Green & Houlihan, 2006; Green & Oakley, 2001).

The fall of Communism in 1989 significantly impacted the international sport landscape (Riordan, 1995). While China was not affected, the East German system dissolved[1] and the other European Communist countries were faced with a choice of 'how sharply they should break with the past and adopt a pattern of sport based on market relations' (Riordan, 1995, p. 24). To date, few researchers have examined the consequences of the fall on former Communist countries' national elite sport systems. Two exceptions are Girginov and Sandanski's (2008) study on Bulgaria, and Petracovschi and Terrets' (2013) study on Romania, both of which describe the difficulties the countries experienced with regard to professionalisation and private financing of elite sport. The Bulgarian case study identified three phases that affected the elite sport system between 1989 and 2000: the shrinking of the sport system, especially the number of sport organisations and the athlete population; the insulation of national sport organisations, mainly because they lacked state support; and the expansion of elite sport through development and innovation strategies that individual sport organisations implemented.

With relevance to how WAG in both former Communist and non-Communist countries has developed since 1989, what has changed is that a large proportion of coaches from former Communist countries have found employment around the globe. While statistics of the exodus are not available, qualitative investigations demonstrate what the transfer of Communist WAG expertise has meant for both the emigrating coaches and the receiving clubs and gymnasts (Kerr & Obel, 2018). Further, what we can observe is that the competition landscape has changed since 1989. While Romanian and Russian gymnasts continue to perform well at international events, their dominance is not as strong. Today, gymnasts from around the globe successfully participate in highest international competitions.

In this chapter, the purpose is to examine the development of WAG systems since 1989 through the inclusion of six case study countries – Australia, Brazil, Italy, Romania, Russia, and the Netherlands. Specifically, we pose the following questions: How did the fall of Communism reduce Romania's and Russia's WAG dominance? How did the Australian, Brazilian, Italian, and Dutch WAG governing bodies develop their systems to gain competitive ground? And lastly, what have the two former Communist countries done to reinvent their WAG systems since 1989? To answer these questions, we adopt glocalisation thinking (Robertson, 1994; 1995). Our theoretical starting point is Giulianotti and Robertson's (2012) argument that sports governing bodies and stakeholders do not simply follow global trends, but must develop innovative methods to remain competitive (for similar arguments, see Collins & Bailey, 2013; Green & Oakley, 2001; Maguire, 1994). Specific to WAG, we recognise the global influence the Communist WAG system continues to have, but assume that all national governing bodies develop and implement local measures to produce competitive success.

Glocalisation theory and WAG

Scholars critical of the concept of globalisation developed glocalisation theory (e.g., Ferguson, 1992; Scholte, 2008). Robertson (1994; 1995), a key proponent of glocalisation, critiqued globalisation theory for being ambiguous, elusive, and even redundant because he felt the conception neglected how local conditions, events, processes, and activities diversify societies. Robertson (1995, p. 25) even went as far as to write that globalisation mystifies cultural homogenisation, and the idea that 'bigger is better', obliterating 'locality – even history'. In arguing that localising forces and heterogenisation are features of life, Robertson (1995) moved beyond global homogenisation and universalisation to blend the terms 'global' and 'local' with 'glocal'.

Robertson (1995) understood glocalisation as a social process (rather than an abstract category), through which communities develop according to global and local trends and standards. He argued that 'glocalisation projects' represent the continuous 'features of contemporary globalisation', capturing how individuals, social groups, and communities interpret, shape, and decontextualise global phenomena to suit their everyday activities (Robertson, 1994; 1995). Such glocal 'action-reaction' processes generate 'homegrown' activities (Collins & Bailey, 2013), which have particular relevance for sport since, on the one hand, international governing bodies such as the International Olympic Committee (IOC) and international and continental (sport-specific) governing bodies (e.g., International Gymnastics Federation; European Gymnastics Federation) significantly shape domestic policies and systems (Houlihan, 2009). On the other hand, research has pointed to how local historical, socio-cultural, and political conditions and events, government mentalities, financial conditions, and developmental activities influence local practices (Barker-Ruchti et al., 2017; Giulianotti & Robertson, 2012).

With regard to sport, Giulianotti and Robertson have led glocalisation research. Their work has examined the development of football game identity and the emergence of transnational sport corporations (Giulianotti & Robertson, 2004); fanship (Giulianotti & Robertson, 2006) migration of football players (Giulianotti & Robertson, 2007); and the development of Asian sport (Giulianotti & Robertson, 2006, 2012). With regard to gymnastics, researchers have recently adopted the glocalisation perspective to examine the sportisation of parkour[2] in New Zealand and Italy (Puddle, Wheaton, & Thorpe, 2018; Sterchele & Ferrero Camoletto, 2017), and Chinese sport and gymnastics governing bodies' reactions to gymnastics developments since the 1950s (Zheng, Tan, & Bairner, 2017). This latter research demonstrates how Chinese gymnastics predominantly developed in relation to USSR gymnastics. This adoption process was at times passive, that is, was globalising as Soviet influence extensively shaped Chinese policy domains. At other times, the Chinese responses were more participative, which involved the Chinese gymnastics governing body actively influencing the International Federation of Gymnastics – FIG. A third response, which took place during the Chinese Cultural Revolution (1966–1976), was conflicting, as Mao Zedong's governance halted all gymnastics activities. Zheng and colleagues' study is exemplary in demonstrating how local conditions and events (e.g., Chinese Cultural Revolution), governmental processes (e.g., international influence through representation at FIG), and developmental activities (e.g., training camps in the USSR) shaped local gymnastics operations, and importantly, affected gymnasts' competitive success during different phases of Chinese gymnastics developments.

Against this glocalisation background, the six case study country authors included in this chapter collected materials to chronologise the conditions, events, processes, and activities that influenced their countries' WAG systems. The materials included information on governance and structure of WAG; financing; number and demographics of the elite gymnast population; competitive success at major events; coach population; and other relevant information as to the state of WAG prior and since the fall of Communism. The information was collated through the authors' expert knowledge of WAG in the case countries; publicly available documents; informal interviews with relevant WAG stakeholders; and scientific and media texts. To collate the materials, the first author created Table 4.1, which presents developments reported by the case country authors to have shaped WAG prior to and since the fall of Communism.

Based on the information in Table 4.1, we present below the six countries' developments prior to 1989 and since the fall of Communism. In the first section, we cluster the Communist and non-Communist countries to sketch their distinctive situations. In the second section, our aim is to highlight the local events and conditions that have shaped WAG developments since 1989. We begin with Australia as a state-managed system; move to Romania and Russia as former state-managed systems; and then Brazil and the Netherlands as systems receiving limited and temporary state support. Lastly, we present Italy, as this country's development was the most heterogeneous.

WAG prior to 1989

Prior to 1989, the WAG systems in the two Communist and four non-Communist countries differed. As mentioned at the outset of this chapter, the Romanian and Soviet systems constituted state-governed and state-funded *regimes* (Riordan, 2003). In Australia, Brazil, Italy, and the Netherlands, (elite) sport did not have the characteristics of a regime. Rather, individual institutions (e.g. clubs), mostly through volunteers, offered sport activities and in some cases elite sport training. Yet, as the global sporting arms race gained importance (Grix & Carmichael, 2012; Houlihan & Zheng, 2013), Communist sport success motivated non-Communist governments to

Table 4.1 Conditions and events that have shaped the six countries' WAG development prior to and since 1989

Country	Prior to 1989	Since 1989
Australia	- State forms Australian Institute of Sport (AIS) in 1981 - Performance increases from 1980s onwards - AIS hires Chinese coach Ju Ping Tian in 1983 - Australian Gymnastics Federation invests in networking and coach education from 1980s onwards	- Western Australian Institute of Sport hires 1st Soviet coach (Andrei Rodionenko) in 1993. Other state institutes follow suit - Opie Report into AIS gymnast allegations of abuse in 1995 - AIS replaces Ju Ping Tian with American Peggy Liddick in 1997 - Gymnasts reach best ever results 2003–2010 (3rd team 2003 World Championships (WC); 3rd individual 2005 WC; 6th team 2008 Olympic Games (OG); 1st individual apparatus 2010 WC) - Performance declines post-2010; team does not qualify for 2016 OG - Romanian-American Mihai Brestyan replaces Peggy Liddick in 2017
Brazil	- Brazilian Gymnastics Confederation (BGC) is established in 1978 - First gymnast participates in WC in 1980 - Coach population is mostly Brazilian	- Ukrainian coach Iryna Illyashenko arrives in 1999 - Gymnasts reach major success at 2001 WC (2nd floor); since 2004, team qualification - Ukrainian coaches Oleg and Nadia Ostapenko arrive in 2001 through IOC's Olympic Solidarity Programme - BGC establishes the training facility 'Curitiba Training Centre' and Russian coach Alexander Alexandrov is hired in 2000 - BGC closes centralised training facility in 2008 - Elite gymnast population reduces - Brazilian Olympic Committee and Ministry of Sport initiate an intense renewal process towards 2016 OG. Implementation of Brazil Medal Plan - 2016 OG success confirms 2008 success - Brazilian Olympic Committee hires Valeri Liukin in 2018

Country	Prior to 1989	Since 1989
Italy	- Italian Gymnastics Federation (FGI) is established in 1869, the first sport federation in Italy - WAG follows a de-centralised organisational structure - First international success at 1950 (2nd individual WC; 3rd team) - Brixia Brescia (BB) is founded in 1984 by Enrico Casella	- Project 'Brixia Integral Development' is launched in 1990 - Government changes sport from self- to state-dependency in 2000 - FGI president Riccardo Agabio implements Gymnastics for All and Olympic Gymnastics structure (no funding) - FGI choses BB as main elite training centre. Enrico Casella is hired as head coach - Casella becomes national coach in 2004. Success follows (1st team WC 2006; 1st individual WC 2006) - Sponsors invest in BB - FGI starts a marketing and advertising campaign in 2011
Romania	- WAG is state-funded - Gymnasts reach significant international success starting in 1976 - Media mystifies and heroises gymnasts - Government funds stop from 1989 onwards - Exodus of coaches during 1990s	- Performance success continues at 2004, 2008, and 2012 OG - Famous coaches Octavian Bellu and Mariana Bitang create success and sacrifice mirage - Media scrutinises WAG practices and de-mystifies gymnasts - Maria Olaru publishes *The Price of Gold* in 2016 - Non-qualification for 2016 OG
Russia	- Sports Federation of USSR regulates WAG - Many influential coaches (e.g., Yuri Shtuckman, Leonid Arkayev, and Andrei Rodionenko) - Extensive competitive success since 1952	- Coach emigration and closing of training centres during 1990s - Continued competitive success - Vladimir Putin issues plan to rebuild national sport infrastructure in 2006 - Some influential coaches educated by earlier experts (e.g., Vladislav Rotstorotski, Alexander Alexandrov) remain or return to Russia post-2006 - Corporate sponsorship deal with VTB Bank since 2006

Country	Prior to 1989	Since 1989
The Netherlands	- WAG follows a centralised WAG system since 1978 - Some international participation during 1970s - Arrival of coaches Eva Bartha from Hungary in 1972; Albert and Lisa Asarjan from Romania in 1976; and Boris Orlov from the USSR in 1985 (the latter coach through an exchange programme with the USSR Gymnastics Federation)	- National training centre 'Papendal' is closed in 1992 - Some international participation during 1990s - 'Golden generation' of gymnasts from 2002 to 2005 - Royal Dutch Gymnastics Federation forms regional, national, and talent centres in 2008 - OG marketing campaign #OrangeElegance in 2012 - Abuse charges through Simone Heitinga and Stasja Kohler's biography; report in magazine *Heroes* and other reports in 2013 - Gymnasts achieve significant success at 2016 OG (7th team; 1st beam) - OG marketing campaign #TheForceIsGrace since 2016

develop elite sport (Green & Oakley, 2001). The Australian government was the earliest in adopting strategies, and has most closely followed and implemented state-managed sport policies (Green & Oakley, 2001; Houlihan, 2002). Specific to WAG, the formation of the Australian Institute of Sport (AIS) in 1981 resulted in the hiring in 1983 of Chinese coach Ju Ping Tian,[3] who developed a national elite WAG performance progression programme. While not overly distinctive, the programme's demand for precision reflected Chinese and Russian approaches to gymnastics. With the implementation of this programme, the then Australian Gymnastics Federation began to invest in networking and coach education, bringing British expert coaches to Australia for workshops and sending Australian coaches to the USSR to learn (Kerr & Cervin, 2016).

In Brazil and Italy, the Communist influence had few effects. WAG followed a de-centralised structure and no national sport policies were implemented. A first development towards Communist WAG occurred in Italy in 1984 through the founding of one elite training centre – Brixia Brescia. In the Netherlands, despite a de-centralised organisation of sport (Waardenburg & van Bottenburg, 2013), Communist influence was evident from the 1970s onwards through the Dutch Sports Federation's creation of the national sport centre 'Papendal' in 1971, elite gymnasts being obliged to train there and live with billet families from 1976 onwards (Waardenburg & van Bottenburg, 2013); and the reception of coaches from Hungary, Romania, and the USSR from 1972 onwards.

WAG since 1989

Since the fall of Communism in 1989, the six case countries' national WAG's systems have changed significantly. While the global acceptance of a state-governed and state-financed system and the pixie-style model continued to influence countries' efforts to systematise this sport, a number of specific local events and conditions heterogenised the six countries' WAG developments. In Australia, two key local events and conditions compromised the state-governed and state-funded system established during the 1990s. First, as the Communist coaches hired by state sport institutes began to develop successful gymnasts (Kerr & Obel, 2018), the state and club coaches did not want to lose their 'investments' to the centralised AIS because this would have changed the gymnasts' affiliations and cut the state institute funding attached to these athletes. Second, in 1995, AIS gymnasts accused coaches of abuse. While the resulting Opie Report did not find evidence for the allegations, the accusations and inquiry damaged the AIS programme and the then national coach Ju Ping Tian (Varney, 1999). In this context of state institute dissatisfaction of having to pass on their successful gymnasts and AIS criticism, support for a de-centralised national programme grew and became implemented in the later 1990s, a change, which produced the best ever WAG results between 2003 and 2010. Since 2010, success has stalled, however, and Gymnastics Australia is today hoping that the recruitment of Romanian-American Mihai Brestyan, and the performance progression programme that he has implemented, will revitalise WAG.

For Romanian and now Russian WAG, the key local condition that troubled these two countries post-1989 was ceased state governance and state funding (Riordan, 1995). As an immediate consequence, coaches and gymnasts lost their livelihoods and were forced, or took the opportunity, to emigrate (Riordan, 1995). The lack of funding also closed training centres and (boarding) schools, and ended coach education, research, and talent identification procedures, and financial assistance for athletes. In Romania, although performance success continued for some years, and the two key coaches Octavian Bellu and Mariana Bitang kept the country's WAG invincibility mirage alive through continued national and international media attention, the sport's downfall moved the media discourse from supremacy to disappointment and indignation. This country's failure to qualify for the 2016 Olympic Games, coupled with former gymnast Maria Olaru's (2016) book *The Price of Gold*, which described the physical and emotional violence practised by Octavian Bellu and Mariana Bitang, changed the local representation of gymnasts.

In Russia, it was not until President Putin's 2006 directive to rebuild elite sport that some infrastructure was restored, influential coaches kept and even brought home, and the existing, although reduced, gymnast population cultivated more systematically. The directive also secured a sponsorship deal between the Russian Gymnastics Federation and the country's largest partly state-owned consumer bank VTB. Putin's 2006 government directive and the sponsorship deal with VTB Bank have contributed to revitalising this country's WAG system; however, as the sponsorship is top-heavy, and local government support remains insecure, existing funding is insufficient to filter down to cover the needs at grassroots level WAG.

More long term, a domestic condition that continues to concern Romanian and Russian WAG is the free market economy that these countries have adopted since 1989. As Girginov and Sandanski (2008) and Petracovschi and Terret (2013) have demonstrated through their Bulgarian and Romanian case studies, adopting consumer and marketing thinking after a long history of state governance is difficult. Moreover, sport participation now relies on consumer choice, rather than Communist ideologies of state service and rewards, a condition that increasing costs of participation and the sport's loss of popularity complicate. Today, in addition to a lack of state management and funding, Romanian WAG suffers an image crisis, has a reduced elite gymnast population, and is led by very few and mostly aged coaches. Efforts to reinvent the elite sport and WAG systems will continue to challenge this country's sport organisations (Petracovschi & Terret, 2013). Similarly, Russian WAG popularity and population are today much lower than prior to 1989, and this country continues to risk decline if stakeholders cannot develop additional strategies to maintain and improve its WAG operations.

In contrast to the former Communist countries' decline of WAG, Brazil, Italy, and the Netherlands have since 1989 increasingly developed their WAG systems. In many ways, these efforts reflect the global sporting flow from East to West that has shaped elite sport systems around the globe (Green & Collins, 2008; Green & Houlihan, 2006; Green & Oakley, 2001). In Brazil, the development of WAG began through the hiring of Soviet-trained coaches, before and particularly since the establishment of the 'Curitiba Training Centre' in 2000, and the Brazilian Olympic Committee and Ministry of Sport's intense elite sport investment leading up to the 2016 Olympic Games, which included the athlete funding scheme Brazil Medal Plan. These Communist-informed measures have brought competitive success since 2001. Two domestic events and conditions have complicated Brazilian WAG activities. First, in 2008, gymnasts alleged to have experienced abuse by stakeholders of the Brazilian Gymnastics Confederation and Curitiba Training Centre coaches, which resulted in a change in presidency and Technical Committee, and led to the closure of the Curitiba national training facility and dispersal of gymnasts back to their clubs (Molinari, Costa, Monteiro, & Nunomura, 2018). Second, the Brazilian Gymnastics Confederation has since 1989 placed limited focus on developing upcoming gymnast populations and their own coaches. At the 2016 Olympic Games, the elite gymnast population was small and relied on gymnasts who have been in WAG since 2001 and the lack of employment opportunities provided to Brazilian coaches has resulted in coach emigration (Nunomura & Oliveira, 2012). While the lack of gymnast development is today changing (only one gymnast is from the 2001 generation), the consequence of the coach emigration continues to mean that Brazilian WAG relies on the costly employment of foreign coaches. The Brazilian Olympic Committee's latest recruitment of Russian-American Valeri Liukin, who has coached several Olympic champions, continues this trend of hoping that first-generation Soviet-trained coaches improve WAG performance.

In the Netherlands, the efforts in the 1970s to systematise WAG were initially stalled by financial problems and missing competitive success. With the closure of Papendal in 1992, the distribution of gymnasts back to their home clubs and gymnast retirement created modest success during the 1990s. Through the creative work of a number of coaches employed by individual clubs, WAG regained momentum, producing a 'golden generation' of gymnasts from 2002 to 2005. In response, the Royal Dutch Gymnastics Federation (KNGU) restructured WAG in 2008. With regional, national, and talent development centres in place, competitive results flourished and KNGU used the opportunity to initiate the 2012 Olympic Games campaign #OrangeElegance. Allegations of abuse, through Simone Heitinga and Stasja Kohler's biography and media reports, overshadowed these developments. Several coaches implicated in the allegations were fired and serious and heated discussions about elite WAG and child-friendly elite gymnastics training followed. Today, Dutch WAG success continues, with KNGU running a further social media campaign, the 2020 Olympic Games #TheForceIsGrace campaign.

In Italy, the development of WAG was more heterogeneous than in Brazil and the Netherlands. In the first 10 years following 1989, the country's national governing body, the Italian Gymnastics Federation (FGI), was autonomous from the state and self-supported. The project Brixia Integral Development, which the gymnastics club Brixia Brescia initiated and funded in 1990, was a grassroots project to develop elite WAG led by Enrico Casella. This project was crucial in advancing Brixia Brescia to a permanent, although modest, WAG training facility and develop elite-level success. With this success, particularly Vanessa Ferrari's World Championship title in 2006, and Italy's transformation to a state-dependent sport support system from 2000 onwards, the FGI began to co-finance the training facility. This included the employment of Enrico Casella as the national head coach in 2004, who implemented a scientific approach and athlete-centred pedagogy to train elite gymnasts. Moreover, the FGI's Gymnastics for All and Olympic Gymnastics campaigns to increase the Italian WAG population (starting in 2000), as well as the MTV reality television show that was broadcasted for five seasons (starting in 2011), and their own online TV channel (starting in 2017) to generate sponsorship deals, have made WAG more visible. Today, despite limited funds, Italy's WAG success continues and Brexia Brescia is recognised as an International Academy, where federations and clubs from all over the world meet to develop skills and knowledge (Brixia International Academy FGI, 2018).

Conclusion

This chapter aimed to examine the development of WAG systems in Australia, Brazil, Italy, Romania, Russia, and the Netherlands since 1989 using glocalisation theory. Our results demonstrate that the Communist WAG system influenced the four sampled non-Communist countries to adopt measures to develop this sport. In Australia, Brazil, and the Netherlands, the adopted development strategies most closely reflected Romanian and Russian WAG regime characteristics. This homogenisation process entailed what a number of scholars have named a global WAG flow from East to West (Green & Collins, 2008; Green & Houlihan, 2006; Green & Oakley, 2001). Italy's efforts to develop WAG stand out for being less driven by Communist thinking. By adopting strategies specific to this country's financial context, building local coaching expertise, and investing in popularising WAG, this country has developed a WAG system that produces competitive success, has a sustainable WAG athlete and coach population, has acquired funds for their elite operations, and has developed an internationally recognised training facility.

Our results demonstrate how local events and conditions have heterogenised WAG systems and continue to pose specific domestic challenges. The acquisition of funds and cases of abuse stand out as common such challenges. In terms of funding, our chapter outlined different funding systems and the domestic challenges these pose because of insufficiency, purpose, and funder–receiver relationships. A response to the challenge of insufficient funding, as adopted by Italy and the Netherlands, was to implement innovative popularising strategies. In the former Communist countries, where stakeholders have not yet accustomed to a free market economy, marketing and sponsorship funding is either limited or non-existent, and will continue to need innovation. In terms of abuse, cases that generated inquiries and significant media attention were reported in Australia, Brazil, Romania, and the Netherlands. In these countries, the abuse cases affected local affairs, and, similar to financial challenges, will continue to require organisations to develop preventative measures. It is a situation that demonstrates how uncritical reflection of dominant practices (i.e., pixie-style model of WAG) can have undesired consequences (Collins & Bailey, 2013). While some WAG organisations have started to distance themselves from the Communist WAG system, and its pixie-style model in particular (e.g., Sweden), more critical reflection of these understandings, and development of local strategies to safeguard gymnasts, are necessary to reinvent WAG.

In conclusion, our results have shown how the fall of Communism in 1989 has de-centred Romanian and Russian WAG and how the strategies adopted by the included non-Communist countries diversified the international WAG landscape. Regardless of decline or gain, however, our chapter has demonstrated that the developments within each of the six countries' WAG systems evolved in interaction with global and local events and conditions. Thus, while sport policy research outlines factors that create successful sport systems, it is crucial that sport organisations acknowledge local events and conditions, and are prepared for domestic reactions, when developing their sport systems.

Notes

1 We acknowledge that the unification of East and West Germany integrated some Communist sport system characteristics (Volkwein & Haag, 1994).
2 While parkour is not a traditional gymnastics discipline, international and national gymnastics governing bodies have adopted parkour as an additional gymnastics discipline (e.g., FIG; Gymnastics NZ; Swedish Gymnastics Federation).
3 Zheng, Tan, and Bairner (2017) write that the Chinese gymnastics coaches of the 1970s were trained by Soviet coaches through training camps and other forms of exchange. As Ju Ping Tian was national women's coach from 1981 to 1983, she undoubtedly was influenced by Soviet gymnastics experts.

References

Barker-Ruchti, N. (2009). Ballerinas and pixies: A genealogy of the changing female gymnastics body. *International Journal of the History of Sport*, 26(1), 45–62.

Barker-Ruchti, N. (2011). *Women's artistic gymnastics: An (auto-)ethnographic journey*. Basel: Gesowip.

Barker-Ruchti, N., Schubring, A., Aarresola, O., Kerr, R., Grahn, K., & McMahon, J. (2017). Producing success: A critical analysis of athlete development governance in six countries. *International Journal of Sport Policy and Politics*, 10(2), 215–234.

Brixia International Academy FGI (Producer). (2018). Brixia. Retrieved from https://www.brixiagym.it/it/pages/detail/id/6/international-academy-f.g.i..html.

Cervin, G. (2017). *A balance of power: Women's artistic gymnastics during the Cold War and its aftermath*. PhD thesis, University of Western Australia.

Collins, D., & Bailey, R. (2013). 'Scienciness' and the allure of second-hand strategy in talent identification and development. *International Journal of Sport Policy and Politics*, 5(2), 183–191.

Ferguson, M. (1992). The mythology about globalization. *European Journal of Communication*, 7(1), 69.

Girginov, V., & Sandanski, I. (2008). Understanding the changing nature of sports organisations in transforming societies. *Sport Management Review*, 11(1), 21–50.

Giulianotti, R., & Robertson, R. (2004). The globalization of football: a study in the glocalization of the 'serious life'. *The British Journal of Sociology*, 55(4), 545–568.

Giulianotti, R., & Robertson, R. (2006). Glocalization, globalization and migration: The case of Scottish football supporters in North America. *International Sociology*, 21(2), 171–198.

Giulianotti, R., & Robertson, R. (2007). Forms of glocalization: Globalization and the migration strategies of Scottish football fans in North America. *Sociology*, 41(1), 133–152.

Giulianotti, R., & Robertson, R. (2012). Glocalization and sport in Asia: Diverse perspectives and future possibilities. *Sociology of Sport Journal*, 29(4), 433–454.

Green, M., & Collins, S. (2008). Policy, politics and path dependency: Sport development in Australia and Finland. *Sport Management Review*, 11(3), 225–251.

Green, M., & Houlihan, B. (2006). Governmentality, modernization, and the 'disciplining' of national sporting organizations: Athletics in Australia and the United Kingdom. *Sociology of Sport Journal*, 23(1), 47.

Green, M., & Oakley, B. (2001). Elite sport development systems and playing to win: uniformity and diversity in international approaches. *Leisure Studies*, 20(4), 247–267.

Grix, J., & Carmichael, F. (2012). Why do governments invest in elite sport? A polemic. *International Journal of Sport Policy and Politics*, 4(1), 73–90.

Houlihan, B. (1994). *Sport and international politics*. New York and London: Harvester Wheatsheaf.

Houlihan, B. (2002). *Sport, policy and politics: A comparative analysis*. London: Routledge.

Houlihan, B. (2009). Mechanisms of international influence on domestic elite sport policy. *International Journal of Sport Policy and Politics*, 1(1), 51–69.

Houlihan, B., & Zheng, J. (2013). The Olympics and elite sport policy: Where will it all end? *The International Journal of the History of Sport*, 30(4), 338–355.

Kerr, R. (2006). The impact of Nadia Comaneci on the sport of women's artistic gymnastics. *Sporting Traditions*, 23(1), 87–102.

Kerr, R., & Cervin, G. (2016). An ironic imbalance: Coaching opportunities and gender in women's artistic gymnastics in Australia and New Zealand. *The International Journal of the History of Sport*, 33(17), 2139–2152.

Kerr, R., & Obel, C. (2018). The migration of gymnastics coaches from the Former Soviet Union to New Zealand: An actor–network theory perspective. *Leisure Studies*, 37(5), 615–627.

Kerr, R., Barker-Ruchti, N., Schubring, A., Cervin, G., & Nunomura, M. (2017). Coming of age: Coaches transforming the pixie-style model of coaching in women's artistic gymnastics. *Sports Coaching Review*, 8(1), 7–24.

Maguire, J. (1994). Sport, identity politics, and globalization: Diminishing contrasts and increasing varieties. *Sociology of Sport Journal*, 11(4), 398–427.

Molinari, C. I., Costa, V. R., Monteiro, K. O. F. F., & Nunomura, M. (2018). Critical analysis of the performance of women's artistic gymnastics in Brazil in the 2004–2016 Olympic cycles. *Science of Gymnastics Journal*, 10(3), 453–466.

Nunomura, M., & Oliveira, M. S. (2012). Centre of excellence for women artistic gymnastics: The Brazilian coaches' perspective. *Motriz: Revista de Educação Física*, 18(2), 378–392.

Olaru, M. (2016). *Pretul Aurului. Sinceritate Incomoda (The price of gold. Uncomfortable sincerity)*. Bucharest: Editura Vremea Bucureşti.

Petracovschi, S., & Terret, T. (2013). From best to worst? Romania and its nostalgia for Olympic successes. *The International Journal of the History of Sport*, 30(7), 774–788.

Puddle, D., Wheaton, B., & Thorpe, H. (2018). The glocalization of parkour: a New Zealand/Aotearoa case study. *Sport in Society*, 22(10), 1724–1741.

Riordan, J. (1993). Rewriting Soviet sports history. *Journal of Sports History*, 20(3), 247–258.

Riordan, J. (1995). From Communist forum to Capitalist market: East European sport in transition. *European Physical Education Review*, 1(1), 15–26.

Riordan, J. (2003). The Soviet Union and Eastern Europe. In J. Riordan & A. Krüger (Eds.), *European culture in sport: Examining the nations and the regions*. Bristol: Intellect.

Riordan, J. (2007). The impact of communism on sport. *Historical Social Research/Historische Sozialforschung*, 32(1), 110–115.

Robertson, R. (1994). Globalisation or glocalisation? *Journal of International Communication*, 1(1), 33–52.

Robertson, R. (1995). Glocalization: Time-space and homogeneity-heterogeneity. *Global Modernities*, 2, 25–45.

Scholte, J. A. (2008). Defining globalisation. *World Economy*, 31(11), 1471–1502.

Sterchele, D., & Ferrero Camoletto, R. (2017). Governing bodies or managing freedom? Subcultural struggles, national sport systems and the glocalised institutionalisation of parkour. *International Journal of Sport Policy and Politics*, 9(1), 89–105.

Waardenburg, M., & van Bottenburg, M. (2013). Sport policy in the Netherlands. *International Journal of Sport Policy and Politics*, 5(3), 465–475.

Varney, W. (1999). Legitimation and limitations: How the Opie Report on women's gymnastics missed its mark. *Sporting Traditions*, 15(2), 73–90.

Volkwein, K., & Haag, H. R. (1994). Sport in unified Germany: The merging of two different sport systems. *Journal of Sport and Social Issues*, 18(2), 183–193.

Zheng, J., Tan, T.-C., & Bairner, A. (2017). Responding to globalisation: The case of elite artistic gymnastics in China. *International Review for the Sociology of Sport*, 54(5), 536–556.

Part II

The gymnast experience

Jenny's story Part II: An unexpected event

James Pope

What happened was, Frank slapped me, really hard. And it really threw me. I mean, I never thought Frank was violent, but I now think he was, a lot of the coaches were really, when you think about it. Up to then, even after I'd made a mess of some routine, right from the first time he shouted, we'd always make up, and maybe I even enjoyed the comfort of that make up. My God, it sounds a bit weird, doesn't it? Frank would hold me sometimes, like hold my shoulders hard and look at me and tell me what I had to do, after he'd yelled at me, and it would be calm, and I do remember I felt so safe with him. This can get deep. I don't know if I want go there.

That kind of making up, I don't know if that was a good thing. He'd stare right into my eyes, and it wasn't an apology really, more like an admonishment, when you think about it. But I think I was so immersed in his world that I felt he cared about me.

'Jen, come on! Get it right! The regionals are only a month away. There's no point doing half the job, is there?'

His big arms would hold me and it felt like he'd always be there for me, so the shouting wasn't a bad thing at all – it was for my own good. And all the coaches shouted anyway. I wanted to do well, there's no doubt about that. It might have been a kind of love, like I said before, maybe a childish kind of love. I'd been with him since I was eight, and when you think back, I spent more time with him than I did with my own dad. And obviously, I knew I needed him to help me win – he knew how to make me good. He'd been successful in the past, which is why my mum was so pleased he took me on. So you don't throw that opportunity away.

But … the slap. I mean, it was pretty common for coaches to slap gymnasts' legs to get them to position themselves better – more like correcting a bad position, not a punishment, not violent. Or at least that's how we saw it back then, and I don't think anyone complained. So I don't know why this time was different from 'normal'.

I think I was 12 or 13. I'd been getting very good, I knew that. My body was strong, and I was winning things. I'd got to national level, and I could sometimes feel how amazing my body was, that sense of flow, you know, when all your work is rewarded with a perfect exercise. I began to feel maybe a bit superior to some of the other girls who only did a bit of netball or whatever. At secondary school, there were some girls who had started hanging around the playground looking sexy, even at 13, and I could see they looked at me and I knew they wanted to take the mickey, maybe they even wanted to bully me because I really didn't hang out with them at all, and I never got into trouble with teachers. But they didn't bully me because, at school, if you're good at sport, you're liked – teachers like you, boys like you. You had a status. I felt great about myself without having to try. Which is ironic, isn't it? Because I was working so hard at the gym!

Mum talked to me about weight – I knew that some girls in the sport were encouraged to stay young, in their bodies, so they would starve themselves. I knew there were drug supplements to hold off puberty, because girls could perform better if they stayed small. I must admit I never felt like I had to go that far, but we did talk about my weight. I just had to watch what I ate. I might have been lucky – I was naturally small, and I was naturally slim, so I had a good body for artistic gymnastics. The muscles come, you get strong. And I was growing up, getting my shape, you know, although at that stage I wasn't feeling sexy or anything like that. I just felt good about myself. I was confident.

But Frank sometimes could knock me back a bit, as I've said. And I think that's how this incident happened. I'd been on beam, practising flic layouts, and I just couldn't stick. I did it over and over again, and I really was trying, trying, trying, but I wasn't getting it, and I was hurting. Then, as he would sometimes do, he shouted loudly, and instead of being shocked, or crying, or pushing through the pain, this time for some reason I just stopped and turned my back on him. In my head I was yelling, 'I'm not doing that again! It's too much!' I don't know where it came from. Maybe I'd been building it up for a while, but I defied him. Then he went, 'You're useless! Get it right!' And he slapped me across the back of my thighs, like he'd done before. But this time, it felt much harder, and it made me furious. Teenage hormones and adrenaline made me brave and I turned back round and just stood there looking straight at him.

I remember the look on his face, like he was going to really hit me, not just a slap. For a split second I was scared. It was weird. He looked at me for a second or two, and then yelled at the absolute top of his voice, 'Either do the work, or quit!' I felt the gym go quiet around us – everyone had heard, and I could feel all their eyes on me. Then *I* felt terrible and I nearly burst into tears, but something held that back. I was angry and humiliated and nearly in tears, all at the same time. But I still didn't move.

'OK, you're wasting my time. Go home.' And that was all he said. He walked off, as if nothing had happened. And I had lost all my bravado and I said nothing more, and I wanted to disappear into a hole.

What had I done? What had just happened? I remember thinking I must have done something terrible. But on the other hand, he'd just destroyed me in front of everyone, and I didn't want to be with him anymore. I hated him in that moment, I know I did. And yet, I felt ashamed. Was it for my own good, because he cared so much about me? Was it my fault he was so angry? But do you slap and yell at someone you care about? I couldn't process it then.

I see now that the shouting and the slaps were a form of control, for sure – but of course, then I didn't see that at all. I guess I just saw it as an explosion of stress in both of us. I couldn't get the movement right and he was super-motivated for me, and I was disappointed in myself, and we both got angry, and he slapped me harder than usual. I felt a mixture of anger and then sadness, almost as if I'd hurt *him*. That was it – I'd hurt *him*, by making him angry and then by making him blow up.

I sat in the changing room until it was the regular time to leave. Frank didn't come to find me. Mum picked me up from the session, as always, and I did notice that Frank was as friendly to her as ever. But I didn't want to talk to Mum, all the way home. When we got in, my dad must have noticed I was quieter than usual. 'Hello, you – what you been up to?' he said.

I said something like, 'Just been to the gym as always. Duhhh.' You know, stroppy teenager stock attitude.

'I know that! Madam! Just asking …?! You look a bit glum. You OK?'

I might have blushed. I felt my face go hot. Why was I blushing? I must have known something wasn't right. Frank hitting me and chewing me up like that was something different, but I didn't understand it properly then. But I knew enough to know I couldn't tell Dad what had really happened. So I said, 'I fell when I was doing a flic-flac. My leg's really sore and I couldn't finish the session properly.'

Now Mum got involved. 'Really? How did you manage that?' She was smiling, obviously thinking I'd made a hash of the routine. I played along, and I know I was relieved she'd bought my version.

'I don't know! It was going well and suddenly I was face down on the mat. I felt so stupid. Frank just laughed.'

'Well, at least he laughed …!' said Dad, finding it funny too.

'Weren't you concentrating?' Mum said, always the one to bring it back to my performance. 'You can't succeed unless you take this seriously.'

'Of course!' I was angry now. 'Why do you always have to assume I'm not working hard enough? You have no idea how tough this is!' I don't think I was really angry with her, was I? Or perhaps I was – she was, is, a lovely mum but she did also prod me, and I wanted to please her, of course I did. Dad was pretty laid back about it, just happy if I was happy – but Mum wanted me to do well, and she understood what it took to succeed. Even if I'd told her there and then that Frank had properly hit me, she wouldn't have believed it.

And do you know what? I didn't believe it. By the time Mum had become the target of my anger and I'd stomped up to my room in a mood, I'd stopped thinking about Frank, and I was blaming my mum for being so pushy. But no matter how much Mum wanted me to do well, she wasn't to blame for Frank. I just didn't see it, because, in a way, in gymnastics, his behaviour was *so* normal, and I had no idea what would come next.

Chapter 5

Living with stories of gymnastics in higher education

Carly Stewart and Michele Carbinatto

A testimony to gymnastics experience

We begin with a story. A former gymnast, Emily, was invited to respond to the following questions in a sports sociology lecture with Carly: What does gymnastics mean to you? How would you describe what it feels like to those who don't know? What makes it gymnastics and not something else? Emily responded immediately with a broad smile on her face; 'it's nice to be asked, because I find it really difficult to respond to some of the papers [focused on women's artistic gymnastics] that we read as part of the degree, because that's not my experience of it'. The moment caught me, causing me to shift uncomfortably in my seat, to sit forward and listen. I had often drawn attention to gymnastics in sociology of sport teaching and suspect elsewhere others had too (in psychology and health modules perhaps). In doing so, I'd always assumed a critical coalition with gymnasts, and with non-gymnasts something of 'the shock factor' to draw them in and rouse a response. After all, the literature does paint a rather harrowing picture of the culture of gymnastics and its consequences. I felt passionate about the topic despite not being a gymnast myself. The spectacle and horror of gymnastics often made for a 'good' story and certainly for important discussion in the classroom. But perhaps I'd not been engaging gymnasts as embodied listeners on a critical or emotional level as I'd assumed. Perhaps gymnasts carried stories of gymnasts in their bodies in ways I had not understood. From this, we (Carly and Michele) posed a simple research question: How do former gymnasts who are now in sport-related higher education live with their stories of gymnastics?

Gymnastics stories as companions

Frank (2010, p. 1) proposes ways to think about and study stories so that we can 'live better with the stories that surround and circulate through our lives'. To begin, we must view stories as social actors working with people, for people and on people; that they are able to bring people together and pull them apart. Some lives are made good by stories and some lives are endangered by stories. Frank's (2010, p. 42) point is that stories go beyond linguistics and are 'semiotic-material companions' (as if they are living things) in our lives. For Frank (2010) the goal in studying them is to improve the terms of that companionship that we humans have with them.

This said, stories can be good harmonious companions for human beings in that stories take care of bodies and bodies reciprocally enable stories to be. Emily's enthusiastic jolt to answer the question in the opening story indicates some capacity in which her gymnastics story is a good companion and her testimony is to an unrecognised or suppressed body truth as lived (Frank, 2013). She wanted to call out the nature of that companionship! Alternatively, they can be bad companions – ones which may be retained but resented. It is possible that the haunting stories of the USA gymnasts who were sexually abused (see Chapter 6), for example, may be bad companions; albeit ones that they now need, to give them a place in the healing process, but also resent because the story requires them to fit a 'victim' image that others expect as part of the story. Ryan's (2000) exposé of gymnasts (and figure skaters) illuminates how stories offer to be good companions of gymnasts who receive them, the possibility of the Olympic dream for example, yet too often become bad once highlighting the dangers of these stories. Understanding the variety of companion relations that gymnasts can have with gymnastics stories in their lives can help us to understand their long-term effects (Kuhlin, Barker-Ruchti, & Stewart, 2019).

It is important to understand that for Frank (2010) effective stories perform themselves into bodies and for good companionship to occur there must be harmonious assimilation between bodies and stories. To observe this process in gymnastics is to understand that gymnasts seek out experiences that can be told as stories (see Ryan's 2000 account of the Olympic dream) and this in turn shapes normative principles and conduct in the gymnastics world. Much literature reviewed in this book points toward the dedicated commitment of gymnasts to fulfil the obligations of the powerful coach and to respect the rules in a silent work ethic (see Burke, 2001). This commitment is instilled in childhood and sustained throughout gymnastics careers by all of the stories of gymnastics they listen to. Gymnastics stories are then templates for experience that lead them to choices that are unchosen.

Understanding how gymnastics stories continue to be good or bad companions in gymnasts' lives after serious gymnastics careers are over is not well understood, particularly for the non-elite. One possible pathway for gymnasts to follow is sport-related higher education, perhaps with the aim of sustaining sporting selves and identities (see Sparkes et al., 2007; Coakley & Donnelly, 1999). Little is known about how these former gymnasts live with their stories of gymnastics, helping them to see what's possible and what's not in this setting. This chapter aims to explore the stories of five former non-elite gymnasts, all of whom are currently studying sport-related higher education in the UK. More widely, we hope to contribute to an agenda that concerns 'older' gymnast development (defined by Barker-Ruchti et al., 2016 as those over the age of 20 years). We conclude by reflecting upon what we can learn from studying the companionship gymnasts have with their stories including ways to find more liveable relationships with them.

A brief note on approach and methods

This study took a socio-narratological approach (Frank, 2010) in order to elicit and analyse stories and storytelling of five gymnasts who were either now retired and at university or continuing to practise gymnastics at university in the UK. A defining characteristic of narrative research more generally is that it views human beings as storytellers and directs analytical attention to the story as a site for investigation itself (Smith & Sparkes, 2009; Sparkes & Smith, 2014). In this sense stories can be a *resource* and *topic* for those interested in them (Plummer, 2001) and researchers may be concerned with the *whats* and *hows* of storytelling for analytical purposes (Smith & Sparkes, 2009). Turning our attention to the stories as a resource we sought further insights into the lived experiences of gymnasts across a variety of contexts and situations as they are remembered and reassembled through storytelling (Frank, 2010). Thematically, we asked what do narratives of gymnastics disclose about the lived experience of gymnastics? For Frank (2010) lived experiential disclosures originate in the practice of storytelling and therefore whilst our analysis was primarily biographical it was also a work of applied phenomenology orientated to existential meaning. Following Max van Manen (2016) we acknowledge that biographical material in a story *can* be a rich resource for lived experiential material, if examined as such. This said we deliberately turn our attention to experiential dimensions and thematic distinctions to describe and frame some common aspects of lived gymnastics experience (van Manen, 1998; 2016).

However in doing this, we recognise that stories are not simply repositories for memory; instead they are the process of performing memory in action, reassembling lives both collectively and individually (Frank, 2010). Thus we are guided principally by Frank's (2010, p. 71) dialogical narrative analysis which studies 'the mirroring between what is told – the story's content – and what happens as a result of telling that story – its effects'. Described as a method of questioning, Frank poses a set of questions that initiate such analyses. These include the following which are emphasised in our analysis: What does the story make narratable? Who is holding their own in the story? What is the effect of people being caught up in their own stories? What is the force of fear in the story, and what animates desire? How does a story help people to remember who they are?

Table 5.1 Sample of gymnasts

Name (pseudonym)	Discipline	Brief biography
Jo	Artistic	21 years old, an active member of the university gymnastics club, competes in university competitions
Sophie	Acrobatics	21 years old, not a member of the university club but occasionally attends a local circus club
Emily	Artistic	20 years old, no longer participates at university
Ella	Rhythmic	20 years old, an active member of the university gymnastics club, competes and choreographs for the team
Lauren	Acrobatics	19 years old, no longer participates and has only been retired for four months

In total we interviewed five female gymnasts (see Table 5.1) for 2–3 interviews, each lasting for approximately 2–4 hours. We asked, 'tell us about gymnastics in your life'. Further questions and prompts were used to invite rich in-depth responses in semi-structured and unstructured conversational interviews including 'What was it like to be a gymnast before university?' 'Tell us what it felt like to do gymnastics, and tell us how it feels now'. 'What does gymnastics mean to you now and where do you see it in the future?' We were guided by the questions of storytelling practice and thought about the ways gymnastics stories were companions to varied extents.

Findings

'Going upside down!' Stories animated with desire

When asked to tell us about gymnastics, the gymnasts spoke of their gymnastics pasts and immediately of what was pleasurable or fun. Thematically, holding onto gymnastics as a good companion was about achieving moments of gymnastics experience where the body is harmoniously synced with the world. Jo, who still participates in gymnastics at university described:

> When you learn something new and you do it without any support and you just feel 'Oh wow! I just did that!' and … You see, when I won you

did get a buzz, but that didn't make me any happier than if I did a skill really well, for the first time (...) Now I feel ... if I don't do gym for a while I miss going upside down! That sounds really funny, I miss being on my hands and not my feet and I think that's one reason I do it.

Sophie, who chooses not to do gymnastics at university, similarly describes the feelings she gets:

> The most enjoyable thing: Once you accomplish a new skill it is really rewarding, because you tend to try for quite a while before you master it. Then when you finally get it, it's really exciting and you just want to learn more (...) but now I'm a little bit older and I would like to get back into doing it – obviously not as hard core as I did before, but I still love it and I've been doing handstands this morning!

For van Manen (1998, p. 3) these experiential descriptions denote 'liveable relations' with the body, where it is not a detached curiosity but feeling well in an unbroken unity of existence in the world. All gymnasts in our study spoke enthusiastically of the smooth perfected movements that they sought. In addition, pleasure in their stories concerned reassembling moments when they experienced the admiring look of others at school as positive and of intensifying their subjectivity as gymnasts:

> I liked the feel of accomplishing something that was quite scary; people were like 'Wow! That's really cool!' (...) 'I'm a gymnast! Yes, me and my friends were "The Gymnasts!"' (...) I liked it because it was such a big thing at school, being one of the gymnasts was quite a cool thing to be. But I wasn't popular, kind of thing, I was just a gymnast. But that was my label.
>
> (Jo)

> All the kids were just 'Oh, I want to be like Lauren when I'm older! I want to be Lauren's partner!' so I felt good in that way, so I had motivation to be what I was, to constantly keep training and keep performing to these people. And we had shows in our club, so all the parents could come and watch and they were just 'Wow! I want my child to be like you when they're older'. And it was so good. (...)
>
> (Lauren)

Frank (2010) stresses that what stories do are to teach us who we are; they make us knowable. Gymnastics stories call out to gymnasts to act on their gymnastics identity. These moments animate desire, and as such stories are good companions where they reassemble gymnastics bodies and identities individually and collectively in an act of performing memory.

Stories compel because they express in narrative form what begins in bodies (Frank, 2010). Other ways stories were animated with desire related to appreciation of other gymnastics bodies that stirred an affective response (van Manen, 1998). The gymnasts recalled feelings of intense motivation or desire when seeing gymnastics on TV. Sophie states:

> I love watching it on the TV and I feel myself doing it with them, when they're doing certain moves I'm almost like ... you know what it feels like (...) Yes, and whenever I watch it on TV I'm straight on my laptop looking for adult gymnastics classes and straight away it makes me want to get straight back into it.

Similarly Jo describes:

> It makes me want to do it – a lot! I'm like 'Oh!' I really have a drive but then when I go and do it in the gym; I get a bit frustrated because I know I could do that once and now I can't do it anymore. Stuff we do at gym, I could have done that for fun, like straddle levers and up and down, and I could do that all the time, when I could ... And I just can't do it anymore and it's so frustrating, because I know I can!

Fear and desire are the complementary mirror opposites of a single whole in storytelling. Jo's story animates the interplay of fear and desire, not with emotions that precede the stories, but as performed and shaped by the telling. For Jo and others storytelling shifted from remembering and reassembling lived experience of doing gymnastics past to doing gymnastics in the present as decidedly different. The fear gymnasts hold through storytelling is related to gymnastics bodies that are no longer able to do what they once could. Thematically, these experiential descriptions are of moments when their wellness or unity with the world is broken and of discovering, as it were, their own bodies anew (van Manen, 1998). Jo explains:

> When you're trying to do something and you just feel as if you've got ankle weights on and you can't do anything. Yes, it's really strange.

This is important because people remember by telling stories of times past in response to the needs in the present (Frank, 2010). In essence gymnasts reassembled memories of lived experience in order to contemplate gymnastics still being part of their lives, and to different ends. For Sophie, Lauren, and Emily who do not participate in university gymnastics, telling gymnastics stories animated fear of what and who they no longer were:

> Yes, I think I surprised myself with how much I could still do, but yes, there were definitely things I couldn't do that I could when I was

younger, and that's what I wanted to try to learn again. Try to get back to what I used to do. Especially with Artistic, like the apparatus, there were things I hadn't done since I was really young and I thought 'Oh, let's give that a go'. But I felt I couldn't do it without a bit of help (...) I don't know, because I wanted to join the university team when I came here but I just didn't really get on with it. It was not what I ... It's like I said about adult gymnastics, it's so different from what I've always done.

(Sophie)

University gymnastics was an organic entity without a coach that allowed them to be autonomous in their training and take leadership roles. Both Jo and Ella reflected upon how other gymnasts, like Sophie and Lauren, are not always comfortable with the independence required in university gymnastics:

We had a girl who was amazing; she used to be in the Great Britain training squad when she was younger and she left. She was still amazing, 10 times better than any of us, but she left because she felt like she wasn't ... She just couldn't do it anymore. But we were 'Well, none of us can. It's fine!' but she just couldn't cope with it.

(Jo)

Jo explained how gymnastics is about accepting loss, that you can't be what you once were, but to enjoy the challenge and fun of trying to complete the same skills. Like Jo, Ella is also involved in university gymnastics and recalls having switched disciplines from rhythmic to artistic; 'I just do it to have fun now. I've developed from what I had before, from artistic, so I'm just happy, contented'. Ella, who is a rhythmic gymnast, choreographs routines for artistic university competitions and Jo often led training sessions. They developed independence, self-responsibility, and enjoyment (Barker-Ruchti et al., 2016). We might suggest that Jo and Ella are able to accommodate different body-self relationships in stories where desire to do gymnastics weighs as heavily or more heavily that than fear of not being able to do it.

'I'm getting quite upset by it.' Holding their own when stories are trouble

Gymnasts' stories as bad companions, causing trouble, were also apparent where experiences of physical, psychological, and emotional pain carry significant weight and have visible affects in the present. Telling such stories *enact* realities that had previously been silenced, bringing them into being again. The gymnasts can be described as 'holding their own' as they aspire to become successful gymnasts and try to avoid threats to the value of self as being not good or strong enough (Frank, 2010, p. 77). They are 'caught up' in their own stories of gymnastics that require certain actions of them. However, the gymnasts' stories also make narratable the moral existence of a group of people in close proximity caught up in their own stories – the coaches – assembled as characters for evaluation:

> At the time I enjoyed it, until a certain point when it was too much. The conditioning part of it was OK, I liked that, I liked the feeling of the pain. But then being forced by the coaches to do something you don't want to do in that training sense and you just don't want to do it; and they shout at you until you do it. And that's awful. They make you do press-ups if you didn't do it right, or didn't do it at all. How scary is that! (…) I was learning Tsukahara on the vault – it's a half vault with a back somersault off and I wouldn't do the somersault. And they said 'You're going to do it. Every time you don't do it, you're going to do 10 press ups, then 100 press ups and then 1,000 press ups, if you don't do it.' And I didn't do it the first time, and I did 10 press ups. And she said 'You're going to do it this time!' and she shouted at me, and I did it and she said 'It wasn't so hard, was it?' And I was in tears and I was (imitates weeping) 'Oh, I didn't want to do it!'
>
> (Jo)

> They [coaches] seemed really old when I was there, but they must not have been as old as I thought they were! They were quite scary actually. It was only as I got older that I actually started to like them; because I just used to be really scared of them, when you were younger, they were really strict. As I said, they seemed really old to me, and they were really scary. But we did get on well; otherwise I don't think I would have stayed. I used to cry quite a lot, I remember that was quite a big part of it, crying because my coach had slapped me round the head or something! Yes, it was quite funny when you look back at it (…) Yes, if you couldn't do something just being made to do it again and again and again, even though you could be crying and just exhausted, being made to do something. I remember one time on the beam I did a Shushunova jump and I landed in the beam and I scratched all the inside of my thighs and I was just too scared to do it. And my coach just made me stand there until I did it again. (…)
>
> (Sophie)

Thematically, we might infer that gymnasts' bodies are rendered as instruments for performance ends. Coaches seem to sometimes 'forget', in a manner of speaking, that there is a person attached to the body (van Manen, 1998):

> The stretching, the flexibility side is horrible. Absolutely horrible! It's borderline, I know some coaches who've been investigated for cruelty. Not in my club, but some coaches have, because it's such a fine line

between what you can and can't do to a person. The way you get stretched is crazy (...) you get pushed to the point where you cry, because it's that painful, but you have to if you want to be flexible, you just have to push your body.

Is it quite normal, for gymnasts to cry?

Yes, it is very normal. All gymnasts go through the stage of 'you have to get flexible to be a good gymnast'. So you do get stretched.

(Lauren)

One gymnast, Emily, breaks down and starts to cry as she talks to us about this: 'I'm getting quite upset by it, not living up to people's expectations, the coaches, they make you feel so little about yourself.' She explains that what caused her to cry was remembering a specific moment, 'being told you are clearly not bothering when you feel you are trying hard, it's like a stab to the heart'. However, Emily's emotional response reminds us that we are never totally objectified, that we cannot separate our bodies from our sense of self. In this moment Emily's gymnastics story is a bad companion reassembled as a painful experience in which her meaningfully integrated body and self-intentions were misunderstood.

There are other occasions where gymnastics stories cause trouble. These relate to body appreciation. Van Manen (1998, p. 11) recognises that 'many people seem to live in peace with the shape and nature of some parts of their body and in a certain discord with other parts'. Gymnasts felt distaste towards their muscular shoulders in sleeveless dresses or tops. They were also aware of their relatively short height in socialising contexts. Their stories are animated with fears regarding the meanings of their body shapes to others. Sophie illuminates yet again the interplay of desire and fear in her story as she contemplates returning to gymnastics:

No, I don't want ... I already feel I'm too big, so I just want to ... I don't know, I'm scared that it will just come back again and I'll be the massive muscly person! But, no, it is something, a good way to get the body that I want, but I'd have to stop at a certain level. I don't want to get too muscly. I'm very aware of my arms and my shoulders, and I think being short as well, you can't – it's quite hard being short, you can't carry it off as well (...) the other thing is it makes me look really young. A lot of people think I'm about 16 and I think that's to do with my height as well, and I think that's another reason that I hate being short; because a lot of people – no one believes me when I tell them. I get ID'd everywhere.

Thematically, arms, shoulders, and height were consistently brought to the fore in gymnasts' stories. These have not been alluded to in the gymnastics literature thus far, and deserve further attention framed by stories that teach us gendered ways of knowing ourselves.

Finally, to return to the point that stories are a process of memory in action, we return to the overarching aim. Given the pleasures and the pains we had listened to, how did gymnasts make sense of their gymnastics stories in their lives now? We asked, given the choice, would they do it again? Sophie's response illustrates the process of sense-making that all gymnasts performed answering this question, highlighting a lack of narrative resources available to make sense of it. Sophie reassembled her memories of the past in the needs of the present:

> I don't really know why I carried on going. I did enjoy it, obviously, there were good parts and bad parts and obviously when we started winning things and doing really well, that gives you satisfaction, you want to keep going. You wouldn't just quit. I think you work so hard towards something that you want to see it through to the end and there's always something, the next competition to prepare for and then ... Obviously the friends that I made when I was there, we were all really close friends, so that was nice. I don't think you can actually understand it unless you've been there. Because I don't really ... when I think back now, I don't know how I put up with all that, but I think when you're younger you just accept it as 'that's what it is'. I really don't know. I can't actually wrap my head around why.

Reflections on studying stories in gymnastics

In this chapter we presented a dialogical narrative analysis that asked questions of the work that gymnastics stories do in the lives of five former non-elite gymnasts currently studying higher education in the UK. In doing so we contribute to the gymnastics literature by bringing a socio-narratological approach to understanding the lives of gymnasts' as storied and specifically 'older gymnasts' whose voices are relatively neglected in research (Barker-Ruchti et al., 2016). Here we reflect upon what we can learn from studying gymnasts' stories in this way, and of finding ways to assist gymnasts and others to live well with their stories.

First we point to the importance of telling these stories to give gymnasts a voice to make them narratable in a context where gymnasts' stories have been typically characterised by silences or secrecy. Making gymnasts' lives narratable through research may be seen as an enactment of resistance that makes them claimsworthy or put another way gives them a sense of who they are (the same might be said of similar other forms of stories in this book) (Frank, 2010). Emily's testimony that opened the chapter is illustrative of this process and all gymnasts' expressed appreciation at the chance to talk about their experiences in depth for the first time. Importantly our study has pointed towards the ways in which stories are good companions in the lives of gymnasts; something we don't often hear about. All five gymnasts exercised self-regard and value in their stories, shedding some light on which ones are companions that they need and want in present moments of their lives and those which they don't. We found that good moment's animated desire to continue with gymnastics through recollections of liveable experiential relationships with the body (van Manen, 1998; Carbinatto et al., 2017). Supporting Barker-Ruchti and colleagues (2016), having fun and executing skills effortlessly is the centre-piece of maintaining a liveable relationship with gymnastics. However we found that their stories animated a co-existing fear of not being able to restore a former gymnastic body-self, particularly where body experience and situated experience were not harmonious. In effect stories expressed feelings of being 'out of step' with the body. While van Manen (1998) suggests that it is unlikely that anyone will ever achieve consistent and lasting wholeness of body and self, we should be reflectively engaged in questioning how to live well with the body in different contexts. For Frank (2010) this is about living well with stories.

Frank proposes that living well with stories is to first recognise that stories are out of control; they take on lives of their own. It would be difficult for a caring gymnastics coach, or a parent, or anyone concerned about gymnastics to read gymnasts' emotional responses and not take pause. However, Frank cautions that listeners can find themselves caught up in a one-sided story that excludes consideration of other perspectives. This is important where the counter to gymnasts' holding their own becomes the threat against which coaches must hold their own. To this end stories are too effective at demonising rather than opening up dialogue. We urge readers, gymnasts and coaches in particular, to think *with* and *about* stories. This said, keeping with Frank's suggestions for living well with stories, we need *more* stories of gymnastics and in particular we need *other* stories from coaches in order for better dialogue between the two. We also need *different* gymnastics stories which imagine entirely altered conditions based on a different set of principles (e.g. of a different model of coaching success). The stories of Jo and Ella, for example, go some way to answering this need in creating new stories of the older gymnast at university. Old gymnastics stories take their place in the past, resonating still but no longer with power to set parameters for the future. Universities can provide the setting and place in which new stories of gymnastics are told and retold. The ethical problem with gymnastics stories, as literature would suggest, is that high stakes apocalyptic stories (destructive ones) have been reframed to be everyday ones in the world of gymnastics (Frank, 2010).

This said further research on the grounds of narrative ethics is needed to ensure that all stories are told and everybody hears everybody else's stories. We need to ask, how are coaches holding their own? And, can they acknowledge what's at stake? From a socio-narratological perspective narrative researchers should be as 'narrative bees' (A. W. Frank, personal communication, September 17, 2014); picking up stories of gymnasts 'here' and taking them to coaches 'there', and so forth, to connect stories of gymnastics that are otherwise isolated. Stories which attract other stories, Frank (2010) suggests, leverage change faster.

References

Barker-Ruchti, N., Kerr, R., Schubring, A., Cervin, G., & Nunomura, M. (2016). 'Gymnasts are like wine, they get better with age': Becoming and developing adult women's artistic gymnasts. *Quest*, 69(3), 348–365.
Burke, M. (2001). Obeying until it hurts: coach-athlete relationships. *Journal of the Philosophy of Sport*, 28(2), 227–240.
Carbinatto, M. V., Chaves, A., Moreira, T., & Nunomura, M. (2017). Pedagogia do esporte e motivação: discussão à luz da opinião de ginastas. *Revista Brasileira de Educação Física e Esporte*, 31(2), 433–446.
Coakley, J., & Donnelly, P. (Eds). (1999). *Inside sports*. New York, NY: Routledge.
Frank, A. W. (2010). *Letting stories breathe: A socio-narratology*. Chicago, IL: University of Chicago Press.
Frank, A. W. (2013). *The wounded storyteller: Body, illness and ethics*. Chicago, IL: University of Chicago Press.
Kuhlin, F., Barker-Ruchti, N., & Stewart, C. (2019). Long-term impact of the coach-athlete relationship on development, health, and wellbeing: Stories from a figure skater. *Sports Coaching Review*. doi:10.1080/21640629.2019.1620016.
Plummer, K. (2001). *Documents of life 2*. London, England: Sage.
Ryan, J. (2000). *Little girls in pretty boxes: The making and breaking of elite gymnasts and figure skaters* (2nd edn). New York: Warner.
Smith, B., & Sparkes, A. C. (2009). Narrative analysis and sport and exercise psychology: Understanding lives in diverse ways. *Psychology of Sport and Exercise*, 10, 279–288.
Sparkes, A. C., & Smith, B. (2014). *Qualitative research methods in sport, exercise and health*. Oxon, England: Routledge.
Sparkes, A. C., Partington, E., & Brown, D. H. K. (2007). Bodies as bearers of value: the transmission of jock culture via the 'Twelve Commandments'. *Sport, Education and Society*, 12(3), 295–316.
van Manen, M. (1998). Modalities of body experience in health and illness. *Qualitative Health Research: An International Interdisciplinary Journal*, 8(1), 7–24.
van Manen, M. (2016). *Researching lived experience* (2nd edn). London, England: Routledge.

Chapter 6

Media narratives of gymnasts' abusive experiences
Keep smiling and point your toes

Ashley Stirling, Alexia Tam, Aalaya Milne and Gretchen Kerr

Introduction

In her opening event on the uneven bars at the 1976 Olympic Games, Nadia Comaneci awed the judges and was the first gymnast in Olympic history to receive a perfect score of 10. By the end of the Games, Nadia accrued seven perfect scores, four on uneven bars and three on balance beam, symbolising and inspiring a pursuit of gymnastic perfection (Bruce, 2007). Since the era of Nadia Comaneci and her perfect 10, Olympic all-around individual champions such as Mary Lou Retton (United States), Lilia Podkopayeva (Ukraine), Simona Amanar (Romania), Svetlana Boginskaya (Soviet Union), and Simone Biles (United States) continue to be celebrated for their athleticism, artistry, focus, poise, and accomplishments. Following their example, young gymnasts all over the world are pushing themselves to reach their full potential in the pursuit of the Olympic dream (Howells, 2017; Winter, 2019). But, while the outward performances of successful gymnasts are adored by many, their experiences behind the scenes are far from the perfect image of the silent smiling gymnast we see standing on the podium.

Soon after Nadia's famous performance at the 1976 Olympics, at the height of her fame and at the young age of 15 years, she made a suicide attempt. While hospitalised, she reportedly claimed that she was 'glad because I didn't have to go to the gym' (Salon, 2019). In addition to pressures to fend off puberty and maintain a pre-pubescent body, Nadia faced harsh psychological and physical treatment by her coaches, and was exploited by the state (Ryan, 1995). Behind the stoic picture of perfection presented by Nadia while performing was another far-from-perfect story.

Twenty years after Nadia became known to the world, Joan Ryan, a sports columnist for the *San Francisco Chronicle*, published the book *Little Girls in Pretty Boxes*, a journalistic account of the physical and psychological problems behind the making of elite gymnasts and figure skaters. This text presents a collection of disturbing narratives gleaned from almost one hundred interviews of female gymnasts and figure skaters. These young, elite, female athletes told stories of pressures by coaches, judges, and administrators to maintain the ideal pre-pubescent body shape, pressures they responded to with food deprivation and other disordered eating patterns. Stories also reflect a requirement to be obedient and compliant to the coaches' instructions and demands, even when these demands reflected psychologically or physically abusive coaching behaviours. These female gymnasts became accustomed to berating, derogatory, humiliating, and degrading comments and threats from coaches. To be 'successful', these athletes learned to stay silent – tolerate the abuse, and not complain when in pain from injury or starvation. In the most extreme cases, the pressures and demands placed upon these young athletes resulted in catastrophic injury and deaths as in the cases of Christy Henrich who died from anorexia nervosa and Julissa D'Anne who was left paralysed from a vaulting accident and subsequently died. As Ryan (1995, p. 14) stated:

> The bottom line is clear: There have been enough suicide attempts, enough eating disorders, enough broken bodies, enough regretful parents and enough bitter young women to warrant a serious re-evaluation of what is done to produce Olympic champions. Those who work in these sports know the tragedies all too well. If the federations and coaches truly care about the athletes and not simply about the fame and prestige that comes from trotting tough little champions up to the medal stand, they know it is past time to lay the problems on the table, examine them and work out a way to keep their sports from damaging so many young lives.

Shortly after this book was released, Dominique Moceanu, who at the age of 14 was the youngest member of the gold-medal-winning US gymnastics team at the 1996 Olympics, received widespread media attention when she legally emancipated herself from her then father-coach at the age of 17, whom she described as violent and manipulative (Shipley, 1998). A decade later, she made the following public accusation of her US Olympic team coaches Béla Károlyi and Márta Károlyi of emotional and physical abuse:

> It was verbal and emotional abuses running rampant. The adults around the sport should have spoken up more when they saw this toxic culture … Calling my father, to enforce physical punishment on me, was the scariest thing of it all. I was terrified every time I went to the gym – my coaches would threaten me, that if I didn't perform well enough, to their liking, they would call my father …
>
> (Garsd, 2018)

The stories revealed in Ryan's book and the athletes' testimonies of the late 1990s expose several forms of child abuse and exploitation. Twenty years later, with the passage of time, advancements in child protection, and the international spread of the #MeToo movement, one would expect that gymnasts' stories today would be different from those presented in Ryan's book. The purpose of this chapter is to address more recent stories of female artistic gymnasts' experiences in the sport.

Methodology

This chapter presents a thematic analysis of recent gymnast narratives from media content (e.g., news articles, public testimonies, videos) focusing on the voices of gymnasts and the discourse of sexual and psychological harm experienced from persons in positions of authority and trust. Thematic analysis allows us to identify patterns in the gymnast narratives, which provides us with a rich understanding of their experience, emotion, and the meaning that the gymnasts have attached to relationships and events (Bochner, 2014; Smith, 2016). Thematic analysis is a method designed for identifying patterns and interpreting the importance of those patterns (Braun, Clarke, & Weate, 2016). Through this methodological lens, the gymnasts' stories are not merely interpreted as a way of telling someone (or oneself) about one's life, but rather they are the means by which identities and individual realities are socially constructed and fashioned (Rosenweld & Ochberg, 1992).

The six-step process for thematic analysis (Braun & Clarke, 2006) was employed to review stories from various media sources, and main themes were categorised focusing on core overarching patterns. The stories shared within each theme were then collectively analysed by focusing on common experiences expressed across gymnasts and interpreted in light of previous research (Lieblich, Tuval-Mashiach, & Zilber, 1998; Sparkes & Smith, 2014). Stories were collected from various online sources, including articles from various news outlets and public access impact statements from the gymnasts involved in the Larry Nassar case. Sources included in this analysis must have included a direct statement from a gymnast. Further, with the current focus on sexual violence in North America, particularly gymnastics, the media included in this analysis is specific to the USA and Canada.

An analysis of the stories shared through various media sources resulted in themes we have labelled: tumbling in silence, the façade, invisible scars, and the journey towards healing. Each theme will be addressed in turn.

Tumbling in silence

One of the most striking themes emerging from the analysis was the suffering the female artistic gymnasts experience in silence. Breaking the silence on years of sexual abuse, an American former gymnast whose coach was found guilty of rape of a child and indecent assault and battery on a person over 14, has shared her story to ESPN News. The gymnast begins with:

> It had been three years since we started having sex when the man who would later be convicted of raping me took me to an abortion clinic. He had scheduled the appointment for after my 18th birthday so that I wouldn't need a parent to sign their permission for the procedure ... I had my follow-up appointment scheduled for a week later, and during recovery you're not supposed to have sex. But the night before I was supposed to go, he forced me to have sex with him because he 'just couldn't wait that long'.

She continued to say:

> For two or three weeks in July, he and two other coaches would run a gymnastics camp. It was usually held on a college campus, and we'd train during the day, stay in dorm rooms at night and do some normal summer camp things when we weren't in the gym, such as campfires and talent shows. But it was far from a wholesome camp experience, at least for me. Once you became a junior counselor around age 14, you were a part of the staff, and although you still trained during the day, you were allowed to hang out with the coaches at night, drinking and playing games that included things like strip poker and group showers. And that sexual environment often carried over to the daytime workouts. Once, I finished a tumbling pass at camp and was walking past the coach when he turned to another coach and said, in front of me, 'It's taking all of my willpower not to go after that one'. I was 14 years old, walking past him in a leotard ... This gymnastics camp was billed by our coaches as something special – you're part of it, and it's a family. Whatever happens here stays here. And if people didn't subscribe to this and stopped coming to the camp, they would be shunned. God, you didn't want to be outside the circle ... We were trained to say that nothing bothered us and not show any sign of fear or pain. It all clouded my ability to see that what was happening with this coach was wrong.
>
> (Anonymous, 2016)

Another recent example of this theme of suffering in silence is illustrated through the stories of female artistic gymnasts who were repeatedly sexually abused by Dr Larry Nassar, former USA Gymnastics and Michigan State University doctor. When one of these gymnasts, Mattie Larson, came forward and shared her story, she described the abuse occurring over years, beginning at the age of 14. She also maintained silence about her abuse:

> All I wanted to do as a kid was go to the Olympics. I was at the height of my career at 19 and the Olympics were just one year away, and I just couldn't take any more of the abuse. I was broken. Larry, my coaches, and USA Gymnastics turned the sport I fell in love with as a kid into

my personal living hell ... The first time I distinctly remember Larry abusing me was at my first U.S. national championships in Minnesota. I was 14 and ended up not being able to compete because of an extremely painful hip injury ... My injury was very close to my pelvic bone so when Larry put his fingers in my vagina for the first time, I innocently thought it was some sort of internal treatment for that specific injury. Almost each and every time I received treatment from Larry from that moment on he would molest me ... no matter what Larry was supposed to be treating on me over the years, usually my ankles or my knees, his fingers always seemed to find their way inside of me ... People have asked me why I didn't tell anyone back then. There are many reasons. At the time it hadn't quite registered to me that I was being molested ...

Here's this man who was supposed to be the most renowned doctor in the U.S. gymnastics community, was also charismatic, and one of the only nice adults I had in my life at the time. He would even give us candy or junk food, which is completely forbidden. I just couldn't comprehend that someone like him could do something so awful. On top of that, who was I going to tell? Certainly not my coaches who I was afraid of. I also didn't tell my fellow teammates ... In the midst of all these adults who I was scared of, Larry, you were the only one I trusted. In the end, you turned out to be the scariest monster of all.

(Larson, 2018)

A gymnast may interact with many individuals in an authoritative position on a regular basis, including coaches, parents, and physicians. When young athletes are dependent on persons in positions of power in sport and build close and trusting relationships with these authority figures, these athletes are placed in a position of vulnerability to unwanted and/or coerced sexual activity, otherwise described as athlete sexual abuse (Brackenridge, Bishopp, Moussalli, & Tapp, 2008). A significant body of research exists in sport and non-sport literature on risk factors to sexual abuse including: perpetrator characteristics such as being male, older than the victim, and with ascribed authority; victim characteristics such as being female, trust in and commitment to the perpetrator; and characteristics of the environment including access to young people, and access to private settings (Brackenridge, 1997). Many of these risk factors are salient within the sport of women's artistic gymnastics and were mentioned in the gymnasts' narratives of their abuses. For example, in both narratives the abuser was an older male with well-recognised credentials and a strong reputation, he gained the trust of the gymnasts, and had easy access to the gymnasts with meetings occurring in private locations.

Struggling to comprehend how, at the time, the gymnasts did not recognise or label the interactions as sexual abuse, the gymnasts seem to go out of their way to justify why they had so much trust in the authority figure and how they previously did not want to see his actions for what they were. This phenomena by which a predator develops trust and secures secrecy and then violates trust is referred to as the 'grooming process' (Finkelhor, 1984). Drawing on the work of Leberg (1997), Brackenridge and Fasting (2005) described different types of grooming that occur in sport. Exemplified in the gymnasts' narratives, physical grooming was demonstrated when inappropriate touching was presented as friendly interactions or legitimate medical treatment (as discussed in later chapters); psychological grooming occurred as a result of the coach/physician establishing trust and rapport by providing comfort and candy to the gymnasts; and socially, the abusers' reputation within the sport and medical community provided him with unquestioned power within USA Gymnastics. Specific examinations of the grooming process of sexual exploitation in sport have suggested four stages: 1) Targeting a potential victim, 2) Building trust and friendship, 3) Developing isolation, control, and loyalty, and 4) Initiation of sexual abuse and securing secrecy (Cense & Brackenridge, 2001). Likewise, Toftegaard Neilson (2001) proposed a grooming process model for sexual abuse in sport, including three interrelated phases: confidence, seduction, and abuse. Both grooming and the medicalisation and science of high performance sport are addressed further in later chapters of this book.

The narratives presented epitomise the grooming process. In the first case, the coach gained the trust of the gymnast by allowing her to hang out with the coaches at night and by including her in drinking games. This occurred at a special elite and isolated training camp where the gymnasts felt privileged to have the opportunity to be trained by the reputable coach and understood that they were not to communicate any of the camp activities with others. Similarly, Nassar gained the trust of the gymnasts and developed rapport by showing them kindness, providing consolation when the gymnasts were upset about the psychological and physical abuse they suffered in training, and offering them food that was otherwise restricted by coaches. It is no wonder that the gymnasts had difficulty labelling his 'treatments' as abusive when he had previously demonstrated care and kindness. Moreover, even when some of the gymnasts told others, including other adults, about their concerns regarding Nassar's treatments, the responses were to diminish the gymnasts' concerns citing the exemplary reputation of Nassar. This supports the previous work of Kirby, Greaves, and Hankivsky (2002) who coined the term 'dome of silence' to refer to the cultural influences that may prevent female athletes from speaking about their experiences of sexual abuse in sport.

In the gymnasts' narratives, there seems to be a passionate intentionality in sharing their stories so that other gymnasts will not stay silent and have to endure the same experiences. As stated by Grace French (2018), 'It has taken time to find my voice, but I speak now for that little girl who sat terrified in his office, afraid to speak up, because maybe it really was "treatment"'.

The façade

Female artistic gymnasts are commonly portrayed as smiling, focused, physically and mentally strong, poised, and competent young people. But, behind this portrayal, gymnasts often experience unhappiness, a loss of autonomy, a fragile sense of self, and a vulnerable body image. The notion of a façade is exemplified with the story below.

> What people don't realize is the sheer muscle it takes in order to face the world with a smile on. To stay focused with the task at hand on any given day and to try and hold on to even a shred of the former me that my friends and family know and love. Those people see the fleeting good moments from what an otherwise ugly reality that has been this past year of my life. They don't see the frustrating the exhaustion, the sadness, the emotional and physical trauma that haunts my every day and every move.
> (Riethman, 2018)

It has been speculated that the unhappiness and fragile sense of self may arise from ongoing psychologically abusive behaviours such as demeaning and belittling criticisms, including negative comments about the body (Kavanagh, Brown, & Jones, 2017; Pinheiro, Pimenta, Resende, & Malcolm, 2014; Yabe et al., 2018).

Michelle Kaeser, a provincial level Canadian artistic gymnast, spoke out about the verbal abuse she faced from her coach when she failed to devote full energy to her performance:

> There's no arguing; you just do what the coaches tell you. That's how it works. The sport demands a blind obedience and obtains it because the athletes are too young and indoctrinated to challenge authority. My floor music started, a ridiculous upbeat samba number that I hated. It was [the coach's] choice, of course. 'It's the perfect fit for your personality,' she decided, although I was deep into grunge by then, spending my off-time worshipping Kurt Cobain's ghost. I moved through the routine, arrived at the cat leap and, to spite her for her spite, just half-assed it. No height, knees low, sloppy arms. 'STOP!' she screamed. 'Stop the music.' The gym went quiet. 'What the hell was that?' she asked, her face in this memory like a growling beast's. Suddenly, the pockets of spit that were forever hovering at the corners of her mouth hung down her face like long lengths of drool, stalactites of saliva. Then came the yelling. Everyone in the gym turned to watch, to see whose turn it was to bear the brunt of her rage. You get screamed at over and over and over as a gymnast, but it never stops being humiliating. So I was crying – I was always crying, everyone was always crying.
> (Kaeser, 2018)

Jamie Dantzscher, member of the bronze-medal-winning American artistic gymnastic team at the 2000 Olympics in Sydney, described her coach's engagement in harmful practices that encouraged disordered eating behaviours as follows:

> My coaches weighed me every day, called me fat, and told me I needed to lose weight. At fifteen years old, I started making myself throw up after meals. When I told someone at USA Gymnastics that I was starving myself and throwing up meals, their only response was, 'I don't care how you do it, just get the weight off'. When I started my period at sixteen years old, my coach said it was because I had too much body fat and ordered me to lose weight so I wouldn't menstruate anymore.
> (Dantzscher, 2018)

In 2019 Katelyn Ohashi, former artistic gymnast who competed for the University of California, came forward to speak about her troubles with body image. 'As gymnasts, our bodies are constantly being seen in these minimal clothing leotards. I felt so uncomfortable looking in the mirror. I felt uncomfortable walking back into the gym, like there were eyes just targeted at me,' she said. 'I hated taking pictures. I hated everything about myself.' Ohashi said that the comments from coaches or jokes she made with friends about skipping meals to lose weight wore away at her mental health. 'You start normalizing things because that's what you know and you grow up surrounded by people that are going through the same thing as you, so it becomes what you expect almost,' she said. 'But when you look back on it, I do think it's a form of abuse. It was common, especially in the elite world' (Sanderson, 2019).

Speaking out against British Gymnastics about the emotional and psychological abuse witnessed at the hands of a coach, a parent claimed:

> Comments were made to parents [by the coach] such as 'how do you let your kid get that fucking fat?', 'why does she even bother coming?' … One of the worst instances I have witnessed, was during stretching at the beginning of a session. A gymnast was lying in a box split and her splits were particularly high [her hips were at least a foot from the ground]. Without warning [the coach] forcibly pushed her hips down and she hit the floor in a box split, [the coach] then sat on top of the gymnast, who was clearly in tremendous amounts of pain, and held her hips to the ground for a timed minute. At the end of the stretch [the coach] got off and walked away while the gymnast hid her tears.
> (Kelner, 2017)

Supporting Pinheiro and colleagues' (2012) finding that all the gymnasts they interviewed had competed at least once while in pain or injured, Rebecca

Seal, a former gymnast who became a journalist, describes some of her training-induced injuries and the instructions she received from her coach to use laughter as a façade for the pain:

> During my very short gymnastics career, I fell headfirst onto and then off innumerable vaults. I missed my grip on the asymmetric bars. I cut my palms when I was nine, again on the bars, and one of my coaches packed the blisters with chalk and covered them with surgical tape before lifting me back up to the bar. I slipped catastrophically on the beam – one leg on either side, not pretty. I once back-flipped on to my head, hurt my wrists by repeatedly turning them inwards when back-flipping, twisted my ankle, hurt my knees, hips and back, and pulled countless muscles. One of my coaches, a wonderful man, used to say 'laugh when it hurts'. Needless to say, we all laughed a lot.
>
> (Seal, 2005)

Also consistent with the narratives of the gymnasts, it has been reported in previous research that emotional abuse occurs commonly in sport and often in public spaces with other coaches, parents, and athletes present (Yabe et al., 2018). In a study by Stirling and Kerr (2014), including former female gymnasts, it was reported that athletes often perceived emotionally abusive coaching practices to be a necessary component of the training process. Furthermore, Pinheiro and colleagues (2012) suggest that athletes accepted various forms of abuse as normal in sport. They highlight that from an early age gymnasts are immersed in a culture that normalises risk, pain, injury, and abuse. Gymnasts have reported that parents, other athletes, and sport administrators have witnessed the abusive behaviours, yet, rarely intervened. This is consistent with the tone and messaging of the narratives reviewed – all in some way highlighting a common discourse of psychological harm.

Within the gymnasts' narratives, reflections on coach pressures, critical comments, body image, and disordered eating behaviours are so intertwined, highlighting the strong interrelation between the coaches' weight-related comments and the disordered eating behaviours of artistic gymnasts (Pinheiro et al., 2012). The emphasis placed on weight and aesthetic appearance of a female gymnast is linked with a higher risk for eating disorders (Bloodworth, McNamee, & Tan, 2017; Stewart, Schiavon, & Bellotto, 2017; Sundgot-Borgen & Torstveit, 2010) and has caused eating disorders to occur 6 to 10 times more often in female athletes as opposed to male athletes (Schaal et al., 2011). Eating disorders, like other forms of psychological harm in sport, are seen as 'part of the game' and are often overlooked, however, these result in physical and psychological injuries, both in the short and long term (Fields, Collins, & Comstock, 2007).

Bloodworth et al. (2017) found that among female gymnasts, food monitoring was treated as a discipline used to attain success in the sport.

Gymnasts also reported having the ability to control the regimented dietary customs, which is theorised as being an expression of autonomy (Bloodworth et al., 2017), one of the few areas of their sport experiences in which autonomy can be expressed (Warriner & Lavallee, 2008).

Smits, Jacobs, and Knoppers (2017) reported that at the elite level, decisions were made for the female gymnasts. This loss of autonomy made it particularly difficult to file a complaint about a case of harm. Learning to defer decision-making to their coaches and keep their opinions to themselves was beneficial for keeping coaches happy and when coaches are happy, there is less likelihood of abuse. Finally, gymnasts also felt as though they needed to make a sacrifice in order to succeed, and part of this sacrifice was to accept the abusive behaviours.

Invisible scars

Although the gymnasts may have retired from competing in the sport of artistic gymnastics, unfortunately the effects of their harmful experiences are not easily left behind. Gymnasts' narratives highlight the long-lasting impact of their experiences of sexual and psychological harm. Jamie Dantzscher described the lasting influence of the harm she experienced during her time as a gymnast:

> In college, I began therapy for my eating disorders and the overwhelming abuse I suffered from my elite career. I felt lost for most of my twenties, engaged in a pattern of self-destructive behaviors. My threshold for pain and abuse had been built up so high that I would stay in relationships with men who abused me physically and emotionally … I watched my friends and family members settle into their careers and get married and start families, and I couldn't figure out why I couldn't get my life together. I became so severely depressed that I wanted to take my own life. Thanks to good friends and family, I was able to come out of my depression and discover the determination to get my life on track and never fall back into the same self-destructive patterns. Even now, I still feel strangely disconnected from what happened to me. I can only comprehend the heinousness of what Larry did to me through other survivors' stories. But I finally understand that I subconsciously registered his abuse, along with the emotional abuse of my coaches, because it seeped into other areas of my life and echoed through my relationships, self-destructive behavior, anxiety, and depression.
>
> (Dantzscher, 2018)

Emily Meinke talked about the lasting impact of her experiences of sexual abuse at the hands of team physician Larry Nassar:

So how did these experiences affect my life? Following the abuse by Larry I went through a string of abusive relationships, men taking advantage of me and abusing me in every way possible, sexually, physically, and emotionally. It wasn't until I reached my 30s that I was able to stand up for myself, realizing the pattern of abuse was destroying my life. I battle anorexia and bulimia as I struggle with body image and self confidence always. Intimacy continues to be a challenge in my marriage. For years I felt so incredibly alone and confused.

(Meinke, 2018)

Sara Tank Ornelas, who trained under Béla Károlyi, attributed her ongoing, post-retirement injuries and body-image issues to her coaches' emotionally abusive training. She speculated that her struggles with 'horrible arthritis' and low self-esteem were due to the nature of her training environment: 'I think it's a habit from being called fat and told I had a big butt' (Weiss & Mohr, 2018).

The long-term effects of sexual and psychological harm experienced as an artistic gymnast are consistent across the gymnasts' stories as well as with the negative effects reported in previous research. Some of the long-term outcomes of sexual abuse include post-traumatic stress disorder, developmental effects, strained relationships including marital and parental relations, eating disorders, and low self-esteem (Wolfe, 2007). Furthermore, athletes may drop out of sport and suffer from mental illnesses such as anxiety, depression, or suicide due to experiences of sexual abuse and harassment in relations with authority figures in sport (Fasting, Brackenridge, & Walseth, 2007). Kavanagh and colleagues (2017) described the coping process to experiences of psychological violence in sport as including coping in the moment, coping over time, and post-experience coping. When coping in the moment, athletes try to avoid impacting their performance and suppress any reaction they might have. Avoidance, support seeking, and dropping out of sport are common coping mechanisms over time for athletes who have experienced emotional abuse. Once athletes have had time to process their abusive experience, athletes make meaning of the incidents.

The importance of their stories

Although sharing stories as victims of sexual and psychological harm, the gymnasts' narratives present a clear and consistent discourse of perseverance and a recognition of the importance of sharing their stories so that future gymnasts will not have the same experiences. Jordyn Weiber, former American artistic gymnast, 2012 gold-medal Olympic team member and current gymnastics coach, made the following statement:

> Even though I am a victim I do not and will not live my life as one. I am an Olympian. Despite being abused, I worked so hard and managed to

achieve my goal. But I want everyone, especially the media, to know that despite my athletic achievements, I am one of the over 140 women and survivors whose story is important. Our pain is all the same, and our stories are all important.

(Wieber, 2018)

Natalie Woodland, a former member of the US National Gymnastics Team, stated, 'I may seem like a lamb on the outside but I'm a lion on the inside … I'm finally realizing I'm not alone and my story is important, and I have a right to be heard' (Woodland, 2018). Similarly, Jamie Dantzscher, a 2000 Olympian, looked at Nassar as she said: 'Your days of manipulation are over … We have a voice. We have the power now.' Jamie further speaks about her desires to protect young gymnasts from the experiences she had endured herself:

After graduating from UCLA with a degree in psychology, I coached gymnastics at various summer camps and gyms. I enjoyed being a positive coach and wanted to inspire young gymnasts no matter what level they were going to achieve. I was determined to never be a coach who took their love for gymnastics away from them. I wanted them to never experience the twisted, harmful world I grew up in.

(Dantzscher, 2018)

Aly Raisman, also a victim of Larry Nassar, speaks about regaining power in her impact statement:

Imagine feeling like you have no power and no voice. Well, you know what, Larry, I have both power and voice, and I am only beginning to just use them […] The survivors are here, standing tall, and we are not going anywhere.

(Raisman, 2018)

Gwen Anderson, a former gymnast, also speaks about moving forward after her abuse:

We are going to move forward, we are going to live our best lives, because we are fighters and we are strong. We overcome impossible odds, because that's what we were trained to do, because that's what we know how to do – because we are gymnasts.

(Anderson, 2018)

In reading the narratives, the gymnasts present a sense of purpose in their stories, inspiring a call for change within the sport of gymnastics. Notably, both the gymnasts' expression of these narratives as well as the associated presentation and interpretation is occurring during a period of heighted societal focus on the #MeToo movement and breaking the silence on women's experiences of violence in a range of domains (Kaplan, 2018; Kaufman, 2018), including sport. Given the feelings of isolation expressed in response to their experiences of abuse, this discourse of unison and solidarity in many ways reflects the gymnasts taking control of an experience that was previously outside their control. Their stories may be interpreted as active attempts to re-appraise their experiences of harm and develop new stories of strength and autonomy. It was interesting to see the gymnasts acknowledge how over time their understanding of their experiences of sexual and psychological harm were evolving in light of hearing the stories shared by others. 'I can only comprehend the heinousness of what Larry did to me through other survivors' stories.' Through their narratives it is also clear how their emotional responses to their own experiences have also evolved from disgust and fear to a more mature articulation of anger. Fasting and colleagues (2017) reported common behavioural responses to abuse including passivity, avoidance, direct confrontation and challenging the perpetrator verbally or through writing, and confrontation with humour (Fasting et al., 2007). This research also shows that older victims are more likely to use direct confrontation rather than the younger victims who most commonly respond with passivity.

Further reinforcing this interpretation of the gymnasts' narratives, the following concluding statement was made by Emily Meinke as a part of her testimony at the trial of Larry Nassar:

> I want to take a moment to speak about a disturbing trend that's taking place in our society and how we collectively process information regarding claims of sexual abuse ... Hypothetically, if an equal number of male gymnasts expressed similar concerns of abuse, including collegiate level gymnasts and even former Olympians, do you think it would have taken this long for someone in a position of power to take action and effect change? ... In my opinion there's a glaring double standard and it's time that we examine the roots of these inconsistencies and make a conscious effort to make significant changes so that it never, ever happens again to any child. This is a revolution and it's about time we hold the power.
>
> (Meinke, 2018)

Racheal Denhollander, the first woman to publicly accuse Larry Nassar, states:

> [We are] Women and girls who have banded together to fight for themselves because no one else would do it. Women and girls who

carry scars that will never fully heal but who have made the choice to place the guilt and shame on the only person to whom it belongs, the abuser.

(Denhollander, 2018)

Having opportunities to be heard is an important step in the process of healing from abuse but far more is needed, not only to safeguard future female gymnasts from harm but to ensure positive developmental benefits are reaped and the athletes' love for the sport is nurtured. Further, numerous questions remain pertaining to former artistic gymnasts who have experienced abuse, including: how many survivors require and/or receive mental health supports post-trauma?; how many survivors will continue to suffer from their experiences?; and how do we account for the suffering of the survivors' family members who either did not know about the abuse or did not heed potential warning signs?

Denhollander's (2018) testimony is also significant as it calls upon others to enact their responsibilities to ensure the safety and protection from harm of young athletes:

But may the horror expressed in this courtroom over the last seven days be motivation for anyone and everyone no matter the context to take responsibility if they have failed in protecting a child, to understand the incredible failures that led to this week and to do it better the next time.

Denhollander's call for 'anyone and everyone' to take responsibility for child protection and 'to do better the next time' sounds uncomfortably similar to the call Ryan made in 1995 (p. 14):

since those charged with protecting young athletes so often fail in their responsibility, it is time the government drops the fantasy that certain sports are merely games and takes a hard look at legislation aimed at protecting elite child athletes.

The gymnasts' narratives of abuse highlight the failure of adults in positions of authority and trust over young female gymnasts to take preventative measures, to look for warning signs, and to heed the voices of gymnasts who expressed concern. Since the emergence of the Nassar case, steps towards legislation in the US have begun with the establishment of the US Center for SafeSport which provides education, outreach, and an independent avenue through which to report concerns about sexual abuse within Olympic and Paralympic movements. Time will tell how effective this Center will be and hopefully in the near future, the mandate of the Center will expand to address other forms of abuse and will open its doors to pre-Olympic/Paralympic athletes.

Conclusion

The narrative analysis presented in this chapter is the production of discourses of harm experienced by female artistic gymnasts from persons in positions of authority and trust in women's artistic gymnastics. Gymnasts' stories of sexual and psychological harm, obedience and silence, long-lasting invisible scars, as well as a recognised importance of sharing their stories are presented through the gymnasts' voices. Former gymnasts are once again speaking out, sharing the troubling nature of their experiences, and questioning why it is acceptable that this trauma be endured on the path to achieve gymnastic success. One would think that Ryan's 1995 book, coupled with so many high-profile testimonies of abuse from Olympic gymnasts in the latter quarter of the twentieth century, would have been a powerful wake-up call for adults in positions of trust and authority in women's artistic gymnastics to do better. Whatever interventions were put in place, if any, at that time, have proven to be insufficient to protect gymnasts, as indicated by more recent cases of abuse. One is left to wonder whether this moment in time, with the recent testimonies of female artistic gymnasts' experiences of abuse, will be any different than when Ryan raised alarm bells about abuse in women's gymnastics. Perhaps the widespread and severe sanctions imposed on adults in positions of authority and trust and the institutions to which they belong in the Nassar case will make a difference this time. And, perhaps the broader effects of the #MeToo movement will also add help to ensure the athletes' voices are heard this time.

Further research is required on the gendered-based experience of harm addressing the insightful and provocative question posed by Emily Meinke about the double standard for athlete protection and the need for timely change for girls and women. We need to explore ways to have gymnasts' voices heard in an ongoing manner and not just after a crisis occurs. Further, we must acknowledge and listen to gymnasts' stories as they evolve over time as we may learn how to better support them and other athletes as they heal. Others have called for the inclusion of athletes' voices (Barker-Ruchti & Schubring, 2016), but, to date, stories of female artistic gymnasts' voices being solicited and heard are absent. What mechanisms could be incorporated to enable athletes to be active agents in their experiences rather than passive, obedient, and silent participants? How might adults in positions of power and trust be enabled to use that power and trust to not only protect athletes from harm but ensure athletes have a fulfilling and nurturing experience? While our understanding of violence in sport has come a long way, there is still much research required to advance our understanding of women's and girls' sporting experiences and effective strategies for safeguarding the welfare of all athletes in the sport domain.

References

Anderson, G. (August, 2018). Lansing Statement January 17th 2018 – Gwen Anderson. Retrieved online from https://inourownwords.us/2018/08/08/gwenanderson/.

Anonymous. (December, 2016). I was raped by my gymnastics coach; 'We were trained to say nothing bothered us'. *ESPN News*. Retrieved online from https://abcnews.go.com/Sports/raped-gymnastics-coach-trained-bothered-us/story?id=44218997.

Barker-Ruchti, N., & Schubring, A. (2016). Moving into and out of high-performance sport: the cultural learning of an artistic gymnast. *Physical Education & Sport Pedagogy*, 21(1), 69–80.

Bloodworth, A., McNamee, M., & Tan, J. (2017). Autonomy, eating disorders and elite gymnastics: ethical and conceptual issues. *Sport, Education and Society*, 22(8), 878–889.

Bochner, A. (2014). *Coming to narrative*. Walnut Creek, CA: Lefty Coat Press.

Brackenridge, C. H. (1997). 'He owned me basically ...' Women's experience of sexual abuse in sport. *International Review for the Sociology of Sport*, 32, 115–130.

Brackenridge, C. H., & Fasting, K. (2005). The grooming process in sport: Case studies of sexual harassment and abuse. *Auto/Biography*, 13, 33–52.

Brackenridge, C., Bishopp, D., Moussalli, S., & Tapp, J. (2008). The characteristics of sexual abuse in sport: A multidimensional scaling analysis of events described in media reports. *International Journal of Sport and Exercise Psychology*, 6(4), 385–406.

Braun, V., & Clarke, V. (2006). Using thematic analysis in psychology. *Qualitative Research in Psychology*, 3(2), 77–101.

Braun, V., Clarke, V., & Weate, P. (2016). Using thematic analysis in sport and exercise research. In B. Smith & A. C. Sparkes (Eds.), *Routledge handbook of qualitative research in sport & exercise* (pp. 191–205). New York: Routledge.

Bruce, D. (2007). *Nadia Comaneci: The perfect 10*. Retrieved online from https://www.amazon.com/dp/055705026X/ref=rdr_ext_tmb.

Cense, M., & Brackenridge, C. (2001). Temporal and developmental risk factors for sexual harassment and abuse in sport. *European Physical Education Review*, 7, 61–79.

Dantzscher, J. (August, 2018). Book excerpt: 'Little Girls in Pretty Boxes' with new forward by Olympic gymnast Jamie Dantzscher. *ESPN W*. Retrieved online from http://www.espn.com/espnw/culture/article/24300690/little-girls-pretty-boxes-new-forward-olympic-gymnast-jamie-dantzscher.

Denhollander, R. (August, 2018). Lansing Statement January 24th 2018 – Rachel Denhollander. Retrieved online from https://inourownwords.us/2018/08/29/rachael-denhollander/.

Fasting, K., Brackenridge, C., & Walseth, K. (2007). Women athletes' personal responses to sexual harassment in sport. *Journal of Applied Sport Psychology*, 19(4), 419–433.

Fields, S. K., Collins, C. L., & Comstock, R. D. (2007). Conflict on the courts: A review of sports-related violence literature. *Trauma, Violence, and Abuse*, 8(4), 359–369.

Finkelhor, D. (1984). *Child sexual abuse: New theory and research*. New York: Free Press.

French, G. (August, 2018). Lansing Statement January 24th 2018 – Grace French. Retrieved online from https://inourownwords.us/2018/10/01/grace-french/.

Garsd, J. (January, 2018). Gold medalist Dominique Moceanu warned us 10 years ago about abuse in USA Gymnastics. *PRI's The World*. Retrieved online from https://www.pri.org/stories/2018-01-25/gold-medalist-dominique-moceanu-warned-us-10-years-ago-about-abuse-usa-gymnastics.

Howells, K. (2017). Butterflies, magic carpets, and scary wild animals: An intervention with a young gymnast. *Case Studies in Sport & Exercise Psychology*, 1, 26–37.

Kaeser, M. (February, 2018). Don't fear failure: Why quitting gymnastics taught me the true meaning of success. *The Globe and Mail*. Retrieved online from https://www.theglobeandmail.com/opinion/michelle-kaeser-failure-is-golden-too/article37828663/.

Kaplan, K. (2018). After Alyssa Milano's #MeToo tweet, Google searches about sexual assault hit record high. Retrieved from https://www.latimes.com/science/sciencenow/la-sci-sn-metoo-google-searches-20181221-story.html.

Kaufman, Z. D. (August, 2018). When sexual abuse is common knowledge – But no one speaks up. *Boston Globe*. Retrieved from https://papers.ssrn.com/sol3/papers.cfm?abstract_id=3225992.

Kavanagh, E., Brown, L., & Jones, I. (2017). Elite athletes' experience of coping with emotional abuse in the coach–athlete relationship. *Journal of Applied Sport Psychology*, 29(4), 402–417.

Kelner, M. (July, 2017). British Gymnastics failed to suspend coach for emotional and physical abuse. *The Guardian*. Retrieved online from https://www.theguardian.com/sport/2017/jul/14/british-gymnastics-alleged-emotional-physical-abuse.

Kirby, S., Greaves, L., & Hankivsky, O. (2002). Women under the dome of silence: Sexual harassment and abuse of female athletes. *Canadian Woman Studies*, 21(3), 132–138.

Larson, M. (August, 2018). Lansing Statement January 23rd 2018 – Mattie Larson. Retrieved online from https://inourownwords.us/2018/08/28/mattie-larson/.

Leberg, E. (1997). *Understanding child molesters: Taking charge*. London: Sage.

Lieblich, A., Tuval-Mashiach, R., & Zilber, T. (1998). *Narrative research: Reading, analysis, and interpretation (applied social research methods)*. Thousand Oaks: Sage.

Meinke, E. (August, 2018). Lansing Statement January 23rd 2018 – Emily Meinke. Retrieved online from https://inourownwords.us/2018/08/29/emily-meinke/.

Pinheiro, M. C., Pimenta, N., Resende, R., & Malcolm, D. (2012). Gymnastics and child abuse: An analysis of former international Portuguese female artistic gymnasts. *Sport, Education and Society*, 19(4), 435–450.

Raisman, A. (August, 2018). Lansing Statement January 19th 2018 – Aly Raisman. Retrieved online from https://inourownwords.us/2018/08/10/alexandra-raisman/.

Riethman, S. (August, 2018). Lansing Statement January 23rd 2018 – Sterling Riethman. Retrieved online from https://inourownwords.us/2018/08/29/sterling-riethman/

Rosenwald, G. C., & Ochberg, R. L. (Eds). (1992). *Storied lives: The cultural politics of self-understanding*. New Haven, CT: Yale University Press.

Ryan, J. (1995). *Little girls in pretty boxes: The making and breaking of elite gymnasts and figure skaters*. London: The Women's Press Ltd.

Salon, E. (March, 2019). Nadia Comaneci – Romania's national treasure. Retrieved online from https://www.science-a2z.com/nadia-comaneci-romanias-national-treasure/8/.

Sanderson, A. (April, 2019). How walking away from elite gymnastics helped me reclaim my joy. *Think: Opinion, Analysis, Essays*. Retrieved online from https://www.nbcnews.com/think/opinion/elite-gymnastics-culture-cruel-ucla-s-ncaa-gymnastics-program-helped-ncna996491.

Schaal, K., Tafflet, M., Nassif, H., Thibault, V., Pichard, C., Alcotte, M., ... Toussaint, J. F. (2011). Psychological balance in high level athletes: Gender-based differences and sport-specific patterns. *PLoS ONE, 6*(5).

Seal, R. (December, 2005). Growing pains. *The Guardian*. Retrieved online from https://www.theguardian.com/sport/2005/dec/04/features.sport19.

Shipley, A. (October, 1998). Moceanu is declared a legal adult. *The Washington Post*. Retrieved online from https://www.washingtonpost.com/archive/sports/1998/10/29/moceanu-is-declared-a-legal-adult/262702a3-ee62-484d-ab38-8dacf95f35bf/?noredirect=on&utm_term=.ba1d3774c4a0.

Smith, B. (2016). Narrative analysis in sport and exercise: How can it be done? In B. Smith & A. C. Sparkes (Eds.), *Routledge handbook of qualitative research in sport & exercise* (pp. 260–273). New York, NY: Routledge.

Smits, F., Jacobs, F., & Knoppers, A. (2017). 'Everything revolves around gymnastics': Athletes and parents make sense of elite youth sport. *Sport in Society, 20*(1), 66–83.

Sparkes, A. C., & Smith, B. (2014). *Qualitative research methods in sport, exercise and health: From process to product*. New York: Routledge.

Stewart, C., Schiavon, L. M., & Bellotto, M. L. (2017). Knowledge, nutrition and coaching pedagogy: A perspective from female Brazilian Olympic gymnasts. *Sport, Education and Society, 22*(4), 511–527.

Stirling, A. E., & Kerr, G. (2014). Initiating and sustaining emotional abuse in the coach-athlete relationship: An ecological transactional model of vulnerability. *Journal of Aggression, Maltreatment & Trauma, 23*(2), 116–125.

Sundgot-Borgen, J., & Torstveit, M. K. (2010). Aspects of disordered eating continuum in elite high intensity sports. *Scandinavian Journal of Medicine and Science in Sports, 20*, 112–121.

Toftegaard Neilson, J. (2001). The forbidden zone: Intimacy, sexual relations and misconduct in the relationship between coaches and athletes . *International Review for the Sociology of Sport, 36*, 165–182.

Warriner, K., & Lavallee, D. (2008). The retirement experience of elite female gymnasts: Self identity and the physical self. *Journal of Applied Sport Psychology, 20*, 301–317.

Weiss, M., & Mohr, H. (February, 2018). U.S. gymnasts speak of eating disorders, emotional abuse, training on broken bones. *The Associated Press*. Retrieved online from https://globalnews.ca/news/4045312/usa-gymnastics-abuse-victims/.

Wieber, J. (August, 2018). Lansing Statement January 18th 2018 – Jordon Wieber. Retrieved online from https://inourownwords.us/2018/08/10/jordon-wieber/.

Winter, R. D. (2019). The pursuit of excellence and the perils of perfectionism. In B. Hemmings, N. J. Watson, & A. Parker (Eds.), *Sport, psychology & Christianity: Welfare, performance and consultancy*. New York: Routledge.

Wolfe, V. V. (2007). Child sexual abuse. In E. J. Mash & R. A. Barkley (Eds.), *Assessment of childhood disorders* (4th edn) (pp. 685–748). New York, NY: Guilford Press.

Woodland, N. (August, 2018). Lansing Statement January 23rd 2018 – Natalie Woodland. Retrieved online from https://inourownwords.us/2018/08/28/natalie-woodland/.

Yabe, Y., Hagiwara, Y., Sekiguchi, T., Momma, H., Tsuchiya, M., Kuroki, K., ... Nagatomi, R. (2018). The characteristics of coaches that verbally or physically abuse young athletes. *The Tohoku Journal of Experimental Medicine, 244*(4), 297–304.

Chapter 7

Trampoline gymnasts' body narratives of the leotard
A seamless fit?

Rhiannon Lord and Carly Stewart

Introduction

The concerns that scholars have about female gymnasts are, in one way or another, related to the young female body at risk of harm. These concerns are well documented and include serious medical, psychological, and developmental problems such as debilitating injuries (Edouard et al., 2018), stunted growth and maturation (Caine, Bass, & Daly, 2003), body dissatisfaction/consciousness and disordered eating (De Bruin, Oudejans, & Bakker, 2007; Neves et al., 2017), and retirement difficulties (Kerr & Dacyshyn, 2000). As discussed by several other authors contained in this book, often these problems are inextricably linked with harmful training practices and abuses that pervade gymnastics culture and which are normalised (Pinheiro, Pimenta, Resende, & Malcolm, 2014; Smits, Jacobs, & Knoppers, 2017). Amidst this wealth of literature, critical socio-cultural scholars of gymnastics point towards the narrowly defined gymnastic body ideal – young, lean (thin but muscular), hyper-feminine (and inherently heterosexual) – as a central concern whereby it drives harmful and abusive practices with serious consequences (e.g. see Barker-Ruchti, 2009; Stewart, Schiavon, & Bellotto, 2017).

A discerning feature of the female gymnast body ideal is that it is young and lean with no fat or adult curves. It is a body accentuated by a seamless fit with the leotard; a skin-tight suit, v-cut at the crotch exposing the leg, thighs, and buttocks of the gymnast and a regulated requirement of competitions (Fédération Internationale de Gymnastique [FIG], 2016). Surprisingly, the leotard is given relatively little direct academic attention despite some scholars prioritising the physical body as the site of study in order to explain or theorise socially and culturally driven problems in gymnastics (e.g. Barker-Ruchti, 2009, Barker-Ruchti & Tinning, 2010, Weber & Barker-Ruchti, 2012). A justification given for the necessity of leotards is that they are essential for coaches and judges to be able to observe gymnasts' bodies for performance faults (such as bent legs) or activation of muscles (Barker-Ruchti and Tinning, 2010) and yet the same is argument is not made for male gymnasts who wear full-length stirrups or shorts that are not skin-tight. The naturalisation of socially constructed bodies that perpetuate gendered structures in sport is perhaps visible nowhere more so than in gymnastics (McMahon, 2017) and concerns about gender have been attributed explicitly to risk of violence inflicted upon female gymnasts (Barker-Ructhi, Schubring, & Stewart, forthcoming). The leotard as a crucial component for the construction of ideal bodies at risk of harm in gymnastics would seem to be a critical point for scholarly analysis yet it is, in our opinion, often overlooked and not given the attention it deserves.

Crucially, we suggest that a lack of critical attention given to the leotard reflects some noticeable gaps in the socio-cultural gymnastics literature that focuses directly upon the subjective experiences of gymnasts and the relationships they form with their bodies and with the bodies of others in their environment, and their associated multiple senses of self and identities over time. It might be said that gymnasts' fleshy and intimately lived bodies (as opposed to abstract, fragmented, measured, theoretical bodies) have been an absent presence in a plethora of literature about them. This chapter draws upon the 'body narratives' (Sparkes, 1999) of trampoline gymnasts narrated during ethnographic fieldwork. Trampoline gymnastics is a sub discipline of women's artistic gymnastics and it is governed by the same uniform rules and so leotard requirements are the same in the code of points for artistic gymnasts and trampoline gymnasts. These body narratives illuminate how the body is socialised in a subcultural career process over time and encounters moments of bodily agency for and against the social and gendered conventions of gymnastics culture. To conclude we offer thoughts concerning possibilities for subverting gender structures which may lead to serious bodily practices and harms.

Gymnasts' bodies as an absent presence

This chapter is framed by works which seek to centralise and recognise the importance of the body and embodiment as central issues in the social sciences and humanities. From this perspective there is general scholarly agreement that theorising about the body has tended to be disembodied and has operated to distance us from everyday experiences of ordinary people (Frank, 2010; 2013; Sparkes, 1997; 1999; Shilling, 2012). We observe this to be the case in gymnastics literature where, with a few exceptions, the bodies of gymnasts as subjectively experienced have tended to be overlooked or filtered out through disembodied theoretical frameworks. There is perhaps good explanation for this based upon what the literature tells us about the types of 'body-selves' female gymnasts are. Put simply, the term 'body-self' is the relationship between the body and a sense of self (Frank, 2013; Sparkes, 1999). Firstly, gymnasts operate in a highly disciplined and controlled environment, rarely afforded a voice and so accessing gymnasts' experiences is difficult. They are often silenced. Second, and relatedly, gymnasts are typically young and/or lacking maturity, which makes gaining access to them more difficult where coach-gymnast power relations are observed to be highly unequal reflecting patriarchal structures.

Barker-Ruchti and Tinning (2010) illustrate these points in their work. As one of the few exceptions that does centralise the body theoretically, they focus upon the subjective realities of elite artistic gymnasts in Australia, providing powerful insights into how these gymnasts' are shaped: their bodies produced through disciplinary power. Adopting a feminist Foucauldian framework they draw attention to networks of power and modes of objectification that classify, discipline, and normalise gymnasts who, they observe, have very little autonomy. From this perspective, dominant social, cultural, and historical gymnastic discourses are internalised or inscribed into the bodies of female gymnasts, and subsequently taken into their sense of themselves as selves, their corresponding actions and behaviours. Two key areas in which this can be seen are first in bodies that are objectified and endure pain and suffering to achieve high levels of control and performance, and second in gender identities heavily shaped by the feminine beauty body ideal. Concerning the leotard, Barker-Ruchti and Tinning (2010) note the 'tight and scanty training outfits exposed the body to the coaches' (p. 240) 'partially hid the gymnasts' muscular torso and arms and emphasised the feminine body-line' (p. 246). Less however is said about the gymnast's embodied experiences of the leotard.

There are works which have been able to access the gymnast voice and provide insightful data on first-hand experiences where the abused, pained, and troubled body implicitly speaks *through* the stories collected and is connected to socio-cultural structures or sociological, psychological, or developmental theories for understanding (e.g. Pinheiro et al., 2014; Kerr & Dacyshyn, 2000; Stirling & Kerr, 2013). Kerr and Dacyshyn (2000) in Canada for example explore identity formation through experience of transition to retirement, highlighting one important but challenging developmental task for adolescent gymnasts is of achieving a level of body acceptance in a culture where food, appearance, and weight are so prominent. Further they argue that gymnasts are also denied the freedom to experience their bodies and associated biopsychosocial changes associated with puberty (where it is often delayed). This results in gymnasts deferring identity crises and halting full identity development until retirement. Lavallee and Robinson (2007) focus similarly on retirement transition in the UK illuminating body-centred concerns as closely tied to formation of identity. Such works on transition into retirement illuminate the role of the body in the process of ongoing reflexive identity formation where the former gymnastic body-self is disrupted. We know less however about the processes of body-self formation in the gymnasts' career over time from their perspective.

How, for example, do they develop their body-selves at and through key points in their careers? What are the key moments in a gymnastic career that integrate the body-self or change it? What are the conditions that shape whether a gymnast constructs an identity that is risky or healthy?

In summary, works have advanced certain ways of understanding the gymnastic body but these have heavily theorised about it and not intimately connected to it as it is lived in flesh and blood (Leder, 1990). Against this backdrop we suggest that the lived experiences of gymnasts, the ways in which they experience their bodies, and how these shape identities and selves over time in the gymnastic career require more attention. In order to do this, we take the approach that narrative ways of knowing can enhance our understanding of ways in which body-self relationships develop over time (Sparkes, 1999).

Hearing the body-self in body narratives

This section proceeds on the premise that subjectivity and selfhood are deeply rooted in the body, that psychology and physiology are intimately linked. As Eakin (1999) notes, it is only when the link between body and self is disrupted we may experience an identity crisis and grasp that these are normally invisibly linked and functioning in our lives. For example, this might happen if we experience a serious life-changing injury or illness akin to understanding *injury to my body* as *injury to me*. Alternatively, body image issues might be conceptualised similarly as a crisis of identity where biology and psychic elements are disturbed. This is a model of embodied selfhood (Eakin 1999; 2008).

The notion of body-self and narrative are linked in the coming together in the reflexive telling, listening, and reading of life stories to make sense of experience and construct meaning in a coherent (orderly) manner (Sparkes, 1999; Smith & Sparkes, 2002). In stories people are often trying to figure out who they are in the practice of narrative identifying where narrative and identity formation are inextricably linked (Frank, 2000; Eakin, 1999; 2008). Therefore narrative is not merely a literary form but a mode of phenomenological and cognitive self-experience, an integral part of self (Eakin, 1999). Similarly for Frank (2010, p. 42) there is no important difference between stories and materials in the form of 'machines, architectural arrangements, bodies and all the rest'. This said stories perform themselves into bodies and bodies can be materialised stories. This said people tell stories *through* their bodies and as researchers we can attempt to hear individuals' bodily experience speaking in stories (Becker, 1997).

However, adopting a model of the embodied self requires that we give the relation between individuals' experience and representation of it more examination than it is usually afforded in disembodied models of self.

Eakin (1999, p. 100) notes there is an often misleading distinction between 'experience and expression' 'content and form'. Frank (2010) elaborates that this conventional mimetic understanding of stories suggests that people have experiences and then tell stories about those experiences i.e. life happens and is now represented in the stories. Rejecting this understanding puts stories before experiences; because we have stories we have experience. This said stories must not be regarded as a clear window through which those receiving the story can see the world it describes. Instead it is a sketched window, drawn from culture, worth looking at. Stories are, therefore, simultaneously personal and social. This is important because stories shape what becomes experience, and humans may seek out experiences (including dangerous ones) that can be told as stories. Body narratives then, according to Sparkes (1999, p. 126), 'allow us to explore the relationships between the embodied self and the wider society that structures and shapes stories available to particular individuals and groups', like gymnasts.

Body problems and (inter)actions as a lens

In order to make sense of the ways in which the trampoline gymnasts in our study experience their bodies, we refer specifically to the work of Arthur Frank (1991; 2013) who takes a phenomenological starting point to focus on the body as a problem for *itself*, as it is embodied, within a social context. The body-self must respond to these problems and through *action* and asking itself four core questions as it does so:

1 Control: How predictable will my performance be? Can I reliably predict how my body will function? Can I control its functioning?
2 Desire: Am I lacking or producing desire?
3 Relation to others: Am I monadic and closed in upon myself or dyadic and existing in relation to others?
4 Relation to self: Am I associated with my own being, my surface, or am I disassociated from corporeality?

Styles of ideal or typical body usage emerge as the body responds to all four of these questions. Here we focus upon two discrete styles (of four in total) as they relate to our data and analysis:

The disciplined body is concerned primarily with the question of control. It is defined through actions of self-regimentation, for example repetitive sports training, in order to be predictable. The body of a gymnast, for example, may lie at the end of the control continuum where predictability is at its highest expression. Consequently it experiences a crisis when control is lost. It is monadic, lacking desire, and dissociated from itself in these action moments.

The mirroring body is also concerned with control but through the predictability of its appearance. It expresses this through regimes concerned with its surface such as consumption as it seeks to recreate its image in the image of other more desirable bodies; the visual is primary. Where the disciplined body fears disruption to its work routine, the mirroring body fears disfigurement. Like the disciplined body, it too is monadic and closed off from others in these actions but is desiring and always wanting more.

Finally we acknowledge that Frank (1991; 2013) develops Goffman's (1963; 1990) interactionist work. *Impression management* enables individuals to use their bodies to enact particular social roles and identities and (re)construct and/or maintain forms of self-identity, particularly in *front stage regions* where subcultural standards are expected. In contrast, *backstage regions* are used for periods of relaxation and/or practices to inform front stage performances. Moreover, shared understandings of body idioms, that is physical gestures and body decoration, enable an audience to make sense of individuals' (in)authentic performances (Goffman, 1990). In turn, individuals' perceptions of audience responses to their performances reinforce or diminish their sense of self-identity. Importantly, Frank (2013) notes body-selves are not as freely constructed through social interaction as Goffman posited, but they instead shaped by cultural discourses contained in cultural narratives (Frank, 2013). Goffman's ideas have been used relatively widely to understand impression management and identity construction in sport (e.g. Beames and Pike, 2008; Donnelly and Young, 1988), including older gymnasts (Kerr et al., 2018). Frank's typology of body usage, though stemming from medical sociology, has also been applied to small number of cases in sport (e.g. Stewart and Pullen 2014; Sparkes, 2004) but has not yet been applied to gymnastics. We have found that using Frank's (2013) typology in combination with Goffman's (1990) work to be valuable in thinking about the unique combination of types of bodies that gymnasts actively construct in a social context, how these shape career paths and both constitute and contribute to problems gymnasts experience.

A brief note on methods

This chapter draws upon body narratives narrated and performed by 26 competitive trampoline gymnasts, aged 6–21 years old, during an 18-month ethnographic study in one UK trampoline club. A total of 1600 hours of ethnographic fieldwork, comprising of participant observations at training sessions, competitions, and other club events (e.g., social and fundraising events), semi-structured interviews, and focus groups, produced rich detail on gymnasts' embodied experiences as they reflected on and progressed through their trampoline career. In addition, 14 gymnasts provided written accounts of their lived subcultural experiences. A multi-method ethnographic research design enabled us to understand gymnasts' embodied lives within the subcultural context (Brewer, 2000).

Primary researcher Rhiannon Lord (RL) was a coach at the trampoline club prior to and during the research. Pre-existing close connections and rapport with gymnasts and their parents led rich detailed data on gymnasts' lived experiences. Thus, the researcher's subjectivities and biography were not viewed as a hindrance, but central to developing a detailed understanding of gymnasts' experience in a rigorous and ethical way (Smith, 1989) and reflexive activity was undertaken to monitor and examine researcher subjectivity throughout the research process.

Combinations of narrative thematic analysis, structural narrative analysis, and performative narrative analysis (as defined by Sparkes and Smith, 2014) were used to understand and make sense of gymnasts' embodied lives. This three-pronged analytical approach revealed *what* body-selves gymnasts constructed and *how* they are constructed at various points over time.

Constructing a gymnastic body-self and identity

The body is central to the ways in which gymnasts construct a sense of self and identity. In the initial stages of gymnasts' careers, they need to construct a gymnastic body in order to be accepted into the gymnastics subculture. There is a reciprocal relationship between body-selves and culture; the body in-folds culture through the process of mirroring other, better bodies. At the same time bodies out-fold culture to others as a resource for (re)construction of their own body-selves (Frank, 1991; 2013). Gymnasts' own descriptions of their early interactions in the trampoline subculture illustrate the ways in which they mirror other, 'better' gymnastic bodies that are on display to inform their ideas of what it is to be 'a trampolinist', that is what they should look like and how they should behave. The young gymnasts quickly internalise bodies on display and seek to become them. For example:

RL: How did you learn what it was to be a gymnast?
ABBIE: Um, I don't know, like looking at other people probably. Like, I remember seeing Georgia and thinking *that's* what a trampolinist is.
RL: Why Georgia?
ABBIE: She was probably the best in the club at the time. The highest level. She looks like a gymnast, doesn't she? She's so small. She always seems to have a leotard and Milano shorts on even if she has a t-shirt over the top. She always trains hard. She's always here. I think, at the time at least (laughs), I wanted to be like Georgia. Embarrassing now (laughs).

Asked to reflect on that, Abbie remembers:

Well I remember going home and asking my Dad if I could get a leotard and Milano shorts. He wanted me to wait for a bit, to see if I liked club, and I remember getting in a mood about it, so he did order me some stuff online. I know I put a t-shirt over the top, but I always have a leotard on underneath and I always wear my shorts even if I'm coaching … I wanted to fit in and that was the way to do it. I didn't want to look different.

(Abbie, 13 years old; interview)

Abbie's account is illustrative of common acts of consumption the trampolinists reported engaging in. The mirroring body seeks predictability (control) of appearance. Accordingly, it is seen through acts of consumption that enhance the body in an 'endless assimilation of the world's objects to one's own body, and of one's own body to the world's objects' (Frank, 1991, p. 62). Newcomers feel an embodied desire to become other, 'more stylish' bodies by internalising and idealising what they perceive to be the gymnastic ideal and actively consume it. Trampolinists often accessed symbolic objects, for example the leotard, to recreate the external surface of the body in the image of older more established gymnasts via parents' economic capital. The leotard is a core symbol of the gymnastic body-self and identity.

The mirroring body, like the disciplined body, is defined by control and both suffer a crisis when this is lost. New gymnasts are particularly fearful of contingency experienced through the mirroring body, in this case of not fitting in or of looking different from the group. An assimilated appearance helps them to quickly fit in over a short period of time as recorded in field notes:

The new gymnasts came in today. They seemed just as nervous as they did on Tuesday, although they did appear to be a little chattier. It looks as though Abbie is starting to make friends with Amy and Georgia; she joined their group today. She also wore Milano shorts and a leotard underneath her t-shirt, so she blended in quite well. I noticed that Erin also wore a leotard today, which is a little different to her recreational attire.

(Fieldnotes)

There were examples, however, of where newcomers also made *neophyte mistakes* (Donnelly and Young, 1988) during their initial construction of a gymnastic body-self in the training hall setting. Often these were as the result of not mirroring other bodies closely enough in terms of their appearance or what Goffman (1990, p. 34) terms items of expressive equipment or their 'personal front'. For example one interaction captured in field notes illustrates:

Hannah [gymnast] came in, 10 minutes late. She came over to me and Joanna and apologised for being late, she'd been at a netball match. I explained that it was ok and to go and join in with the warm-up on the red bed … Georgia approached us during the break.

GEORGIA [GYMNAST]: Why has Hannah got skorts [combination of short and a skirt] on?
JOANNA [GYMNAST]: She was [at] a netball match or something.
AMY [COACH]: It looks ridiculous, what is it her PE kit?
GEORGIA [GYMNAST]: Yeah why wouldn't you bring your kit with you?
AMY [COACH]: I'll go and speak to her and tell her next time she needs to wear club kit.

(Fieldnotes)

The first competition is a key moment in the gymnasts' career and marks a significant point for the ongoing process of socialisation. Throughout the research, competitions epitomised front region performances where certain standards are embodied and maintained (Goffman, 1990). In the competition hall gymnasts are judged by an audience which includes their peers, coaches, competition judges, and spectators consisting of parents, grandparents, and friends. The body is on display and judged against normative standards of gymnastic culture. In this social context, Frank's body problem of control presents itself. Can I reliably predict how my body will function? Can I control its functioning?

RL: Can you tell me a bit about your first competition?
SOPHIE: It was awful. All those people it was so scary.
RL: But you did really well.
SOPHIE: Yeah but I just remember it as awful.
RL: Why?
SOPHIE: Because everyone watches you. You've got the judges. Even though we practise in the hall, it's still different people judging you. You get judged by other gymnasts and coaches and stuff as well, I guess. And leotards don't help. Like, they're uncomfortable especially when you're not used to them. I remember taking my shorts off and thinking 'oh no'.
RL: Was there anything good about it? Other than getting a medal?
BOTH: Laughs.
SOPHIE: I don't know, it just seemed like after the first one [competition] I was part of the group. They sort of were more friendly. I think it was like they needed to see if I could trampoline properly or something.

(Sophie, 13 years old; interview)

Sophie describes the 'oh no' embodied discomfort of removing her shorts in the competition space to a different audience illuminating a disruptive moment where the body feels out of control in relation to its appearance and dissociated from the self and idealised image it tries to recreate.

Moments of body-self unity

Following the first period in the subcultural career where mirroring and disciplined bodies are developed through regimens of training, appearance, and social conduct we observe a period of increased unification between the body and self, important in creating a stable and enduring athletic identity. We might describe that trampolinists are now embedded into the subculture and have a sense of belonging and that their body narratives speak to a unified body-self and associated identities. These narratives can be characterised as: 'I look like a gymnast', 'I behave like a gymnast', 'I feel like a gymnast', and 'others see me as a gymnast'.

RL: Do you think you look like a gymnast?
RIA: I guess so, yes … like my body … I'm muscly, but not too muscly. Enough to be good on the trampoline. So not like skinny, but not fat either … I think I work hard too. Like I try hard to do things right. Like doing that military sit for like an hour (laughs) and you had to tell me to stop (laughs). Filling in my [training] diary. I don't mess about like Lewis.

(Ria, 9 years old; interview)

Ria's reflections are permeated by action problems concerning predictability of performance and appearance and illustrate the reflexive mixing of ideal mirroring and disciplined types (Frank, 2013). Disciplined gymnastic practice over time, specifically conditioning exercises in this case, enabled her to not only act and feel like a gymnast in front stage training spaces, but also momentarily satisfy a desire to look like a gymnast through a preoccupation with developing musculature or the surface of the body, associated with mirroring bodies. Other narratives of body-self synergy were discussed mainly by older or more competent gymnasts in referring to mastery of skills. In these moments the body is experienced as 'an aspect of the world' (Van Maanen, 1988): pleasurable and in harmony with self. Gymnasts exist in a 'liveable relation' with their bodies:

> There's no other sensation like it. It's like weightlessness, like you're flying through the air. You can feel the air rush against your skin. You can feel your hair get left behind in the air and whip back against your back. There are brief points where you actually feel suspended in the air (the top) and I can't think what else you could possibly do to feel that.
> (Jessica, 20 years old; diary extract)

Collectively unified body-self narratives create a sense of belonging to the trampoline group and the gymnastics subculture more broadly. The unified body-self is essential for the longevity of gymnasts' careers, health, and well-being. Body-self disruption comes in a myriad of forms and has implications for gymnasts' health, well-being, and careers.

Moments of body-self disruption

Mirroring and disciplined body-selves do not cope well when control is lost (Frank, 1991; 2013). One inevitable event that signifies loss of control to the gymnasts in our study is the onset of menstruation which included bodily changes such as the development of breast tissue and broadening of the hips. These moments have been an absent presence in much of the literature. Although they have been highlighted in more recent work (Barker-Ruchti, Kerr, Schubring, Cervin, & Nunomura, 2017), when viewed from an embodied perspective, the feeling of a body out of control in its behaviour, movement, and appearance is not a welcome one. In essence, puberty changes the lived relation gymnasts have with their bodies and disrupts the gymnastic body-self that has been constructed until this point. The body now moves into the consciousness foreground of narratives, and stories *about* or *of* the body are told (Leder, 1990). Gymnasts were particularly conscious of their bodies in a leotard:

EMMA: Well I developed hips which wasn't the greatest thing to happen [laughs] ... hips and no boobs. I don't know I'm just so aware of my bum and hips now, especially in a leotard ... there is something about feeling womanly rather than not. I don't think I ever felt like a child, but I definitely felt different after [puberty], my body was definitely different.

(Emma, 18 years old; interview)

Importantly, gymnasts have limited opportunities for body management in spaces where a tight level on control and discipline exists (Barker-Ruchti & Tinning, 2010). The leotard stood forth as a prominent issue particularly in competition spaces where regulations and dominant practices police adherence; there are reprimands for knickers showing and so many gymnasts choose not to wear any underwear.

NAOMI: Do you remember when Yasmin was competing and ...
SOPHIE: Oh that was awful.
NAOMI: Basically, because she was, you know 'on' [her period], she wanted to wear knickers, but obviously you can't so she'd tried hiding that she was wearing underwear by wearing a thong and everyone could see it. And you're not supposed to wear underwear so people were looking at her for that as well.
SOPHIE: Some people were actually pointing and laughing.

(Focus group)

In these spaces, gymnasts are front region (Goffman, 1990) and their lack of agency in managing their bodies is exacerbated causing body consciousness:

> It's hard to get around it [hiding pubescent changes]. Because you have to wear a leotard in competition. There's no choice. Like, I know it covers you, but at the same time it shows everything (...) like everything! Like, I don't like my bum and hips, but it's hard in a leotard because everyone can see. And, like, boobs as well. Even though the top is most covered, 'cos it's tight it shows them [breasts].
>
> (Naomi, 11 years old; interview)

Despite reflecting upon discomfort felt, the leotard is not contested. Gymnasts quickly dismissed alternatives (e.g., unitard) that did not conform or mirror the expectations and norms of a gymnastic body ideal:

EVA: No. I don't think so (laughs). Could you imagine? Oh no. No. Just no (laughs).
RL: What about leggings?
EVA: You just don't see people wearing leggings, at least not at competitions, can you even do that?
RL: What about in training?
EVA: Maybe in training. No one does though. Well Kirsten used to but she was [pause] well you know, bigger. But, what are they called again? The uni things [unitards] no though, just no.

(Eva, 10 years old; interview)

Repetition of these ideas across gymnasts of different ages indicated that this was more than preoccupation with short-term fashion trends, but part of wider subcultural discourse around an ideal gymnastic body-self. Mirroring bodies are at play and the leotard forms an important part of sustaining a predictable appearance. Data would suggest there are no alterative gymnastic body-selves to internalise.

Concern extends to body practices used to restore control when body-self disruption occurs. We already know that in front stage regions such as training sessions and competitions present limited opportunities for girls to engage with body management when responding to control actions problems. This means that gymnasts typically tried to restore control of appearance through harmful practices in back stage regions such as the home. In a quest to revert to a unified body-self gymnasts body narratives were of discipline and punishment. They engaged in behaviours to look and feeling like a gymnast that included dieting (reduced calorie intake, cutting out food groups or refusing to eat) and excessive exercise:

When I look in the mirror, I always feel bad. I have tried all different types of diets and gone through times where I try not to eat, but it doesn't seem to work and I just end up feeling like crap. Sometimes, even if I look better, I feel worse ... I want to make myself perfect. I've only ever done it for trampolining. I guess I feel pressured to look a certain way, more so in my sport than in general life. I bought a leotard once that was a size too small so that I could aim to fit into it before the comp. I did a lot of extra training ... running ... and stopped eating properly for a while. I know, I know, it was stupid. But I never managed it and I've never really worn it, except for a bit after I'd been ill and I felt okay in it.

(Amy, 16 years old; focus group)

Mirroring bodies fear disfigurement where the visual is primary. Importantly it produces desire, but that desire can never be fulfilled. We should be concerned with Amy's eating practices, and other gymnasts who have developed these lived relationships to their bodies. Viewed through Frank's (2013) theoretical framework what counts for these bodies is sustaining the image today, at the expense of other realities such as serious illness or even death. Frank (2013) notes that amidst consumer culture we are all mirroring bodies at one time of another, however developing and inhabiting ideal styles of monadic mirroring body usage as gymnasts typically do is concerning.

Reflections and concluding thoughts

In this chapter we have sought to understand the lived experiences of gymnasts and the ways in which they experience their bodies, in relation to identities and selves – the embodied self – over time in the trampoline gymnastic career. In order to do this, we have employed Frank's (2013) empirically driven theoretical framework which begins with the body; we have tried to hear bodies speaking in stories. Our data illuminates the ways that gymnasts spoke *through* the body as they sought a unified body-self and gymnastic identity, engaging predominantly in mirroring and disciplined styles of body usage and being. However, gymnasts spoke *of* the body as 'out of control' illuminating moments of body-self disruption in the social contexts of managing puberty and keeping up appearances of the gymnastic body ideal across training and competition spaces. In many ways these findings are not surprising, body consciousness and image disorders and eating disorders amongst the gymnast population are well documented. However by paying closer attention to embodied lives we can understand how bodily processes and responses to certain questions of how to act in specific situations outfold through their stories (Frank, 2013), for example in puberty where gymnasts have distinctive problems continuing to be the same sorts of bodies they have been. A focus on gymnastic bodies and their well-documented body problems appears to require new and more self-conscious solutions. Next we will briefly focus our thoughts on the problem of control for female gymnasts and of the implications for practice.

To recall, for Frank (2013) predictability may reach its highest expression in ballet and gymnastics where gymnasts and dancers are expected to maintain control and regain or at least conceal any loss of control as much as possible if mistakes are made. This high level of controlled body usage produces highly disciplined and mirroring bodies that are vulnerable to a loss of control. The gymnasts describe the social problems they experience when they feel they lose control of their bodies, on display, during puberty. They are expected to conceal the contingency of puberty and report a lack of space or being unable to discuss these issues with coaches. The leotard, far from concealing, works to reveal bodily changes and does not help the young female gymnasts in our study resolve this action problem, but instead is stigmatising and accentuates embarrassment for self and others (Goffman, 1990). Our data show that gymnasts feel highly responsible at an early age for how they present themselves and display the signs of their puberty while the gymnastics environment appears to remain indecisive about how to respond. These issues are likely exacerbated by the presence of male coaches who are unwilling to discuss puberty, a female 'problem', and because ideas of ideal gymnasts do not allow for womanly bodies that have gone through puberty. Frank (2013, p. 32) notes that 'as body-selves people interpret their bodies and make choices', that is they have responsibility for their bodies. Gymnasts appear to exercise responsibility by 'passing' or trying to keep puberty from view and seek perfected levels of predictability at whatever cost (e.g. developing eating disorders).

The problems of control in gymnastics are not new and they manifest in many critical discussions from scholars seeking solutions across disciplines and fields of study (e.g. see Kerr et al., 2006; Kerr et al., 2017; Barker-Ruchti et al., 2016). What we contribute here is in line with our theoretical standpoint that takes the lived body of the gymnast as a starting point signalled by a focus on the leotard which is often overlooked. Changing the uniform rules via governing bodies and officials in line with a feminist agenda is a radical but important way to proceed (Barker-Ruchti et al., forthcoming). Not least this agenda is needed to disrupt the inherent gender structures implicit in 'women's' gymnastics that sustain wider binary gender concerns (McMahon, 2017) and in turn contribute to the disruptions that the gymnasts in our study felt. We suggest that expanding representations of the female body should begin with a uniform or dress code that allows the shaping of a more diverse range of fleshy bodies in order to achieve more liveable unified body-selves over time. More immediately finding ways for gymnasts to critically interpret their corporeality and accept degrees of contingency in their embodiment around puberty seems crucial. One way to do this is to offer puberty as a story that can be told and not silenced, expanding the cultural menu of narrative resources available for gymnasts to select from (Sparkes, 1999). Coaches willing to take on a more sustainable coaching agenda in terms of developing healthy gymnasts might actively make space for open conversations or bring puberty stories into in the gymnastics environment.

In closing we hope to have brought attention to the lived body with a focus on the role the leotard plays in how gymnasts experience and live in relation to their bodies in the context of trampoline gymnastics. The body narratives we portray are presented as manifestations of the bodies that tell them and importantly are a media for body-selves to express and reflexively monitor themselves (Sparkes, 1999; Frank, 2013). We should encourage ways for gymnasts to tell and generate new stories. Telling stories according to Frank is an ethical endeavour and researchers and practitioners should look for ways to enable gymnasts to exercise responsibility for bodies *through* stories.

References

Barker-Ruchti, N. (2009). Ballerinas and pixies: A genealogy of the changing female gymnastics body. *The International Journal of the History of Sport*, 26(1), 45–62.

Barker-Ruchti, N., & Tinning, R. (2010). Foucault in leotards: Corporeal discipline in women's artistic gymnastics. *Sociology of Sport Journal*, 27(3), 229–250.

Barker-Ruchti, N., Kerr, R., Schubring, A., Crevin, G., & Nunomura, M. (2017). 'Gymnasts are like wine, they get better with age': Becoming and developing adult women's artistic gymnasts, *Quest*, 69(3), 348–365.

Barker-Ruchti, N., Schubring, A., & Stewart, C. (forthcoming). Gender-based violence in women's artistic gymnastics and implications for prevention and other sports. *Routledge handbook of athlete welfare*. London: Routledge.

Becker, G. (1997). *Disrupted lives: How people create meaning in a chaotic world*. Berkeley: University of California Press.

Brewer, J. (2000). *Ethnography*. Buckingham: McGraw-Hill Education.

Beames, S., & Pike, E. (2008). Goffman goes rock climbing: Using creative fiction to explore the presentation of self in outdoor education. *Australian Journal of Outdoor Education*, 12(2), 3–11.

Caine, D., Bass, S. L., & Daly, R. (2003). Does elite competition inhibit growth and delay maturation in some gymnasts? Quite possibly. *Pediatric Exercise Science*, 15, 360–372.

De Bruin, A. K., Oudejans, R. R., & Bakker, F. C. (2007). Dieting and body image in aesthetic sports: A comparison of Dutch female gymnasts and non-aesthetic sport participants. *Psychology of Sport and Exercise*, 8(4), 507–520.

Donnelly, P., & Young, K. (1988). The construction and confirmation of identity in sport subcultures. *Sociology of Sport Journal*, 5(3), 223–240.

Eakin, P. J. (1999). *How our lives become stories: Making selves*. Ithaca, NY: Cornell University Press.

Eakin, P. J. (2008). *Living autobiographically: How we create identity in narrative*. Ithaca, NY: Cornell University Press.

Edouard, P., Steffen, K., Junge, A., Leglise, M., Soligard, T., & Engebretsen, L. (2018). Gymnastics injury incidence during the 2008, 2012 and 2016 Olympic Games: Analysis of prospectively collected surveillance data from 963 registered gymnasts during Olympic Games. *British Journal of Sports Medicine*, 52(7), 475–481.

Fédération Internationale de Gymnastique. (2016). 2017–2020 code of points: Trampoline gymnastics. Retrieved from: http://www.fig-gymnastics.com/publicdir/rules/files/tra/TRA-CoP_2017-2020-e.pdf.

Frank, A. W. (1991). For a sociology of the body: an analytical review. In M. Featherstone, M. Hepworth, & B. S. Turner (Eds.), *The body: Social process and cultural theory* (pp. 36–102). London: Sage.

Frank, A. W. (2000). Illness and autobiographical work: Dialogue as narrative destabilization. *Qualitative Sociology*, 23(1), 135–156.

Frank, A. W. (2010). *Letting stories breathe: A socio-narratology*. Chicago, IL: University of Chicago Press.

Frank, A. W. (2013). *The wounded storyteller: Body, illness, and ethics*. Chicago, IL: University of Chicago Press.

Goffman, E. (1963). *Stigma: Notes on a spoiled identity*. Englewood Cliffs, NJ: Prentice-Hall.

Goffman, E. (1990). *The presentation of self in everyday life*. London: Penguin.

Kerr, G., & Dacyshyn, A. (2000). The retirement experiences of elite, female gymnasts. *Journal of Applied Sport Psychology*, 12(2), 115–133.

Kerr, G., Berman, E., & De Souza, M. (2006). Disordered eating in women's gymnastics: Perspectives of athletes, coaches, parents, and judges. *Journal of Applied Sport Psychology*, 18(1), 28–43. doi:10.1080/10413200500471301.

Kerr, R., Barker-Ruchti, N., Nunomura, M., Cervin, G., & Schubring, A. (2018). The role of setting in the field: The positioning of older bodies in the field of elite women's gymnastics. *Sociology*, 52(4), 727–743.

Kerr, R., Barker-Ruchti, N., Schubring, A., Crevin, G., & Nunomura, M. (2017). Coming of age: coaches transforming the pixie-style model of coaching in women's artistic gymnastics. *Sport Coaching Review*. doi:10.1080/21640629.2017.1391488.

Lavallee, D., & Robinson, H. K. (2007). In pursuit of an identity: A qualitative exploration of retirement from women's artistic gymnastics. *Psychology of Sport and Exercise*, 8(1), 119–141.

Leder, D. (1990). *The absent body*. Chicago, IL: University of Chicago Press.

McMahon, F. (2017). Gender expectations sustained in the sport of gymnastics. *The Lehigh Review*, 25, Lehigh University.

Neves, C. M., Filgueiras Meireles, J. F., Berbert de Carvalho, P. H., Schubring, A., Barker-Ruchti, N., & Caputo Ferreira, M. E. (2017). Body dissatisfaction in women's artistic gymnastics: A longitudinal study of psychosocial indicators. *Journal of Sports Sciences*, 35(17), 1745–1751.

Pinheiro, M. C., Pimenta, N., Resende, R., & Malcolm, D. (2014). Gymnastics and child abuse: An analysis of former international Portuguese female artistic gymnasts. *Sport, Education and Society*, 19(4), 435–450.

Shilling, C. (2012). *The body and social theory*. London: Sage.

Smith, B., & Sparkes, A. C. (2002). Men, sport, spinal cord injury and the construction of coherence: Narrative practice in action. *Qualitative Research*, 2(2), 143–171.

Smith, J. K. (1989). *The nature of social education enquiry: Empiricism versus interpretation*. New Jersey: Alex Publishing.

Smits, F., Jacobs, F., & Knoppers, A. (2017). 'Everything revolves around gymnastics': athletes and parents make sense of elite youth sport. *Sport in Society*, 20(1), 66–83.

Sparkes, A. C. (1997). Reflections on the socially constructed physical self. In K. R. Fox (Ed.), *The physical self: From motivation to well-being* (pp. 83–110). Champaign IL: Human Kinetics.

Sparkes, A. C. (1999). Exploring body narratives. *Sport, Education and Society*, 4(1), 17–30.

Sparkes, A. C. (2004). Bodies, narratives, selves and autobiography: The example of Lance Armstrong. *Journal of Sport and Social Issues*, 28(4), 397–428.

Sparkes, A. C., & Smith, B. (2014). *Qualitative research methods in sport exercise and health: From process to product*. Oxon: Routledge.

Stewart, C., & Pullen, E. (2014). Monadic, material and mirroring: Female bodies in track athletic culture. *International Review for the Sociology of Sport*, 52(6), 658–678.

Stewart, C., Schiavon, L. M., & Bellotto, M. L. (2017). Knowledge, nutrition and coaching pedagogy: A perspective from female Brazilian Olympic gymnasts. *Sport, Education and Society*, 22(4), 511–527.

Stirling, A. E., & Kerr, G. A. (2013). The perceived effects of elite athletes' experiences of emotional abuse in the coach–athlete relationship. *International Journal of Sport and Exercise Psychology*, 11(1), 87–100.

Weber, J., & Barker-Ruchti, N. (2012). Bending, flirting, floating, flying: A critical analysis of female figures in 1970s gymnastics photographs. *Sociology of Sport Journal*, 29(1), 22–41.

Van Maanen, J. (1988). *Tales of the field: On writing ethnography*. Chicago, IL: University of Chicago Press.

Part III

Coach-athlete relationships

Jenny's story Part III: Worries and pressures

James Pope

So we continued, and I became very good.

I was competing at junior national level, and in the top 10. Frank said I had to work harder to get to the top. He was right. Frank was very strict but he didn't slap me like that again. Maybe I'd overreacted to it anyway? All the coaches were strict, after all; and some of my friends told me worse stories, so I kind of felt lucky I had Frank. And, as I say, he had a reputation, so I knew he could help me go higher. I was beginning to look at international competitions, and Frank said I was good enough. And I believed him – I still had that kind of awestruck feeling about him. He was charismatic, I suppose. And Mum was so positive about him.

On the other hand, it seems like, for quite a while he went cold on me. He seemed annoyed all the time. No more slapping, so that was good … but in a way it was worse that he wasn't nice to me either. It was just work. I hated the training. The training hurt, in your body and in your head. You took it for granted that it hurt, but there was also the fear of pushing yourself into doing things your body didn't want to do. Injuries happened. You could hear about bad ones and be frightened. But, huge but, I loved the competitions. The adrenaline of performing, perfecting a move, and the absolute rush if I won a medal. An unbeatable feeling. An amazing, huge burst of triumphant pleasure. What can I say? I was my own worst enemy, in a way. Frank didn't really have to push me – I pushed myself.

Like I said, I was small, so I was lucky as far as being a gymnast was concerned. Even so I had to keep my weight down. Mum would constantly remind me at meals, but I was already on it. I wasn't skinny, because I was building muscles, but I wasn't really growing like the other girls at school. All the girls at the gym were small, so it was OK when I was with them, and they were my focus. I didn't really have friends as such at school, because I was so busy training. Before school, after school, on Saturdays ... I had Caroline, Caz, a new friend I'd made at the club, but outside of the sport I was a loner really. It seems like I sacrificed something, but I was just so into it that I didn't even notice.

I suppose ... sometimes I did struggle. There was conflict in myself, I guess. Although I was a bit of a celeb at school, I was also a bit of an oddity. If I won something at a regional or national, there would be announcements at school, and of course how could I not love that? But when I heard girls talking about sleep-overs, or parties, I felt odd. I can't say I particularly wanted to go to parties – I was totally immersed in the training and the competitions. But you are aware of yourself. It sounds confusing when I read back what I've written, it seems contradictory. But I wanted the buzz, the muscles, and I couldn't become a girl who was lazy or ate too much, or who smoked.

I was aware too that I was stronger and fitter and more skilful than the others in my year at school, even the boys! In PE I could do everything better than the others. I know I liked being faster than the boys. And I could vault and tumble and somersault in a way the other kids couldn't even dream of! I was a Gymnast! Like a special type of human.

It was a very busy time, and I was in the midst of it. So the really weird stuff almost didn't bother me ... until it did, if you know what I mean. You LOVE what you're doing, and you want to get better, and win things, and you accept behaviour you wouldn't accept outside of that environment.

Frank began wanting photos of us. Not just me. And it's something I've heard of quite a bit. Photos of us in our leotards, showing off our bodies. I think they were for programmes at events, or for promoting the club, and Frank got one of the junior coaches to just snap away as I was going through my moves at training sessions.

But then he started to ask me to pose. 'Just hold that shape, for a moment.' Snap. 'Stretch.' Snap. I kind of liked it. I felt like a bit of a star already and this proved it, right? He would show me the photos, on the camera. I looked great, to me. I looked strong and professional. He seemed to like me more. He was able to flatter me, at the same time as he was cold and strict. As I'm remembering this I can see the problem, but not then. Some of the photos were action shots, and I liked those the best – I could see myself as an athlete, like Khorkina. You'd see photos in magazines and websites of elite gymnasts and they'd look fabulous: strong, muscular, shapely, elegant. And I'd see myself that way. But, as I say, some of the photos Frank wanted were posed. He started doing them himself.

You know the leotard is quite revealing. You're covered, but you're not, if you know what I mean. The guys don't have to show off their bodies like we do. But Frank was focusing on my legs and ... He would say 'this' and 'that' is what the judges would be looking for, and that's one of the reasons the leotards were cut away from the crotch area and up to your hips. He said it was really important for coaches and judges to be able to observe gymnasts' bodies for performance faults. He said he would study the photos to help me improve.

But the photos seemed embarrassing, somehow. It was just a feeling, a sort of being uncomfortable. He would show them to me, scroll through the shots after a session, before my mum came to get me. He would say 'That's it, that's the position we want,' and I'd find myself looking at myself doing a split, and I felt uneasy. No one really liked the leotard anyway – you were made not to wear underwear because you weren't supposed to show your knickers, but that felt like you were somehow exposed. I think we felt we had to look a certain way, in fact, I know that's how we felt. All the imagery of the sport in the media, and even girls' own pictures on social media. And Frank's damn photos didn't help my performance at all, now I think back.

Then again, own worst enemy, like I said before – I'd buy a leotard a size too small, so I'd have to get myself trimmed down to fit it … you don't realise how much your self-image gets warped by what's going on around you. Pressure to fit in.

I started to tighten up, especially if he had the camera. He'd get cold again, angry, cold, shout at me, insult me, then praise me. I was on edge and I couldn't perform for fear of the next thing he'd say. The photos began to get me down. More and more he was taking, and more and more posed, with my legs raised, or split. And he'd get close to my body sometimes. It's true that he never touched me, I never said he did – but sometimes he'd be so close that I could almost feel him.

You see photos on the internet: it's full of photos of gymnasts looking great, and you never think that any abuse is happening. But I begin to wonder if those gymnasts I loved were having this weird relationship with a coach who shouted, slapped them too hard, went cold, insulted their ability, then praised them, then took these close-up photos.

'Can I show my mum and dad these?' I said one evening when he was scrolling through the pictures. I asked innocently, I was literally thinking I looked nice and my parents would like them. 'Oh no,' he said. 'These are official, they've got copyright on them. They belong to the gym. Not me.' And I believed him. I was 14, I guess. What did I know?

We carried on. I must have started to ignore the photos, or I think maybe he eased off, because he knew I was edgy about the posing. I was winning medals, not a gold yet, but beginning to win. I was a star in my own little world. I was approaching the point where I might get to travel abroad. Wow! I was so excited about that. All my awkwardness with Frank vanished once I thought about the possibilities. And I did love the performing – don't forget that. It's obviously easy to criticise Frank, but I loved it, and I just thought Frank was a bit of an odd-bod.

And then, we went up to a national competition, in Edinburgh.

Chapter 8

Power in coach-athlete relationships
The case of women's artistic gymnastics

Sophia Jowett and Svenja Wachsmuth

Introduction

In sport, the coach-athlete relationship is a purposeful relationship at the heart of coaching (Jowett, 2017). While the positive effects of good quality coach-athlete relationships have been acknowledged and evidenced (Davis, Jowett, & Lafrenière, 2013; Felton & Jowett, 2013b), the nature of power in relationships and the impact of power on relationships have yet to be fully understood. This chapter explores the concept of power and its potential effects on both coaches and athletes' outcomes including wellbeing (sense of health, safety, and fulfilment) as well as performance (sense of competence and achievement).

The coach-athlete relationship

The relationship is commonly viewed as a 'two-way street' by coaches and athletes (Antonini Philippe & Seiler, 2006; Jowett & Cockerill, 2003; Wylleman, 2000). Such a description illustrates the mutuality and reciprocity that often exists within this unique partnership and underlines the responsibility, accountability, and dependability shared by both coaches and athletes. This unique coach-athlete relationship is purported to be central to coaching (see Lyle & Cushion, 2017). Coaching becomes a shared context and process within which *both* a coach and an athlete are expected to contribute. Subsequently, their contributions define the effectiveness of coaching and in turn performance success (Jowett, 2017). There are many high-profile examples of coaches and athletes whose partnership defined their success in competitive, high-performance sport. In gymnastics, Aimee Boorman and Simone Biles (USA women's gymnastics team for the Olympics in 2016) have been described as an 'inseparable pair'. Biles offered this description of her relationship with her coach:

> She knows how I feel whenever I walk through the door and what mood I'm in because we've known each other for so long ... There are times

when she has to push me because I'm not pushing myself enough, but everyone needs someone in their life to do that.

(Barron, 2016)

Her coach, Aimee Boorman, reported: 'She has to perform it, and she has to make the choices to home-school and work the extra hours and do the extra flexibility work. That has been her choice. I'm just her guide' (Barron, 2016). This is a powerful example of a coach-athlete relationship that contains dependability – marked by a strong bond, trustworthiness, and consciousness. There is no doubt that there are many factors in athletes' and coaches' careers that play a major role in their success including training plans, technique work, mental training, physiotherapy, and nutrition but one aspect, more than any other, is the coach-athlete relationship. The relationship lays the foundation for coaches' and athletes' personal and interpersonal satisfaction, achievement of goals, and ultimate performance success. Over that past two decades, research has started to unravel the role and significance of this important relationship.

Theoretical and empirical perspectives of the coach-athlete relationship

Since the turn of the century, a number of coach-athlete relationship frameworks have been proposed (see e.g., Poczwardowski et al., 2002; Shepherd, Lee, & Kerr, 2006; Wylleman, 2000); however, one framework that has gained considerable empirical attention is the 3+1Cs model (Jowett & Shanmugam, 2017). This model postulates that the coach-athlete relationship is an interpersonal situation within which coaches' *and* athletes' behaviours (Complementarity), thoughts (Commitment), and feelings (Closeness) are mutually and causally interconnected (Co-orientation). *Complementarity* describes coaches' and athletes' co-operation. This type of co-operation is captured in two ways. First, it is captured in behaviours that are corresponding and hence both coaches and athletes are expected to express and include responsiveness, readiness, receptiveness, easiness, and friendliness. Second, it is captured in behaviours that are reciprocal and hence both coaches and athletes are expected to carry out their unique roles whereby coaches orchestrate, direct, and lead while athletes listen, inquire, learn, filter in information, and execute. *Commitment* defines the intention of the coach and the athlete to maintain a close relationship *over time*. It contains such relational properties as *reliance* on each other for future development and success as well as *loyalty* to each other from season to season, through good and bad times or highs and lows. Commitment is especially important as such events as success and failure, burnout and injury, as well as personal circumstances (e.g., death or illness, divorce or separation, of a relative or significant other) are capable of de-stabilising the bond and future of the relationship by creating uncertainty, friction, or risk. Commitment is the glue that keeps coaches and athletes together over time. *Closeness* refers to the emotional connection or affective bond developed between a coach and an athlete. It contains such relational properties as *trust, respect, appreciation*, interpersonal *liking*, and emotional *caring*. Acknowledging the importance of each athlete and valuing his or her unique contributions, coaches should treat everyone with dignity and respect. Connecting with all athletes in the team or squad, understanding their 'back stories', who they are and what they want to achieve, their needs, wants, and desires, coaches care for their athletes and feel compassionate and empathic toward them. Finally, *Co-orientation* is essentially a 'meeting of the minds' – it captures the degree to which a coach and an athlete understand the relationship they have developed in (dis)similar ways. It reflects a dyad's common ground, similarity, and understanding (see Lorimer & Jowett, 2011).

Research to date has investigated the significance of the relationship and its nature (e.g., Antonini Philippe & Seiler, 2006; Jowett, 2003; Jowett & Cockerill, 2003; Trzaskoma-Biscerdy et al., 2007) as well as its antecedents and consequences (e.g., Adie & Jowett, 2010; Felton & Jowett, 2013b; Hampson & Jowett, 2014; Jowett & Nezlek, 2012; Jowett, Nicolas, & Yang, 2017; Lafrenière, Jowett, Vallerand, & Carbonneau, 2011). Researchers have also attempted to study the role of communication strategies (Rhind & Jowett, 2011; 2012), interpersonal conflict (Wachsmuth, Jowett, & Harwood, 2017; 2018), empathy (empathic understanding: Jowett & Clark-Carter, 2006; empathic accuracy: Lorimer & Jowett, 2010; 2011) and rules (Jowett & Carpenter, 2015) in the coach-athlete relationship. Taken together, evidence suggests that a good *quality* coach-athlete relationship may hold the key to athletes' and coaches' satisfaction (wellbeing) and success (performance). Whereas, *poor* quality coach-athlete relationships may have the capacity to undermine its positive role and thus impact negatively on both performance and wellbeing

Power differentials in the coach-athlete relationship

Coaches and athletes who find themselves in good quality relationships where there is trust and respect (closeness) as well as optimistic future or positive outlook (commitment) and co-operation (complementarity) are more likely to enjoy the journey of developing and growing together within the context of sport (Jowett & Cockerill, 2003; Vella, Oades, & Crowe, 2013). A good quality relationship has the capacity to empower and energise both the coach and the athlete. This sense of empowerment may start with the coach and the role that he or she plays. As described earlier the role of the coach is that of the leader, director, and orchestrator. The coach not only is expected to lead courageously by making tough decisions and taking risks but also is expected to positively influence his/her athletes by engaging and involving them in the coaching process, in the decision making, and making them part of the vision and values of their sport. Good quality relationships help coaches lead and influence their athletes. Coaches who have the capacity to connect with and care about their athletes as well as encourage their hearts are more likely to make athletes feel better about themselves and inspire them to be more than they ever thought possible (Antonini Philippe & Seiler, 2006; Jowett & Cockerill, 2003). The dyadic relationship of Biles and Boorman is a great example of a coach who 'served', empowered, and supported her gymnast to be the very best version of herself. It would seem that Boorman supported Biles to openly voice her thoughts (without fear or intimidation), dream big, and continuously strive to develop by being accountable and responsible for her development and success. Under such conditions, the *power* of the coach is distributed developing a collaborative, inclusive, and athlete-centred environment (see e.g., Jowett, 2017; Kidman & Davis, 2006). Such coaches recognise the influential power inherent in the position of a coach (Mallett & Lara-Bercial, 2016) though they carefully access and manage it in ways that enable and facilitate the athlete to actively be part of the coaching process through working together as one. While 'relational coaching' where the quality of the relationship provides the platform for the above processes to take place sounds simple, it is not always easy to apply (see Jowett & Shanmugam, 2017).

Coaches' primary role is to enhance athletes' performance, motivation, confidence, responsibility autonomy and in this process to make a positive and significant impact on athletes' lives; however, some coaches fall short. One important reason for that is relationships; in this scenario, coaches are unaware or unwilling to grasp the role of relationships as well as the power and influence in relationships. Subsequently, coaches and their athletes find themselves in impersonal coaching environments that are unsafe and toxic underlined by such attitudes as 'if coach doesn't care, then why should I care'. Athletes who experience such environments are more likely to think of their coaches as uncooperative and unsupportive and reflect on their sport with resentment and anger (see D'Arripe-Longueville, Fournier, & Dubois, 1998; Wachsmuth, Jowett, & Harwood, 2017; 2018). These impersonal environments are self/ego-centred characterised by isolation and anxiety, uncertainty or instability, and uneasiness or disharmony.

It is in such impersonal environments that are most likely to find coaches misusing their power by coercing exploiting, abusing, manipulating and mistreating their athletes. In gymnastics, prominent examples of dysfunctional coach-athlete partnerships, in spite of performance successes, can be found in the writings of Joan Ryan. In her book *Little Girls in Pretty Boxes* (Ryan, 1995) the author describes unrelenting coaching practices which would lead athletes to experience anxiety, injuries, and mental health issues lasting beyond the end of their sporting career. Similar accounts have been brought to our attention by athletes, such as Aly Raisman (Jenkins, 2018), speaking up about the emotional, physical, and sexual abuse they had to withstand. The relevant literature has also illustrated that misusing the power inherent in the coaches' role can lead to coaching practices that are less than ideal. Such intrusive, inappropriate, or unacceptable coach behaviours and practices have been connected to negative outcomes both mental (e.g., anxiety, eating disorders, depressive symptoms) and physical (e.g., overuse injuries, chronic pain) (e.g., Cavallerio, Wadey, & Wagstaff, 2016; Krane, Snow, & Greenleaf, 1997; Stirling & Kerr, 2007; 2009; 2013; Tamminen, Holt, & Neely, 2013).

Burke (2001) referred to coaches misusing their power by harassing, abusing, and exploiting their athletes. He stated that 'sport provides the coach with almost unquestionable authority over the athlete' and explained that 'coaches often view their athletes as their possessions' (p. 229). Burke's position was that close and trusting coach-athlete relationships are risky and his proposed solution was that coaches and athletes should keep their distance. However, keeping one's distance from another means that empathy and understanding are undermined denying what coaches and especially athletes want, need, and desire from each other (Jowett & Meek, 2000; Yambor, 1998). Tomlinson and Yorganci (1997), in a similar vein as Burke, argued that 'relations of power and control that characterize all coach-athlete relations' (p. 136) create a climate of perfect exploitation, manipulation, and mistreatment especially around the male coach and female athlete. Their study identified that there is a 'culture of [male] coach domination' (p. 151) where female athletes are powerless to a variety of forms of coach power including discrimination and abuse (see also De Haan & Norman, 2019).

In an attempt to understand the power dynamics of coach-athlete relationships, Drewe (2002) referred to the notion of friendship. She explained that the coach-athlete relationship cannot be compared to 'deep friendships' (Drewe, 2002, p. 175) because there will always be unequal influence and power. The assumption made by Drewe is that the coach determines what is good for the athlete concerning her sport and so 'authoritative assessment remains the prerogative of the coach' (p. 176). However, Drewe (2002) agreed that 'sharing information would seem to be a critical factor in the coach-athlete relationship' (p. 178) and many studies over the years have supported her contention (Antonini Philippe & Seiler, 2006; Jowett, 2003; Jowett & Cockerill, 2003; Jowett & Meek, 2000; Trzaskoma-Bicsérdy et al., 2007). Subsequently, Drewe proposed that on the basis that coaching pivots around inequality and asymmetry between coaches and athletes, 'deep friendships' should be better avoided and 'utility friendships' should be encouraged. However, if coaches and athletes develop a utility relationship, then the nature of connection discussed earlier and its accompanied warmth, compassion, consideration, kindness, supportiveness, identification (i.e., the human touch embraced in understanding the other's feelings and problems) are likely to be absent.

The perspectives offered by Drewe, Burke, Tomlinson, and Yorganci would seem to value the central role of the coach-athlete relationship in coaching. However, at the same time, they would seem to wrestle with issues revolving around (a) the type or nature of relationship that coaches and athletes develop and (b) the power and influence associated with the role of the coach and how coaches' power is being utilised in the relationship. Their characterisations of coach power in coach-athlete interactions include inequality versus equality, dependence versus interdependence, distance versus proximity, trust versus distrust as well as an amalgamation of respect, sharing information, honesty, empathy, and the like. These characterisations of power and the differentials of power that have been discussed would need to be further explored and discovered through sound theory and research and to be understood within the contemporary, twenty-first century, coaching practices and processes and the evolving roles of coaches and athletes.

Characteristics and manifestations of coach power

There is recent evidence, albeit limited, that has attempted to bring to life the concept of power within the context of coaching. From a psychological standpoint, French and Raven (1959) view power as nothing that can be possessed by the individual who aims to influence but is rather ascribed by the one being influenced. An alternative view is that power or more precisely attempts to influence another becomes a property of the members comprising the relationship, namely the coach and the athlete but also a property of their relationship itself (Jowett & Arthur, 2019). Following from the above assumptions, coaches are as powerful as athletes let them be by attributing sources of power, such as knowledge or the capacity to punish and reward, to the coach. This relational understanding of power also implies some kind of dependency between individuals, meaning that coaches are only powerful if they possess something that their athlete desires (e.g., their knowledge, attention, a chance for sporting success) and which they can exchange for receiving control (i.e., power and influence) over the athlete and vice versa.

Within French and Raven's (1959) framework, six distinct sources of power are described: three of these align with the traditional negative connotation of power and have been classified as *anti-social* (legitimate, coercive, reward power) reflecting coaches' formal, ascribed position and capacity to reward or punish, whereas three represent *pro-social* types of power (expert, informational, and referential power) reflecting coaches' ability to influence athletes by being perceived as knowledgeable, well-informed, capable, and efficacious in their coaching role. While athletes usually report multiple sources of coach power, legitimate (athlete perceives that coach has the right to affect him/her) and expert (athlete perceives that the coach has the special and unique knowledge that he/she needs) power are especially relevant for athletes' adherence to coaches' commands (e.g., Gargalianos, Laios, &

Theodorakis, 2003; Konter, 2012; Purdy & Jones, 2011; Rylander, 2014) and are seen as part of the coach-athlete relationship (Antonini Philippe & Seiler, 2006; Jowett & Cockerill, 2003). Nevertheless, individual characteristics such as age, gender, performance status as well as the duration of the coach-athlete relationship significantly influence the power attributed to coaches. For example, research would seem to suggest that younger athletes attribute more power to coaches compared to older, more experienced athletes (Konter, 2012; Turman, 2006), while expert and referential (coach is someone who athlete admires) power of coaches is strongly associated with female athletes and athletes who had been in long-lasting relationships with their coach (Rylander, 2014).

Purdy and Jones (2011) described a coaching environment governed by oppression, unfairness, and dominance in which a high-performing athlete challenged the power dynamics between coaching staff and the group of athletes by refusing to adhere to the determined training regime. Following the example of this athlete, other athletes started undermining the power of their coaches by showing them less respect, trust, and commitment. Purdy and Jones' study illustrates athletes' power to resist the power of their coaches. Moreover, the study highlights that such sources of legitimate and coercive power are limited and less effective. Another piece of research evidence has shown that coaches may be able to exert influence, in this case negative (intimidation and coercion), to lower-status players more easily than to higher-status (more successful) players (e.g., Cruickshank, Collins, & Minten, 2013; Purdy & Jones, 2011; Rylander, 2014).

French and Raven's framework provides a good starting point to explore power; it does not explain the shifts in power (e.g., low-high power or having or not having power) or how power operates in dyads that are established (long-term relationships) or when relationships comprise members that are mature and experienced. Overall, the framework does not provide explanations about (1) how the various sources of power are activated in the process of exerting influence within coaching or within the coach-athlete relationship or (2) how being a more powerful versus a less powerful athlete or coach affects personal (e.g., motivation, confidence, anxiety, dropout, burnout) and interpersonal (e.g., better relationship, team belonginess, social identity, collective efficacy) outcomes. This is because this framework focusses on individuals rather than individuals within two person relationships, like the coach-athlete relationship.

By valuing or acknowledging each other's powers, coaches and athletes empower each other to make a positive and significant difference in their sport (Jowett & Arthur, 2019) and create a relational coaching environment where athletes and coaches are free to be themselves and are open to listen, attend, grasp, notice, and appreciate each other (cf. Jones, Armour, & Potrac, 2002). Such coaching environments, while not reducing coaches' power, grow athletes' power (e.g., feelings of ownership over their personal development). May (1972; cited from Jones et al., 2002) calls this the *nutrient power* of coaches – 'the power to help another person'. Indeed, serial winning coaches have referred to power as a motivational theme in that they can positively influence others (Mallett & Lara-Bercial, 2016). These coaches were described as lifelong learners, confident decision-makers, and leaders who can mobilise athletes. These highly successful coaches used their power to positively influence their athletes by promoting an attitude of 'believe in me, believe in you and believe in us!' Subsequently, the coach-athlete relationship became a true partnership rather than a hierarchy and athletes recognised their coaches' efforts to create inclusivity; they were aware that the final decision-making power resided with their coaches. Not only were they aware of it, they accepted and expected their coaches to make ruthless yet not heartless decisions having the best interest of athletes and the sporting organisation in mind. Mallett and Lara-Bercial termed this set of processes *benevolent dictatorship* highlighting the positive and nourishing power coaches can utilise to support their athletes in becoming the best they can be. Taken together coaches' power over athletes would seem to have two sides: oppressive (negative) and nutrient (and positive) (Clifford & Feezell, 1997).

One aspect that has been missed or neglected from the theoretical work and empirical evidence thus far is athletes' power and more importantly the power athletes (and coaches) have within the context of the coach-athlete relationship. Only few authors have addressed athletes' sources and use of power (e.g., Cruickshank et al., 2013; Purdy, Jones, & Cassidy, 2009) arguing that athletes' sporting success, popularity, as well as their connections with others (i.e., cliques, leadership groups, sport agents), may put them in a place of power – to the extent that they may even hold more power than their coaches. The section below aims to provide an approach to the study of power that is grounded in theoretical and empirical research with the view to generate systematic knowledge and understanding around power in the coach-athlete relationship.

Power in the coach-athlete relationship

According to the philosopher Bernand Russell (1938), 'The fundamental concept in social science is power, in the same sense in which energy is the fundamental concept in physics ... The law of social dynamics are laws which can be stated in terms of power' (p. 22). Despite the importance of power in social interaction, power has never been a focal point for either theoretical or empirical activity within social psychology. In sport psychology, there is some research as outlined earlier but there is a lack of a concerted effort that allows building knowledge and understanding especially as this pertains to the coach-athlete relationship. One of the potential reasons why power has not become a central construct within social psychology including sport psychology literature is its definition and conceptual frameworks to guide research. Simpson and colleagues explained that there are far too many definitions and definitions that do not capture its multidimensional nature adequately and accurately (Simpson, Farrell, Orina, & Rothman, 2015).

It has been suggested that the study of power requires researchers to consider both the *strategies* and the *tactics* used by relationship members to get what they want from one another in order to more fully understand relationship dynamics and outcomes (Reis, Collins, & Berscheid, 2000). Reis et al. (2000) explained that influence strategies are conveyed through the use of influence tactics and can include *coercion, autocracy, reasoning, and manipulation*. The aim of choosing such influence tactics is to help achieve the *agent's (coach or athlete's)* 'higher level goals or objectives' by influencing the *target (coach or athlete's)* within the relationship. In brief, strategies represent higher level goals and interpersonal approaches that the agent may use to try to persuade the target. According to Overall, Fletcher, Simpson, and Sibley (2009), influence strategies exist along two dimensions: *direction* (direct vs. indirect) and *valence* (positive vs. negative). Direct strategies contain overt, visible, and unambiguous attempts to influence another person. In contrast, indirect strategies involve more covert, less visible, and more subtle forms of influence. Positive strategies concern the use of promises or rewards to influence another person, whereas negative strategies revolve around the use of threats or punishments. As in all kinds of relationships, it is important to appreciate the amount and types (e.g., set goals, make decisions, lead, engage, collaborate) of power of coaches and athletes, if we are to fully comprehend and predict the actions of either relationship member and the outcomes as well as the life-course of the coach-athlete relationship.

Simpson and colleagues (2015) conducted a thorough theoretical and empirical review of power and influence both from within and outside the relationship literature. A summary of six most influential theories of power and influence is presented in Table 8.1.

The section below builds on this review to discuss a conceptualisation of power in relationships as put forward by Simpson and colleagues (2015). We discuss this conceptualisation in terms of its application to the coach-athlete relationship as a medium to organise current sport-related research and provide an impetus of theoretical-grounded research in this area.

The dyadic power-social influence model in the coach-athlete relationship

The dyadic model of power and social influence in relationships as proposed by Simpson et al. (2015) integrates and builds on the constructs and principles identified in six major theoretical frameworks reviewed. The model is known as the dyadic power-social influence model (DPSIM). Power within

Table 8.1 Major power theories (taken from Simpson et al., 2015 with permission)

Theory	What is power?	Is power dyadic?	What are the sources or bases of power?	How is power expressed or communicated in interactions?	What are the outcomes of (not) having power?
Social power theory (French & Raven, 1959)	The potential for influence	No	Reward, coercive, legitimate, referent, expert, informational	Through influence processes	
Resource theory (Blood & Wolfe, 1960)	The ability (potential or actual) of an individual to change the behaviour of other members in the social system	Yes; theory considers relative access to resources between partners	Relative access to important or valued resources		
Interdependence theory (Thibaut & Kelley, 1959)	The ability of one person to directly influence the quality of outcomes of another person	Yes; theory considers relative dependence between partners	Relative dependence, fate control, behaviour control, expertise	Through power strategies that elevate one's own power and reduce others' power	The more powerful partner can dictate outcomes for both partners
Dyadic power theory (Rollins & Bahr, 1976)	The ability or potential to influence or control the behaviour of another person	Yes; theory considers relative power, authority, and control between partners	Perception of relative resources and authority	Increased perceived power → increased control attempts → increased power	

Theory	What is power?	Is power dyadic?	What are the sources or bases of power?	How is power expressed or communicated in interactions?	What are the outcomes of (not) having power?
Power within relationships theory (Huston, 1983)	The ability to achieve one's goals by intentionally influencing the partner	Yes; theory considers the traits, relationship norms, and environment of both partners	Reward, coercive, legitimate, referent, expert, informational	Through intentional, deliberate influence tactics	The more powerful partner can dictate outcomes for both partners
Power-approach theory (Keltner et al., 2003)	An individual's relative capacity to modify others' internal states	Yes; theory considers relative access and desire for resources	Holding desired resources, being able to administer punishments	Through providing or withholding resources or Administering punishments	Mood expression, threat sensitivity, automaticity of cognition, approach or inhibition, consistency or coherence of behaviour

this model is defined 'as the ability or capacity to change another person's thoughts, feelings, or behavior so they align with one's own desired preferences, along with the ability or capacity to resist influence attempts imposed by another person' (Simpson et al., 2015, p. 409). It is important to note that this definition of power considers both the agent and target both of whom can influence and resist influence. Subsequently, both coach and athlete are agents and targets of power. There are four sets of constructs that are critical to understanding the operation of power and influence when DPSIM is applied to the coach-athlete relationship: (1) the specific characteristics of the coach and athlete in the relationship (e.g., each person's resources, relationship quality, personality, culture, ethnicity, social class, goals, needs, motives); (2) the type of coach and athlete's power potentially held and used (e.g., French and Raven's (1959) six sources of power: reward, coercive, legitimate, expert, reference, and informational); (3) the type of strategies and their underlying tactics that the coach and/or the athlete is able to deploy (direct/explicit/direct vs indirect/passive to resolve issues/inspire change and using tactics with positive vs negative affect); and (4) the outcomes experienced after influence attempts from the either the coach or athlete or both (e.g., wellbeing, life/sport satisfaction, anxiety, depression, performance success/failure, relationship quality) (see Figure 8.1).

In accordance with the model both the coach and the athlete reside in a social environment (formulated by the sport organisation, its specific club or team culture, embedded in its vision and mission and so on) and they are likely to bring their unique characteristics and resources (personality, goals, motives, needs, desires and so on) to the relationship. These elements form

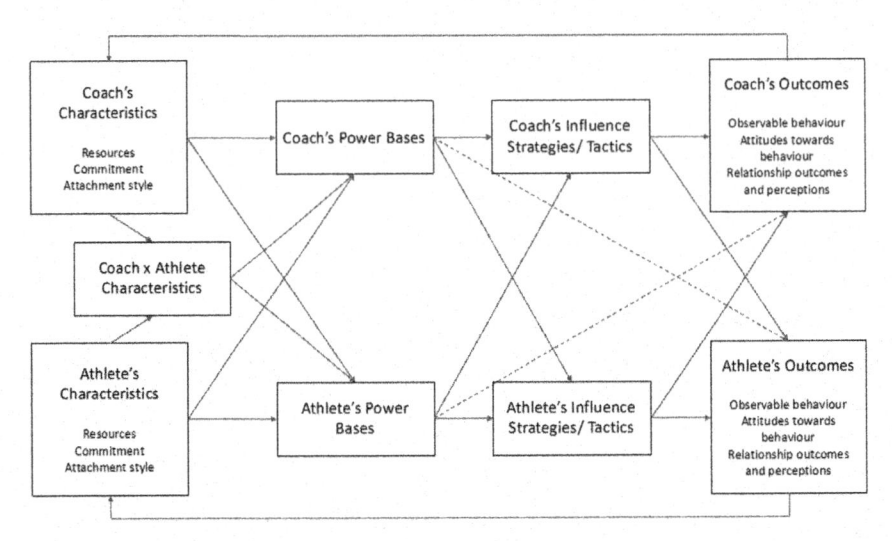

Figure 8.1 The dyadic power–social influence model
Source: taken from Simpson et al., 2015 with permission.

the basis for the type of power that each member has and can use which is likely then to dictate the specific influence strategies and tactics that each member utilises to reach his or her way in decision-making situations. Strategies and tactics utilised affect subsequently attitude and behaviour change as well as important outcomes (e.g., performance, satisfaction). The example that follows illustrates parts of the model.

> A coach and a gymnast have just started working together. The coach operates at the high-performance level of gymnastics; she is accomplished (won a number of accolades with other gymnasts nationally and internationally) and is known for being confident, well informed, knowledgeable, and very interpersonal (caring, understanding, loyal) in her coaching approach. The gymnast has had a successful career as a youth, however, an injury and transitioning to senior level has shaken her confidence though she remains fully committed to her sport and excited for the 'new start'; nonetheless she feels extremely anxious as she desperately wants to impress her coach and do well. According to DSPIM, the coach's and the gymnast's characteristics separately and together affect the sources of power they may be available to them. From the coach's point of view, all sources of power may be available (though due to her characteristics, coercive power may be a source that the coach does not utilise or under-utilise) in any given situation; however, knowing what she knows about the gymnast she may feel that reward and expert power may be the preferred source to influence her. From the gymnast's point of view, some sources may be available (e.g., referent, information) to her than others (e.g., coercion) and her preference may be to utilise information power to influence. In this scenario, the coach enters the relationship able to use different sources of power and thus can communicate in ways that are convincing and influential so that she gets her way in most decision-making discussions with the gymnast.
>
> Subsequently, if the coach and the athlete were to set goals for the foreseeable months or the entire season, the coach would use or may access expert, informational, or potentially reward sources of power while the athlete would choose or access informational and potentially referent power to influence the course of the discussion and decision making. During this process, the coach may use a combination of direct and positive strategies and tactics while the athlete may use indirect and positive strategies leading to influence (e.g., the coach fills the gymnast with confidence and the gymnast accepts the influence on the basis that she feels that the coach has her best interest at heart – she admires her coach and believes she has positive intentions for her) and experience positive outcomes (e.g., I like/trust this coach/gymnast and want to work with her to achieve performance goals) from this process. The outcomes

experienced by the coach may depend on the reaction (positive or negative) of the gymnast and on how important the issue was for her and how hard the coach had to work to influence (types of strategies/ tactics utilised) the gymnast.

If the gymnast is viewed as having fewer sources of power from which she can influence the coach – especially when it comes to decision-making domains that are important to the coach for ensuring progress and development (e.g., intensity, length, content of training, selection of competitions, and attending training camps), then her coach's characteristics and preferences are likely to restrict what she can say and do. However, as their relationship develop over time, the gymnast may gradually assume more domain-specific decision making which may increase her general power in the relationship and as such the opportunity to influence and achieve the outcomes she desires. It is then likely to develop a more equitable relationship and become more dependent on one another because what is good for the gymnast is good for the coach. The gymnast may choose to seize the opportunity to access greater power and not simply 'hand over' her power to the coach (coaches need support from their athletes and athletes have access to resources that coaches may not have). Last but not least, it is important to appreciate that coaches whose role may be seen as that of being the more powerful member in the coach-athlete relationship do not inherently have more power because they have resources. It is the athletes whose role may be seen as that of being the less powerful member in the coach-athlete relationship who usually give their coaches the power.

In summary, this process model outlines that each relationship member (coach & athlete) and relationship characteristics (dyad) affect the capacity and use of each member's potential sources of power, strategies, and tactics, and personal and/or relationship outcomes. Moreover, Simpson and colleagues explain that the broader context (social environment) within which coach-athlete dyads operate may affect the personal characteristics each brings to the relationship. Power, according to the DPSIM, is a dyadic construct and this is captured in the proposed actor and partner effects model (see Figure 8.1). The actor effects are reflected in the parallel lines running from left to right in the centre of the model. *Actor effects* refer to the ways in which an actor's (athlete or coach's) characteristics affect his or her own access to power bases, use of specific influence strategies and tactics, and personal or interpersonal outcomes (statistically controlled for the other relationship member's attributes). The partner effects are reflected in the nonparallel lines running from left to right. *Partner effects* refer to how, for example, an athlete's characteristics affect the coach's access to power bases, use of specific influence strategies, and tactics (statistically controlling for the other relationship member's attributes).

Guided by the proposed model, we would be more likely to generate important knowledge and understanding around such questions as: how do coaches and athletes trade-off the various personal characteristics they contribute to their relationship (e.g., status, roles, needs, desires, closeness) or how do these trade-offs affect the power and influence within relationships as they develop? What happens when the characteristics of an athlete change (e.g., becomes an Olympic champion, suffers from an injury, or underperforms) over the course of a relationship and how may this change the sources of power or influence tactics utilised by the athlete for example? How (when) do the different sources of power (French & Raven, 1959) lead to the deployment of specific strategies and tactics, especially in established coach-athlete relationships, where repeated use of certain tactic (coercion vs. reward) may become ineffective as athletes, for example, assume more domain-specific decision-making roles and become more interdependent (from dependent)? What happens when coaches decide to use certain power bases or sources of power rather than others and how or why they interchange different strategies and tactics over time to generate behaviour change in their athletes with the least negative outcomes for them? Furthermore, there is a need to explore the nature (quality and quantity) of influence strategies and tactics that coaches and athletes employ and how these affect important outcomes including performance and wellbeing.

Alongside the above questions, there are other issues that this area of research would need to consider. First, measures of power and influence in sport psychology are non-existent and more broadly are complicated with measurement challenges. For example, Simpson et al. (2015) explained that self-reports measures have been central to this research but most of these are atheoretical and thus theoretically grounded scales assessing power in relationships are needed. Observations and priming are also measurement methods that can generate useful knowledge around how members communicate and interact to influence one another and make important decisions. Having the right measurement tools would help investigate desired versus actual power balance in the coach-athlete relationships. For example, as noted coaches may have greater power in the relationship than athletes. However, within the relationship coaches and athletes play different roles and have different duties and so athletes by default must possess power in order to engage in decision-making in certain decision domains (e.g., organising daily tasks so to allow for training, attend strength and conditioning sessions or physiotherapy sessions, eat healthily, fully engage in team meetings). The effects of high versus low power within the context of the coach-athlete relationship is critical to understand too. Previous research shows that members who have more power (believe to have more power or are given more power) are less inclined to take the other's perspective, to understand the other and take the other's point of view on board, or read their feelings (Galinksy, Magee, Inesi, & Gruenfeld, 2006; also see Lorimer

& Jowett, 2010). In addition they are less likely to be influenced by the lower power member because their focus is on acting in line with their own beliefs and preferences than those of others (Galinsky, Gruenfeld, & Magee, 2003). In contrast, some other research suggests that the greater power assumed in one's role (coach) can make them more interpersonally sensitive, empathic, understanding to the wants and needs of other's (athlete) who assume less power (cf. Schmid, Mast, Jonas, & Hall, 2009). There is clearly research scope within the context of sport coaching in order to unravel the power dynamics in the coach-athlete relationship.

Power in coach-athlete relationship and psychological safety

The social environment within which the coach-athlete relationship is embedded may shape coaches' and athletes' personal characteristics (e.g., status, goals, preferences) and relationship orientation and quality (e.g., secure or insecure, closeness and commitment) (cf. Simpson et al., 2015) and in turn the power bases or sources of power as well as influence strategies and tactics deployed. With that in mind, we propose here that the presence or absence of 'psychological safety' (Edmondson, 1999) in the environment within which coach-athlete dyads operate may moderate the links of the DPSIM. If coaches and athletes interact within a broader environment that is psychologically safe where they feel safe to be vulnerable, ask questions, point out concerns, feel free to speak up, challenge each other without fear of retaliation in response, or take other interpersonal risks, then the opportunities for growth and development increase as do the opportunities for using coercion and punishment. A coach's characteristics (behaviour, attitudes, values) can be instrumental in building psychological safety and relationship formation (cf. Edmondson, 2004).

From a practical point of view, if coaches wish to create a coaching environment that is psychologically safe where power is reasoned and discussed (as opposed to coerced or forced, manipulated or controlled, dictated or imposed), then there is no cost or risk to speak up. In such a coaching environment athletes don't hold back, don't lack confidence, are not afraid; they are more likely to freely offer their knowledge, insights, information, and ideas. Coaches can create a psychologically safe coaching environment by following these three steps. *First*, set the stage by explaining that the input of athletes in the coaching process is highly valued; your work as a coach and the work of your athlete is inherently interdependent and thus speaking up is critical. *Second*, invite athletes at every opportunity to be open by explaining the importance of their knowledge and the value of their voice. Athletes need to be reminded that coaches have a limited perspective and hence athletes can add to the perspective by potentially helping fill the gaps. *Last*, when athletes offer their views and ideas coaches should respond constructively with thoughtfulness and gratefulness. If coaches appreciate their athletes' courage and resolve for speaking up and for sharing their thoughts and opinions, athletes' confidence will grow. While athletes' openness (as opposed to holding back) means that the value of knowledge is not being lost, not all knowledge or information (opinions, thoughts, suggestions) offered may be accurate or helpful so coaches will have to courteously offer explanations, alternatives, or different perspectives to be considered. Overall, coaches should ensure interactions with their athletes that build psychological safety and minimise power inequalities or distance that may block the free flow of information or knowledge. The notion of creating psychologically safe coaching environments is in line with research conducted within sport psychology around coach empowerment (Duda, 2013), coach autonomy supportive versus controlling behaviours (Bartholomew, Ntoumanis, & Thøgersen-Ntoumani, 2009), and the fulfilment of basic psychological needs in coaching (Felton & Jowett, 2013a; Jowett, Bartholomew, Adie, Yang, Gustafsson, & Jimenez, 2017).

Concluding remarks

In this chapter, we identified the isolated pockets of sport-related research around power as this predominantly is conducted within the (male) coach role. Power in the coach-athlete relationship has never been a focus of sustained theoretical and empirical work within the sport psychology literature. In this chapter we put forward a definition of power and discussed a dyadic power-social influence model. The aim is to provide an impetus for systematic and organised research leading in time to an edifice of empirical knowledge with significant practical applications for coaching. Sport should be a rewarding, fulfilling, and satisfying experience for athletes and coaches alike. Athletes who have been misunderstood, undermined, and undervalued are less likely to view sport as a rewarding, fulfilling, and satisfying experience. A rhythmic gymnast stated: 'People see me as a pair of legs and think that this is all that I am, I need a coach who will see me as a whole person' (Balague, 1998, p. 93). Athletes simply need, want, and desire coaches who care for them (athlete-centred), who are interested in them (inclusive), and can work together with them (coach-athlete centred or collaborative) to achieve performance goals. As the coach-athlete relationship is at the heart of coaching practices and processes, understanding the role and significance of power in this unique relationship would in turn help unravel the many ways coaches and athletes influence one another and their individual and combined outcomes. Finally, this chapter offered practical guidelines for creating an environment that is safe to voice thoughts and opinions and allows to be oneself without fearing negative consequences (e.g., retaliation, intimidation, discrimination). At the heart of a psychological safe coaching environment lies good quality dyadic coach-athlete relationships.

References

Adie, J., & Jowett, S. (2010). Meta-perceptions of the coach-athlete relationship, achievement goals, and intrinsic motivation among sport participants. *Journal of Applied Social Psychology*, 40(11), 2750–2773.

Antonini Philippe, R., & Seiler, R. (2006). Closeness, co-orientation and complementarity in coach-athlete relationships: What male swimmers say about their male coaches. *Psychology of Sport & Exercise*, 7(2), 159–171.

Balague, G. (1999). Understanding identity, value, and meaning when working with elite athletes. *The Sport Psychologist*, 13(1), 89–98.

Barron, D. (2016). Aimee Boorman redefines coaching relationship with Simone Biles. *Houston Chronicle*. Retrieved from https://www.houstonchronicle.com/olympics/article/Aimee-Boorman-redefines-coaching-relationship-8382626.php on 20 January 2020.

Bartholomew, K., Ntoumanis, N., & Thøgersen-Ntoumani, C. (2009). A review of controlling motivational strategies from a self-determination theory perspective: Implications for sports coaches. *International Review of Sport and Exercise Psychology*, 2, 215–233.

Blood, R. O., & Wolfe, D. M. (1960). *Husbands and wives: The dynamics of married living*. New York: Free Press.

Burke, M. (2001). Obeying until it hurts: Coach-athlete relationships. *Journal of the Philosophy of Sport*, 28(2), 227–240.

Cavallerio, F., Wadey, R., & Wagstaff, C. R. (2016). Understanding overuse injuries in rhythmic gymnastics: A 12-month ethnographic study. *Psychology of Sport and Exercise*, 25, 100–109.

Clifford, C., & Feezell, R. M. (1997). *Coaching for character*. Champaign, IL: Human Kinetics.

Cruickshank, A., Collins, D., & Minten, S. (2013). Culture change in a professional sports team: Shaping environmental contexts and regulating power. *International Journal of Sports Science & Coaching*, 8(2), 271–290.

D'Arripe-Longueville, F., Fournier, J. F., & Dubois, A. (1998). The perceived effectiveness of interaction between French judo coaches and elite female athletes. *The Sport Psychologist*, 12, 317–332.

Davis, L., Jowett, S., & Lafrenière, M-AK. (2013). An attachment theory perspective in the examination of relational processes associated with coach-athlete dyads. *Journal of Sport and Exercise Psychology*, 35, 156–167.

de Haan, D., & Norman, L. (2019). Mind the gap: the presence of capital and power in the female athlete–male -coach relationship within elite rowing. *Sport Coaching Review*. doi:10.1080/21640629.2019.1567160.

Drewe, S. B. (2002). The coach-athlete relationship: How close is too close? *Journal of the Philosophy of Sport*, 29(2), 174–181.

Duda, J. L. (2013). The conceptual and empirical foundations of Empowering Coaching^{TM}: Setting the stage for the PAPA project. *International Journal of Sport and Exercise Psychology*, 11(4), 311–318.

Edmondson, A. C. (1999). Psychological safety and learning behavior in work teams. *Administrative Science Quarterly*, 44, 350–383.

Edmondson, A. C. (2004). Learning from mistakes is easier said than done: Group and organizational influences on the detection and correction of human error. *The Journal of Applied Behavioral Science*, 40(1), 66–90.

Felton, L., & Jowett, S. (2013a). 'What do coaches do' and 'how do they relate': Their effects on athletes' psychological needs and functioning. *Scandinavian Journal of Medicine and Sports Sciences,* 23, 130–139.

Felton, L., & Jowett, S. (2013b). Attachment and well-being: The mediating effects of psychological needs satisfaction within the coach-athlete and parent–athlete relational contexts. *Psychology of Sport & Exercise,* 14(1), 57–65.

French, J. R., Raven, B., & Cartwright, D. (1959). The bases of social power. *Classics of Organization Theory,* 7, 311–320.

Galinsky, A. D., Gruenfeld, D. H., & Magee, J. C. (2003). From power to action. *Journal of Personality and Social Psychology,* 85, 453–466.

Galinsky, A. D., Magee, J. C., Inesi, M. E., & Gruenfeld, D. H. (2006). Power and perspectives not taken. *Psychological Science,* 17, 1450–1466.

Gargalianos, D., Laios, A., & Theodorakis, N. (2003). Leadership and power: Two important factors for effective coaching. *International Sports Journal,* 24, 150–154.

Hampson, R., & Jowett, S. (2014). Effects of coach leadership and coach-athlete relationship on collective efficacy. *Scandinavian Journal of Medicine & Science in Sports,* 24, 454–460.

Huston, T. L. (1983). Power. In H. H. Kelley, E. Berscheid, A. Christensen, J. H. Harvey, T. L. Huston, G. Levinger, . . . D. R. Peterson (Eds.), *Close relationships* (pp. 169–219). New York: W. H. Freeman.

Jenkins, S. (2018). Aly Raisman: Conditions at Karolyi Ranch made athletes vulnerable to Nassar. *Washington Post.* Retrieved from https://www.washingtonpost.com/sp orts/olympics/aly-raisman-conditions-at-karolyi-ranch-made-athletes-vulnerable-to-n assar/2018/03/14/6d2dae56-26eb-11e8-874b-d517e912f125_story.html?noredirect=on &utm_term=.9029b16d8b14.

Jones, R. L., Armour, K. M., & Potrac, P. (2002). Understanding the coaching process: A framework for social analysis. *Quest,* 54(1), 34–48.

Jowett, S. (2003). When the 'Honeymoon' is over: a case study of a coach-athlete dyad in crisis. *The Sport Psychologist,* 17, 444–460.

Jowett, S. (2017). Coaching effectiveness: The coach-athlete relationship at its heart. *Current Opinion in Psychology,* 16, 154–158.

Jowett, S., & Arthur, C. (2019). Effective coaching: The links between coach leadership and coach-athlete relationship: From theory to research to practice. In M. Anshel, E. E. Labbe, T. A. Petrie, S. J. Petruzzello, & J. A. Steinfeldt (Eds.), *APA handbook of sport and exercise psychology* (Vol 1; Sport Psychology). London: Blackwells.

Jowett, S., & Carpenter, P. (2015). The concept of rules in the coach-athlete relationship. *Sports Coaching Review,* 4, 1–23.

Jowett, S., & Clark-Carter, D. (2006). Perceptions of empathic accuracy and assumed similarity in the coach-athlete relationship. *British Journal of Social Psychology,* 45(3), 617–637.

Jowett, S., & Cockerill, I. M. (2003). Olympic medallists' perspective of the athlete-coach relationship. *Psychology of Sport and Exercise,* 4, 313–331.

Jowett, S., & Meek, G. A. (2000). The coach-athlete relationship in married couples: An exploratory content analysis. *The Sport Psychologist,* 14(2), 157–175.

Jowett, S., & Nezlek, J. (2012). Relationship interdependence and satisfaction with important outcomes in coach-athlete dyads. *Journal of Social and Personal Relationships,* 29(3), 287–301.

Jowett, S., & Shanmugam, V. (2017). Relational coaching in sport: Its psychological underpinnings and practical effectiveness. In R. Schinke, K. R. McGannon, & B. Smith, *Routledge international handbook of sport psychology*. London: Routledge.

Jowett, S., Bartholomew, K., Adie, J., Yang, X. S., Gustafsson, H., & Jimenez, A. (2017). Motivational processes in the coach-athlete relationship: A multi-cultural self-determination approach. *Psychology of Sport & Exercise*, 32, 143–152.

Jowett, S., Nicolas, M., & Yang, S. (2017). Unravelling the links between coach behaviours and coach-athlete relationships. *European Journal of Sports & Exercise Science*, 5(3), 10–19.

Keltner, D., Gruenfeld, D. H., & Anderson, C. (2003). Power, approach, and inhibition. *Psychological Review*, 110, 265–284. doi:10.1037/0033-295X.110.2.265.

Konter, E. (2012). Leadership power perceptions of soccer coaches and soccer players according to their education. *Journal of Human Kinetics*, 34, 139–146.

Kidman, L., & Davis, W. (2006). Empowerment in coaching. In J. Broadhead & W. Davis (Eds.), *Ecological task analysis perspectives on movement*. Champaign, IL: Human Kinetics.

Krane, V., Snow, J., & Greenleaf, C. A. (1997). Reaching for gold and the price of glory: A motivational case study of an elite gymnast. *The Sport Psychologist*, 11(1), 53–71.

Lafrenière, M.-A. K., Jowett, S., Vallerand, R. J., & Carbonneau, N. (2011). Passion for coaching and the quality of the coach-athlete relationship: The mediating role of coaching behaviors. *Psychology of Sport and Exercise*, 12, 144–152.

Lorimer, R., & Jowett, S. (2010). The influence of role and gender in the empathic accuracy of coaches and athletes. *Psychology of Sport and Exercise*, 11, 206–211.

Lorimer, R., & Jowett, S. (2011). Empathic accuracy, shared cognitive focus, and the assumptions of similarity made by coaches and athletes. *International Journal of Sport Psychology*, 41, 40–49.

Lyle, J., & Cushion, C. (2017). *Sport coaching concepts: A framework for coaching practice*. Routledge: New York.

Mallett, C., & Lara-Bercial, S. (2016). Serial winning coaches: People, vision and environment. In M. Raab, P. Wylleman, R. Seiler, A. M. Elbe, and A. Hatzigeorgiadis (Eds.) *Sport and exercise psychology research: from theory to practice* (pp. 289–322). London: Academic Press (Elsevier).

May, R. (1972). *Power and innocence*. New York: W.W. Norton.

Overall, N. C., Fletcher, G. J., Simpson, J. A., & Sibley, C. G. (2009). Regulating partners in intimate relationships: The costs and benefits of different communication strategies. *Journal of Personality and Social Psychology*, 96(3), 620.

Poczwardowski, A., Barott, J. E., & Henschen, K. P. (2002). The athlete and coach: Their relationship and its meaning. Results of an interpretive study. *International Journal of Sport Psychology*, 33(1), 116–140.

Purdy, L. G., & Jones, R. L. (2011). Choppy waters: Elite rowers' perceptions of coaching. *Sociology of Sport Journal*, 28(3), 329–346.

Purdy, L., Jones, R., & Cassidy, T. (2009). Negotiation and capital: Athletes' use of power in an elite men's rowing program. *Sport, Education and Society*, 14(3), 321–338.

Reis, H. T., Collins, W. A., & Berscheid, E. (2000). The relationship context of human behavior and development. *Psychological Bulletin*, 126(6), 844.

Rhind, D. J., & Jowett, S. (2011). Linking maintenance strategies to the quality of coach-athlete relationships. *International Journal of Sport Psychology*, 42(1), 1–14.

Rhind, D. J., & Jowett, S. (2012a). Development of the Coach-Athlete Relationship Maintenance Questionnaire (CARM-Q). *International Journal of Sports Science and Coaching*, 7(1), 121–138.
Rollins, B. C., & Bahr, S. J. (1976). A theory of power relationships in marriage. *Journal of Marriage and the Family*, 38, 619–627. doi:10.2307/350682.
Russell, B. (1938). *Power: A new social analysis*. London: George Allen & Unwin.
Ryan, J. (1995). *Little girls in pretty boxes*. New York: Doubleday.
Rylander, P. (2014). Coaches' bases of power: Developing some initial knowledge of athletes' compliance with coaches in team sports. *Journal of Applied Sport Psychology*, 27(1), 110–121.
Schmid Mast, M., Jonas, K., & Hall, J. A. (2009). Give a person power and he or she will show interpersonal sensitivity: The phenomenon and its why and when. *Journal of Personality and Social Psychology*, 97(5), 835.
Shepherd, D. J., Lee, B., & Kerr, J. H. (2006). Reversal theory: A suggested way forward for an improved understanding of interpersonal relationships in sport. *Psychology of Sport and Exercise*, 7, 143–157.
Simpson, J. A., Farrell, A. K., Oriña, M. M., & Rothman, A. J. (2015). Power and social influence in relationships. In M. Mikulincer, P. R. Shaver, J. A. Simpson, & J. F. Dividio (Eds.), *APA handbook of personality and social psychology: Interpersonal relations*, 3 (pp. 393–420). Washington, DC: American Psychological Association. doi:10.1037/14344-015.
Stirling, A. E., & Kerr, G. A. (2007). Elite female swimmers' experiences of emotional abuse across time. *Journal of Emotional Abuse*, 7, 89–113.
Stirling, A. E., & Kerr, G. A. (2009). Abused athletes' perceptions of the coach-athlete relationship. *Sport in Society*, 12, 227–239.
Stirling, A. E., & Kerr, G. (2013). The perceived effects of elite athletes' experiences of emotional abuse in the coach-athlete relationship. *International Journal of Sport and Exercise Psychology*, 11(1), 87–100.
Tamminen, K. A., Holt, N. L., & Neely, K. C. (2013). Exploring adversity and the potential for growth among elite female athletes. *Psychology of Sport and Exercise*, 14(1), 28–36.
Thibaut, J. W., & Kelley, H. H. (1959). *The social psychology of groups*. New York: Wiley.
Tomlinson, A., & Yorganci, I. (1997). Male coach/female athlete relations: Gender and power relations in competitive sport. *Journal of Sport & Social Issues*, 21(2), 134–155.
Trzaskoma-Bicsérdy, G., Bognár, J., Révész, L., & Géczi, G. (2007). The coach-athlete relationship in successful Hungarian individual sports. *International Journal of Sports Science & Coaching*, 2(4), 485–495.
Turman, P. D. (2006). Athletes' perception of coach power use and the association between playing status and sport satisfaction. *Communication Research Reports*, 23, 273–282.
Vella, S. A., Oades, L. G., & Crowe, T. P. (2013). The relationship between coach leadership, the coach-athlete relationship, team success, and the positive developmental experiences of adolescent soccer players. *Physical Education and Sport Pedagogy*, 18(5), 549–561.
Wachsmuth, S., Jowett, S., & Harwood, C. (2017). Conflict among athletes and their coaches: What is the theory and research so far? *International Review of Sport and Exercise Psychology*, 10(1), 84–107.

Wachsmuth, S., Jowett, S., & Harwood, C. (2018). On understanding the nature of interpersonal conflict between coaches and athletes. *Journal of Sport Science*, 36(17), 1955–1962.

Wylleman, P. (2000). Interpersonal relationships in sport: Uncharted territory in sport psychology research. *International Journal of Sport Psychology*, 31, 555–572.

Yambor, J. (1998). Coach-athlete issues. In M. A. Thompson, R. A. Vernacchia, and W. E. Moore (Eds.), *Case studies in applied sport psychology: An educational approach* (pp. 115–138). Dubuque, IO: Kendall/Hunt.

Chapter 9

When the coach-athlete relationship influences vulnerability to sexual abuse of women's artistic gymnasts

Gretchen Kerr, Ashley Stirling and Erin Willson

Introduction

The nature and quality of the coach-athlete relationship has been widely acknowledged as influential in an athlete's development (Gervis & Dunn, 2004; Jowett & Cockerill, 2003; Jowett, 2007; LaVoi, 2007). Highly competitive athletes and their coaches spend inordinate amounts of time together, often more so than they do with their parents, family, and friends outside of the sport (Jowett & Cockerill, 2003; Stirling & Kerr, 2009). In addition to the substantial amount of time coaches and athletes spend together, the quality of this relationship is often cited as being a critical determinant for athletic performance and personal development (Jowett & Cockerill, 2003; Jowett & Meek, 2000; Vealey, Armstrong, Comar, & Greenleaf, 1998).

A popular model used in sport and coaching literature to understand the intertwining aspects of the coach-athlete relationship has been developed by Jowett (2007). Specifically, Jowett has found that effective coach-athlete relationships have affective, behavioural, and emotional elements, which are described by her 3 +1Cs model referring to Closeness, Commitment, Complementarity, and Co-operation. Using this framework, a coach-athlete relationship is considered positive if there is a high level or trust and respect, each party is committed to one other and to the same goal, and they act in responsive and friendly ways with one another (Jowett, 2007).

While a significant body of research indicates the potential positive value of coach-athlete relationships for athletic performance and personal development, evidence also indicates the potential for athlete maltreatment to occur within the coach-athlete relationship (Stafford, Alexander, & Fry, 2015). Further, and ironically, the qualities of an effective coach-athlete relationship are similar to the qualities that characterise a coach-athlete relationship in which athletes are vulnerable to maltreatment. Athlete maltreatment, and specifically relational maltreatment, consists of sexual abuse, emotional abuse, physical abuse, and neglect which occur within what is referred to as a critical relationship (Stirling, 2009). A critical relationship is understood as one in which one actor has significant power and influence over the health, safety, well-being of another (Crooks & Wolfe, 2007). Within the child abuse literature, a critical relationship is typically understood as the parent-child relationship, and, in the context of sport, may include the coach-athlete relationship.

Sexual abuse in the coach-athlete relationship

Sexual abuse is the most commonly researched form of maltreatment, in part due to the high-profile media attention garnered by such cases as the Larry Nassar case in the US and the Barry Bennell case in the UK. There are, of course, numerous examples from other countries as no country, type of sport, or sport level is immune from incidents of maltreatment. Sexual abuse can be contact or non-contact, including oral or genital penetration and/or contact, groping, kissing, indecent exposure, online sexual exploitation, and exchange of reward or privilege for sexual favours (Brackenridge, 1997; Stirling, 2009).

Substantial attention has been devoted to understanding risk factors to experiences of athlete sexual abuse. Identified risk factors range from vulnerabilities at the individual level (e.g., being female and younger, athlete with low self-esteem, parental absence), and at the sport or situational level (e.g., access to young people, private training sessions, travelling) (Brackenridge, 1997; 2001). Of these risk factors, the closeness within the coach-athlete relationship as well as the power, authority, trust, and deference afforded to coaches have been highlighted. In this chapter, we adopt a psychological perspective throughout, and submit the proposition that the qualities identified as being critical to healthy and effective coach-athlete relationships are the same qualities that have been identified as increasing the vulnerability of female artistic gymnasts to experiences of sexual violence in the coach-athlete relationship. In the following section, we will address each of the important and well-documented qualities of an effective coach-athlete relationship and demonstrate, by highlighting the relevant research findings, how these same qualities may enhance the likelihood of maltreatment within the coach-athlete relationship. This chapter concludes with the supposition that coaches' misuse of power and inappropriate friendliness increases female artistic gymnasts' vulnerability to maltreatment.

Qualities of effective coach-athlete relationships

Closeness

One of the attributes that is consistently discussed within the literature on coach-athlete relationships is the closeness that exists between the two parties (Jowett, 2007; Jowett & Cockerill, 2003; LaVoi, 2007; Philippe & Seiler, 2006). Jowett described closeness as the emotional tone of the relationship, reflecting the depth of emotional attachment between the coach and athlete.

Closeness is often expressed by athletes and coaches as trust, like, respect, appreciation, belief in one another, and/or care for each other (Jowett & Cockerill, 2003; LaVoi, 2007; Poczwardowski, Barott, & Henschen, 2002). Closeness often develops due to the many hours of working together (Jowett & Cockerill, 2003), and the coach and athlete have a common bond of a shared passion – 'a passion for the sport that has brought them together' (Bergmann Drewe, 2002, p. 175). Highly competitive athletes often refer to their coach as an intimate member of their life, or a close friend, an extension of their family, or a parent-like figure (Brackenridge, Bishopp, Moussalli, & Tapp, 2008; Cense & Brackenridge, 2001).

Within the context of the 3 +1Cs model, Jowett (2007) described closeness as the affective aspect of the relationship, due to the tight emotional bond formed between competitive athletes and their coaches. Alternatively, LaVoi (2007) described closeness as complex phenomena that integrates the cognitive, affective, and behavioural components. Despite the differences in conceptualisations, both researchers found that athletes describe the essential components of closeness as mutual trust and respect (Jowett & Cockerill, 2003; LaVoi, 2007).

The components of closeness have been regarded by athletes as essential requirements in forming a good relationship (Jowett & Cockerill, 2003; Philippe & Seiler, 2006). Athletes have reported that having a close relationship with their coach has enabled open dialogue and communication (Jowett & Cockerill, 2003) and athletes value the ability to talk to their coach about anything – both in sport and in other aspects of their lives, including school and life (LaVoi, 2007). Olympic gold medal gymnast Simone Biles and her coach Aimee Boorman are often cited as having a close relationship, so much so that they have learned to read each other. Boorman is reportedly able to predict how well the training is going to be as soon as Biles walks into the gym (The Associated Press, 2016).

Closeness in positive coach-athlete relationship often extends beyond the sport arena, including diet, academics, and social interests (Stirling & Kerr, 2008). This can help foster a more humanistic approach to coaching, focusing on the athlete from a holistic perspective. Given athletes' desires to have a coach who sees them as a person first and an athlete second, rather than as an instrument for performance success (Jowett & Cockerill, 2003; Philippe & Seiler, 2006), this understanding of non-sport lives appears to be important. Moreover, open communication can include how an athlete is feeling, coach and athlete expectations, and other important aspects that may impact training (LaVoi, 2007). In summary, a close relationship can help to enhance understanding of one another, effectiveness of training, performance improvements, and the well-being of the athletes.

Some athletes have claimed that the elements of closeness can make the difference between an average and an excellent coach-athlete dyad (Philippe & Seiler, 2006). Athletes place high value on coaches who can not only provide instruction of their sport but can communicate feelings of warmth, caring, and genuine interest in their athletes (Jowett & Cockerill, 2003). The social component of the relationship has been considered indispensable, and can also lead to increased motivation, confidence, and the personal development of the athletes (Jowett & Cockerill, 2003; LaVoi, 2007). It is no wonder then, that some athletes describe their relationships with their coaches as having friendship qualities (Philippe & Seiler, 2006).

Alternatively, coach-athlete relationships that lack closeness have reportedly had a negative impact on the success of both parties. Jowett & Cockerill (2003) found that athletes who felt their coaches did not explicitly express interest in the athlete at a personal level had the perception that the coaches did not care about them. Again, this emphasises the importance of the coaches being involved and caring for the athletes in all aspects of life. Moreover, trust can also be necessary for the safety of the athlete, as in a high-risk sport such as gymnastics; athletes who can put trust in their coaches reduce their fears of injuries, especially when learning new techniques (Magyar & Chase, 1996). Therefore, not having a relationship built on trust can impact the health and well-being of the athlete along with her athletic performance.

Ironically, however, a close relationship between coaches and athletes has often been cited as a precipitating factor in cases of athlete maltreatment. Stirling and Kerr (2008) found that athletes discussed the closeness with their coach, regardless of whether they had a positive or negative (abusive) relationship. For example, sexual abuse survivors have expressed feelings of lasting closeness and affection, at times to the extent of loving their abusers (Brackenridge, 1997). Given the sense of closeness, it is common for survivors to express feelings of guilt and remorse for hurting their abusers once they report their abuse (Brackenridge, 1997).

Athletes, and others (athletes' parents, administrators, junior coaches), defer significant authority to coaches. Simply using the term 'coach' rather than a first name adds to the position of authority. Coaches are admired for their expertise and often idolised especially if they have a successful track record of producing top athletes (Tofler, Styer, Micheli, & Herman, 1996). In fact, athletes have commonly referred to coaches as a 'parent-like' figure, or a 'God' (Brackenridge, 1997; Brackenridge et al., 2008; Stirling & Kerr, 2008). Clark reported that the female gymnasts in her study made references to their coaches being God-like as illustrated in the following quote:

> I would just allow it [emotional abuse] to happen because I would never think to tell them they were doing something wrong. It was hard, because they're like God. You're just taught to never question anything they do, or you'll be the one to pay the price for it later.
>
> (Clark, 2017, p. 104)

Successful coaches are far too commonly assumed to 'know what they are doing' and, therefore, are sought after by athletes, and their parents, and, in turn, trusted in an unquestioned manner by athletes, parents, and other adults in the sport arena.

The level of trust that is given to the coaches is arguably one of the most crucial factors within an abusive coach-athlete relationship. Child abuse literature has shown that the most frequent perpetrators of abuse are those who are in a position of care, for example, a parent, or caregiver, someone who the child's welfare depends on, and therefore the child trusts (Erooga, 2012; US Department of Health & Human Services, 2018). Similarly, the athlete is often dependent on and trusts the coach. This can start with trust in the coach from a technical level, and over time, and with positive reinforcements, such as successful performance outcomes, this trust can grow, and can also extend to all areas of the athlete's life (Cense & Brackenridge, 2001). The influence of the coach in the athletes' lives within and outside of sport facilitated a greater level of trust, according to athletes who have experienced abuse, thus enabling coaches to misuse their position of power and exploit the trust athletes have in them (Cense & Brackenridge, 2001; Stirling & Kerr, 2009). While trust has been discussed within positive coach-athlete relationships, the blurring of personal boundaries has been considered a crucial component of the experience of sexual abuse (Brackenridge & Fasting, 2005).

Moreover, the exploitation of trust is a fundamental component of the grooming process that enables sexual abuse to occur. Grooming is the process of slowly gaining the trust of the potential victim, and often those close to the victim (e.g. parents), before systematically breaking down interpersonal barriers prior to committing an actual abusive act (Brackenridge & Fasting, 2005, p. 35). This process can take days, weeks, and even years (Brackenridge & Fasting, 2005). Auwelle et al. (2008) added that grooming can hinder the identification of unacceptable behaviours because it is a gradual process, and at the initial stages, the behaviours are acceptable and only later progress into an area of harm. As Burke (2001) indicated, athletes who have been sexually abused by their coaches often keep the abuse a secret because the athlete trusts the coach and the coach exploits their close relationship by claiming that the secret should be maintained because no one in the outside world would understand their special relationship (Burke, 2001). Sexual abusers work to develop such a strong trust with the athlete that the athlete will keep the abuse a secret because the coach told them to (Burke, 2001).

Commitment

Commitment is the cognitive aspect in Jowett's (2007) 3 +1Cs model that represents the dedication each party has to each other. This construct identifies both the coach's and athlete's intentions to remain a unit over time, and can indicate how motivated the partners are to continue their relationship in the long term (Jowett, 2007; Jowett & Ntoumanis, 2004; Jowett & Nezlek, 2011). Attributes of commitment include 'I feel committed to my coach', 'my sport career is promising with my coach', and 'my coach is committed to me' (Jowett, 2007). A high level of commitment can foster an 'us and we' orientation rather than a 'me and mine' orientation, indicating the belief that the dyad is a working, consolidated unit (Jowett, 2007; Jowett & Meek, 2000). A coach and athlete may experience commitment to one another as they (hopefully) have shared goals of optimising the athlete's potential; however, the motivational bases of each party may differ. As stated previously by numerous researchers (David, 2004; Gervis & Dunn, 2004; Pinheiro, Pimenta, Resende, & Malcolm, 2014), coaches' careers, recognition, incomes, and reputations are dependent upon athletes' performance results, and as such, coaches have a lot to lose if their athletes are not successful.

A high level of commitment, particularly towards one person, can have negative implications. By virtue of closeness and a commitment to one another, athletes can be convinced that their relationship with their coach is unique and a priority, thus enhancing resistance to outside influences and judgements (Burke, 2001). This can be cause for concern because if others express concerns about the health of the athlete within the relationship, the athlete may be more likely to trust the coach than to trust others because of where the loyalty lies (Burke, 2001). Coaches may also take the opportunity to restrict other areas of the athlete's life to establish dominance and commitment and an exclusive focus on the coach-athlete relationship. Coaches may begin to control the athlete's social life, if they can date, what they can spend time doing, all of which can reduce the opportunity to encounter outside influences that may broaden the athlete's perspectives and allow others to monitor the relationship and intervene if needed (Stirling & Kerr, 2009).

Commitments to one another and to the shared goal of sport performance creates a sense of dependency for the athlete on her coach. This dependency is exacerbated when the athlete has developed a singular athletic identity, when, for example, she views herself as a gymnast rather than a person who does gymnastics (Kerr & Dacyshyn, 2000). This is an important distinction because it helps to understand how an athlete views the importance of her athletic career to her sense of self and to others' views of her. A female gymnast with a strong athlete identity who is experiencing abuse may experience personal conflict, torn between who she is, the commitment she has made to herself, to the sport, and to her coach on one hand, while also experiencing harm on the other. Athletes have often expressed fear of negative retributions if they were to reject the coach's advances, including having to leave the sport – their passion – or being abandoned by their coach (Brackenridge, 1997; Cense & Brackenridge, 2001). Athletes have expressed that their biggest fear was not of the violence that was occurring, but of losing the relationship with the coach (Cense & Brackenridge, 2001). Moreover, athletes have rationalised the behaviours as being 'worth it' in order to continue the relationship and their athletic pursuits despite the harm that occurred (Stirling & Kerr, 2009). Coaches can also use the athlete's commitment to their advantage, because they understand the athlete will be compliant and more likely to stay silent out of fear of losing the relationship. In fact, athletes often conceal their experiences of sexual abuse from their friends and family because of the fear of losing their identity and their coach – who is key to their athletic success – should others learn of the abuse. This thinking can be heightened when coaches manipulate their athletes to believe that they would be nothing without the coach (Stirling & Kerr, 2009). As one sexual abuse survivor said, 'I was absolutely dependent upon him [the coach] – he was God – without listening to myself. From 15–19 [years of age] he owned me basically' (Brackenridge, 1997, p. 123).

Complementarity

The third C in Jowett's (2007) 3 +1Cs model is complementarity, which is understood as the interaction between the coach and athlete that is perceived by both parties as cooperative and effective. Complementarity reflects the affiliation motivation of interpersonal behaviours and includes behavioural properties such as being responsive, friendly, and at ease (Jowett & Cockerill, 2003). Traditionally, an effective coach-athlete relationship has been portrayed as authoritarian, perhaps due to the parallels between sport and the military. For example, common references to coaches being 'drill sergeants', media discussions of teams being 'at war' (Kellett, 2002), and the structure of team sports where the coach is a 'central command directing the troops' (Pedersen & Cooke, 2006, p. 422). An authoritarian coach-athlete dyad may be described as a relationship in which the coach plays a directive role and the athlete responds willingly to the directions. In fact, athletes have expressed preferences for coaches 'telling' them what to do as noted in the following quote: 'my role as an athlete was to follow my coach's instructions and my coach's role was to provide me with effective instructions and make me feel good and positive' (Jowett & Cockerill, 2003, p. 323). Researchers indicate that athletes enjoy their passive roles because the coach can take responsibility for the decisions made with the respect to the athlete, while the athlete can solely focus on the physical and performance outcomes of sport (Burke, 2001; Headley-Cooper, 2010).

On the other hand, abused athletes have reported that the normal and expected behaviour during training was that they 'did what they were told, without question' (Stirling & Kerr, 2009). Given the closeness and trust established in the athlete-coach dyad, athletes may feel that the only way to maintain an effective, cooperative, and friendly relationship with their coaches is to comply with the coaches' requests. To raise objections to a coach's behaviours, even if they are inappropriate or criminal, may jeopardise the athlete's key relationship with her coach, let alone her career aspirations as a gymnast. Compliance and normalisation of inappropriate behaviours are important pre-requisites to the grooming process for sexual abuse.

Co-orientation

Co-orientation is the final 'C' in Jowett's (2007) 3+1C model and is understood as the alignment of goals, beliefs, values, and expectations (Jowett & Cockerill, 2003). It is important for coaches and athletes to share mutual goals to ensure the alignment of training plans, expectations, and performance outcomes. For example, if a coach has a goal for a young athlete to make an Olympic team and the athlete is interested only in participating in sport for the social aspects and does not share the coach's goal, training an athlete as if she was going to the Olympics would be unsuccessful, frustrating, a poor use of both the coach's and athlete's time, all of which will create strain on the relationship.

While sharing personal goals and desires can foster co-orientation and ensure athletes and coaches are aligned in their pursuits, research in maltreatment has shown that coaches can exploit these goals to allow for self-serving activities (Burke, 2001). As coaches' careers, incomes, and job security are dependent upon the athlete's success, coaches may use inappropriate measures to ensure performance success even if these measures run contrary to the well-being of the athlete (Donnelly, 1997). For example, in preparation for an important competition, the coach may push the gymnast harder, force her to train longer hours, potentially through injury, while coaching in a more aggressive or tough manner. While these actions may be perceived by the coach as helping the gymnast, they may be physically or emotionally harming the athlete.

Athletes and coaches can value having a deep connection; however, this can also expose the athlete's vulnerabilities and allow for coaches to know what these are. Victims of sexual abuse have often been vulnerable in some way, for example, have low self-esteem, few friends, issues with family life (e.g., a parent dying, parents going through a divorce, poor relationship with family) (Brackenridge, 2001; Cense & Brackenridge, 2001). Abused athletes have expressed that 'it's fantastic to have a coach empathise with you' (Cense & Brackenridge, 2001, p. 68). Athletes who are victims of abuse are frequently seeking someone to care for or understand them, leaving them more susceptible to grooming processes and sexual advances from the coach (Cense & Brackenridge, 2001). Moreover, in an effort to be accepted by the coach, who may be meeting the athlete's psychosocial needs, the athlete may sacrifice her own beliefs and morals to continue receiving these rewards (Waldron & Krane, 2005).

Sharing goals and expectations may benefit the coach-athlete relationship in many ways; however, the fact that the coach is in a position of power may leave the female gymnast vulnerable. For example, a coach may know a gymnast wants to progress in sport, so may manipulate the gymnast by promising success if she succumbs to the coach's desires. Previous researchers have reported that athletes often cooperated with coaches' desires, even sexual desires, for a variety of rewards, including getting extra attention in sport, receiving clothes, or a place on a higher team (Cense & Brackenridge, 2001; Owton & Sparkes, 2017). These patterns are also seen in a variety of domains outside of sport as well. One of those most prominent examples in recent years is the Harvey Weinstein case, where over 80 women came forward with their allegations of sexual exploitation, including the promise of career advancements in return for sexual favours (Moniuszko & Kelly, 2017). In sport, Larry Nassar's abuses of US gymnasts is an important example as he promised therapy to enhance performance while sadly this therapy was a form of sexual abuse. A substantial body of research address the ill effects that can result from a win-at-all-costs approach (Gervis & Dunn, 2004; Waldron & Krane, 2005) and the performance ethic (Van Yperen, Hamstra, & van der Klauw, 2011), both of which can lead to the acceptance of unhealthy, inappropriate, or even criminal behaviours.

Coaches' misuse of their position of power

A wealth of evidence supports the validity of Jowett's 3 +1Cs model for coach-athlete relationships. And yet, the qualities in Jowett's model that characterise an effective coach-athlete relationship are often cited in coach-athlete relationships in which athlete maltreatment occurs. So, what distinguishes a 'healthy' coach-athlete relationship from one in which maltreatment occurs when they both are described with closeness, commitment, complementarity, co-orientation? Could it be that the way in which the coach uses his or her position of power affects whether closeness, for example, is used for positive versus negative purposes? Common to all forms of maltreatment is a power imbalance and a misuse of a position of power (Stirling & Kerr, 2009). A plethora of research findings indicate that a coach has power by virtue of expertise and specialised knowledge, an ascribed position of authority, a track record of success, access to resources, decision-making control over the athlete's training, competitive schedules, and sometimes lives outside of sport (Cense & Brackenridge, 2001; Donnelly, 1997; Stirling & Kerr, 2009). These elements are consistent with French and Raven's (1959) sources of power: legitimate (i.e., authority based on prescribed role); expert (i.e., knowledge of sport and technical skill); reward (i.e., ability to produce success); referent (i.e., charisma, likability, earned respect); and coercive (i.e., the ability to control or influence others). All of these sources of power are typically held by coaches. How these bases of power are used may distinguish whether the 3 +1Cs lead to positive or negative outcomes for the female gymnast.

When a coach and gymnast enter their relationship, they do so on the basis that the coach has the expertise to determine what is good for, or what is needed by, the gymnast for sport performance. In fact, athletes or their parents seek out the coaches who can use their expertise to actualise the athlete's athletic potential and thus advance the athlete's career (Brackenridge, 2001). As a result, the coach-athlete relationship begins with the coach in a position of power and in an authoritative, functional role (Bergmann Drewe, 2002, p. 176). From an early stage in a female gymnast's career, she is conditioned to respect those in a position of authority, including her coaches. Athletes have discussed being in awe of their coach, admiring and idolising them because of their knowledge, expertise, and track record of success (Stirling & Kerr, 2009). Upon successful performances, athletes will often credit their success to the efforts of their coach (Stirling & Kerr, 2009). Additionally, the more success a coach brings to the athlete, the less likely the coach's methods are challenged, thus opening the door for inappropriate or even abusive behaviours to be accepted and justified by athletes and parents alike (Kerr & Stirling, 2012; Stirling & Kerr, 2009; Tomlinson & Yorganci, 1997). Therefore, most of the responsibility for performance success is placed on the coaches, and, with this, the coaches are often given the freedom to produce results through the tactics they see fit, giving the coach ultimate authority. This not only reinforces the unquestioned power the coach has over the athlete, but also indicates the lengths athletes will go to for performance success, even if it means sacrificing their own health and well-being in the process. One gymnast explained the way in which abusive coaching behaviours became accepted and normalised stating 'it was kind of drilled into you ... if you wanted to keep going, then this is what you have to put up with, and everyone put up with it' (Stafford et al., 2015).

Power in the coach-athlete relationship: de-constructing friendships

One consistent theme that runs through the literature on the 3 +1Cs model as well as the maltreatment literature is the friendship that reportedly develops between the coach and athlete. Both athletes and coaches self-report that a friendship develops within this dyad; this is not surprising given the frequent, intense, and emotionally charged interactions that exist between athletes and their coaches. One would expect some degree to friendship to develop, however, the nature of the friendship is an important consideration. Sport philosophers have questioned whether or not it is possible for a coach and athlete to be friends. This question is posed on the basis that fundamental to the development of a friendship is equality, with neither party in the relationship being under the authority of the other (Thomas,

1987, p. 217). Given the previously discussed and well-documented power imbalance that exists within the coach-athlete dyad, the notion of friendship within this relationship is challenged. The authoritative, functional role of the coach in terms of making decisions for and on behalf of the gymnast creates an inherent power imbalance. Further, should one accept that friendships can develop between a gymnast and her coach, then questions arise about conflicts of interests when a coach makes decisions and allocates resources. If it is true that 'only when two individuals allow their feelings about each other to influence how they treat each other that a friendship can exist' (Jollimore, 2000, p. 72), then, to avoid conflicts of interest, friendships should not develop between coach and athlete. It is for these reasons that in other evaluative situations such as employment decisions, career advancement, and jury memberships, friends of the person in question should excuse themselves.

However, given that different types of friendships exist, perhaps a more nuanced look at the coach-gymnast relationship may be warranted. Researchers in this area refer to 'deep' or 'virtue' friendships and 'utility' friendships. Deep friendships are those between equals, in which the parties interact with one another intensely and frequently without being governed by a structure of social conventions. In a deep friendship, there is unconditional love – love based upon who the person is, with all of their strengths and weaknesses (White, 1990). The friendship between romantic or intimate lovers is an example of a deep friendship. On the other hand, utility friendships are those based upon each party being advantageous or useful to the other; in such friendships, the emotions are not as intense as those within a deep friendship. If one can put aside the potential inclination to interpret the word 'utility' as suggestive of manipulation or 'fair-weather friends', utility friendships may be viewed as far more appropriate for the coach-gymnast dyad than deep relationships. After all, the coach-gymnast relationship is characterised by an unequal power imbalance and should not be characterised by intense emotional bonds and unconditional love. A utility friendship recognises power imbalances, allows for the sharing of common goals and a commitment to work together towards common goals, mutual respect, and the sharing of mutual information. We propose that utility relationships should characterise the relationships between coaches and female gymnasts.

In addition to references to friendships, gymnasts often refer to their coach as a member of their family or as a surrogate parent. However, the problematic nature of this is highlighted by one sexual abuse survivor in Brackenridge's (1997) paper:

> I consider it incest – that's what this is all about. Because the time spent, the demands, the friendship, the opportunity ... they are giving you something else no one else can. They're brother, uncle, father ... the child feels safe and will do anything. That's why it's incest.

Again, the depth of the relationship between a coach and gymnast should not replicate that of a gymnast and her parent.

Conclusion

Substantial supporting evidence exists to indicate the importance of closeness, commitment, complementarity, and co-orientation – Jowett's 3 +1Cs model – for effective coach-athlete relationships. A dilemma exists however, as these same qualities are cited by athletes who have experienced maltreatment at the hands of their coaches. For sport researchers and practitioners, this dilemma raises important questions about how the use of the 3 +1Cs model will confidently lead to positive outcomes for the athlete's performance, health, and well-being. In this chapter, we suggest that the ways in which a coach uses his or her bases of power may determine the outcomes of applying the 3 +1Cs model.

Relatedly, we also suggest that there are trends within the vast body of literature on the coach–athlete relationship that need further examination and more complex analyses. For example, common themes within this body of literature include athletes referring to their coaches as friends, members of their family, surrogate parents, or 'Gods'. For the most part, these findings are viewed as positive indications of the close relationship between coaches and athletes that facilitates their work together, as well as the athlete's health and performance. However, given that these references are also characteristic of abusive relationships, perhaps it is time to adopt a more critical view of these descriptors.

References

Auwelle, Y.V., Opdenacker, J., Vertommen, T., Boen, F., Van Niekerk, L., De Martelaer, K., & De Cuyper, B. (2008). Unwanted sexual experiences in sport: Perceptions and reported prevalence among Flemish female student-athletes. *International Journal of Sport and Exercise Psychology*, 6(4), 354–365.

Bergmann Drewe, S. (2002). The coach-athlete relationship: How close is too close? *Journal of the Philosophy of Sport*, XXIX, 174–181.

Brackenridge, C. H. (1997). 'He owned me basically...' Women's experience of sexual abuse in sport. *International Review for the Sociology of Sport*, 32(2), 115–130.

Brackenridge, C. H. (2001). *Spoilsports: Understanding and preventing sexual exploitation in sport*. London: Routledge.

Brackenridge, C., & Fasting, K. (2005). The grooming process in sport: Narratives of sexual harassment and abuse. *Auto/Biography*, 2, 33–52.

Brackenridge, C. H., Bishopp, D., Moussalli, S., & Tapp, J. (2008). The characteristics of sexual abuse in sport: A multidimensional scaling analysis of events described in media reports. *International Journal of Sport and Exercise Psychology*, 6(4), 385–406.

Burke, M. (2001). Obeying until it hurts: Coach-athlete relationships. *Journal of the Philosophy of Sport*, 28(2), 227–240.

Cense, M., & Brackenridge, C. (2001). Temporal and developmental risk factors for sexual harassment and abuse in sport. *European Physical Education Review*, 7(1), 61–79.

Clark, A. (2017). *Coaching abuse experiences in young elite female artistic gymnasts: An ethical appraisal*. Unpublished Master's thesis. Brock University.

Crooks, C., & Wolfe, D. (2007). Child abuse and neglect. In E. J. Mash & R. A. Barkley (Eds.), *Assessment of childhood disorders* (4th edn, pp. 649–684). New York; Gilford Press.

David, P. (2004). *Human rights in youth sport*. London: Routledge.

Donnelly, P. (1997). Child labour, sport labour: Applying child labour laws to sport. *International Review for the Sociology of Sport*, 32(4), 389–406.

Erooga, M. (2012). Understanding and responding to people who sexually abuse children whilst employed in a position of trust. In M. Erooga (Ed.), *creating safer organizations: Practical steps to prevent abuse of children who work with them* (pp. 7–22). London: Wiley-Blackwell.

French, J. R. P., & Raven, B. (1959). The bases of social power. In D. Cartwright (Ed.), *Studies in social power* (pp. 1150–1959). Oxford, England: University of Michigan.

Gervis, M., & Dunn, N. (2004). The emotional abuse of elite child athletes by their coaches. *Child Abuse Review*, 13(3), 215–223. doi:10.1002/car.843.

Headley-Cooper, K. J. (2010). *Coaches' perspectives on athlete-centred coaching* (Master's thesis). University of Toronto, Toronto, ON. Retrieved from https://tspace.library.utoronto.ca/bitstream/1807/24252/1/Headley-Cooper_ Karlene_J_201003_MSc_thesis.pdf.

Jollimore, T. (2000). Friendship without partiality? *Ratio*, XIII(1), 69–82.

Jowett. S. (2005). On repairing and enhancing the coach-athlete relationship. In S. Jowett & M. J. Jones (Eds.), *The psychology of coaching* (pp. 14–26). Leicester: The British Psychological Society. Sport and Exercise Division.

Jowett, S. (2007). Interdependence analysis and the 3+1Cs in the coach athlete relationship. In S. Jowett & D. Lavallee (Eds.), *Social psychology in sport* (pp. 15–27). Champaign, IL: Human Kinetics.

Jowett. S. (2009). Validating coach-athlete relationship measures with the nomological network. *Measurement in Physical Education and Exercise Science*, 13, 35–51.

Jowett, S., & Cockerill, I. M. (2003). Olympic medallists' perspective of the athlete-coach relationship. *Psychology of Sport and Exercise*, 4(4), 313–331. doi:10.1016/S1469-0292(02)00011-0.

Jowett, S., & Meek, G. A. (2000). The coach-athlete relationship in married couples: An exploratory content analysis. *The Sport Psychologist*, 14, 157–175.

Jowett, S., & Nezlek, J. (2011). Relationship interdependence and satisfaction with important outcomes in coach-athlete dyads. *Journal of Social and Personal Relationships*, 29(3), 287–301. doi:10.1177/0265407511420980.

Jowett, S., & Ntoumanis, N. (2004). The coach-athlete relationship questionnaire (CART-Q): Development and initial validation. *Scandinavian Journal of Medicine and Science*, 14, 245–257. doi:10.1046/j.1600–0838.2003.00338.x.

Kellett, P. (2002). Football-as-war, coach-as-general: Analogy, metaphor and management implications. *Football Studies*, 5(1), 60–76.

Kerr, G., & Dacyshyn, A. (2000). The retirement experiences of elite, female gymnasts. *Journal of Applied Sport Psychology*, 12, 115–133.

Kerr, G., & Stirling, A. E. (2012). Parents' reflections on their child's experiences of emotionally abusive coaching practices. *Journal of Applied Sport Psychology, 24*(2), 191–206.

LaVoi, N. (2007). Comment on expanding the interpersonal dimension: Closeness in the coach-athlete relationship. *International Journal of Sports Science & Coaching, 2* (4), 497–512. doi:10.1260/174795407783359632.

Magyar, T., & Chase, M. (1996). Psychological strategies used by competitive gymnasts to overcome the fear of injury. *Technique, 16*(10), 1–5.

Moniuszko, S., & Kelly, C. (2017, October 27). Harvey Weinstein scandal: A complete list of the 87 accusers. *USA Today*. Retrieved from https://www.usatoday.com/story/life/people/2017/10/27/weinstein-scandal-complete-list-accusers/804663001.

Owton, H., & Sparkes, A. (2017). Sexual abuse and the grooming process in sport: Learning from Bella's story. *Sport, Education and Society, 2* 2(6), 732–743.

Pedersen, H. K., & Cooke, N. J. (2006). From battle plans to football plays: Extending military team cognition to football. *International Journal of Sport and Exercise Psychology, 4*(4), 422–446. doi:10.1080/1612197X.2006.9671806.

Philippe, R., & Seiler, R. (2006). Closeness, co-orientation and complementarity in coach-athlete relationships: What male swimmers say about their male coaches. *Psychology of Sport and Exercise, 7*(2), 159–171. doi:10.1016/j.psychsport.2005.08.004.

Pinheiro, M., Pimenta, N., Resende, R., & Malcolm, D. (2014). Gymnastics and child abuse: An analysis of former international Portuguese female artistic gymnasts. *Sport, Education and Society, 19*(4), 435–450.

Poczwardowski, A., Barott, J. E., & Henschen, K. P. (2002). The athlete and coach: Their relationship and its meaning. Results of an interpretive study. *International Journal of Sport Psychology, 33*(1), 116–140.

Stafford, A., Alexander, K., & Fry, D. (2015). 'There was something that wasn't right because that was the only place I ever got treated like that': Children and young people's experiences of emotional harm in sport. *Childhood, 22*(1), 121–137. doi:10.1177/0907568213505625.

Stirling, A. E. (2009). Definition and constituents of maltreatment in sport: Establishing a conceptual framework for research practitioners. *British Journal of Sports Medicine, 43*(14), 1091–1099. doi:10.1136/bjsm.2008.051433.

Stirling, A., & Kerr, G. (2008). Elite female swimmers' experiences of emotional abuse across time. *Journal of Emotional Abuse, 7*, 89–113.

Stirling, A., & Kerr, G. (2009). Abused athletes' perceptions of the coach-athlete relationship. *Sport in Society, 12*(2), 227–239. doi:10.1080/17430430802591019.

The Associated Press. (2016). Olympic gold medalist Simone Biles finds right fit in coach Aimee Boorman. *USA Today*, 12 August.

Thomas, L. (1987). Friendship. *Synthese, 72*, 217–236.

Tofler, I., Strayer, B. K., Micheli, L. J., & Herman, L. R. (1996). Physical and emotional problems of elite female gymnasts. *The New England Journal of Medicine, 335* (4), 281–283.

Tomlinson, A., & Yorganci, I. (1997). Male coach/female athlete relationships: Gender and power relations in competitive sport. *Journal of Sport and Social Issues, 21*(2), 134–155. doi:10.1177/019372397021002003.

US Department of Health& Human Services, Administration for Children and Families, Administration on Children, Youth and Families, Children's Bureau.

(2018). Child maltreatment 2016. Available from https://www.acf.hhs.gov/cb/resea rch-data-technology/statistics-research/child-maltreatment.

Van Yperen, N. W., Hamstra, M., & van der Klauw, M. (2011). To win, or not to lose, at any cost: The impact of achievement goals on cheating. *British Journal of Management*, 2, S5–S15.

Vealey, R., Armstrong, L., Comar, W., & Greenleaf, C. (1998). Influence of perceived coaching behaviours on burnout and competitive anxiety in female college athletes. *Journal of Applied Sport Psychology*, 10(2), 297–318.

Waldron, J. J., & Krane, V. (2005). Whatever it takes: Health compromising behaviours in female athletes. *Quest*, 57, 315–329.

White, P. (1990). Friendship and education. *Journal of Philosophy of Education*, 24(1), 81–91.

Chapter 10

Critical reflections on (adult) coach-(child) athlete 'no touch' discourses in women's artistic gymnastics
Out of touch

Melanie Lang and Joanne McVeigh

Introduction

> One minute you're upside-down, spinning around a bar metres off the ground. The next you're demonstrating perfect balance, somersaulting along a beam no wider than an iphone ...
>
> (British Gymnastics website)

Such is artistic gymnastics – a gravity-defying display of stunts, flips, rotations, pirouettes, and twists and turns, and one of the oldest[1] and most popular Olympic sports (Fédération Internationale de Gymnastique [FIG], 2016). Involving both technical precision and artistic creativity, women's artistic gymnastics (WAG) combines balance, strength, coordination, and control with flexibility, grace, and elegance. But, perhaps more than any other attribute, WAG involves courage – to trust the body's ability to take head over heels, to let go and land safely after a difficult dismount or attempt a skill for the first time, and to overcome fear of the unknown.

Experiencing and coping with fear is both understandable and well placed given the acrobatic nature of the sport. Make no mistake, WAG is a challenging and inherently dangerous sport. Strains, sprains, contusions, and overuse injuries are routine, and serious and traumatic injuries, particularly to the head, neck, and back, are not uncommon as a result of the challenging acrobatic elements that form part of athletes' routines. One study of gymnasts across all disciplines competing at the 2008, 2012, or 2016 Olympics reported the highest rate of injuries was among WAG athletes, with almost 40% of injuries sustained being serious enough to warrant time spent away from the sport (Edouard, Steffen, Junge, Leglise, Soligard, & Engebretsen, 2017). At a non-elite level, data on injury rates among US female college gymnasts across all disciplines suggest an injury rate of 9.22 per 1,000 athlete exposures, with injuries more likely to occur during competition than in training (Kerr, Hayden, Barr, Klossner, & Dompier, 2015), perhaps because of the demands of performing high-risk skills under intense pressure. Thankfully, most injuries reported in this study were relatively minor – ligament sprains (20.3%) and muscle/tendon strains (18.7%) were most common (Kerr, Hayden, et al., 2015) – but more serious injuries have also been recorded. For example, the National Center for Catastrophic Sports Injury Research (NCCSIR) ranks gymnastics as the second most common sport for 'serious or catastrophic'[2] sports injuries among female college athletes (NCCSIR, 2017),[3] and the second leading cause of 'serious or catastrophic' sports injuries among female athletes of all ages (Mueller & Cantu, 2009). Not surprisingly, overcoming fear of injury has been identified as a key issue for artistic gymnasts (Duarte, Nunomura, & Carbinato, 2015).

In addition, developments in gymnastics more broadly, including in WAG, mean that many gymnasts are beginning elite and non-elite training at a younger age and training more intensely than ever before (Caine & Harringe, 2013). USA Gymnastics, for example, recruit talented athletes from age 6 upwards (Caine & Harringe, 2013). The long-term athlete development model adopted by the FIG, entitled the Long-Term Performance Development plan, also recommends girls begin training at age 6 in order to achieve peak elite performance by age 16/17 (Fink, Hofmann, & Ortiz López, 2015). Meanwhile, young gymnasts (aged 7–18 years old) in elite training programmes may train for up to 37 hours per week almost year-round (Caine & Harringe, 2013). At the same time, the skill and difficulty levels across all apparatus have also increased (Russell, 2017). In the past 20 years, apparatus have been modified, allowing athletes to attempt and execute more complex skills; for example, the tops of vaulting tables are now sprung, giving the athlete more flight and elevation for multiple rotations, and the asymmetric bars are higher and more widely spaced apart, thus increasing the momentum and consequential potential to perform complex skills over, off, and between the bars (Russell, 2017). WAG athletes, then, are undergoing intense training regimens and performing more challenging skills at a younger age than ever before on apparatus that have adapted to encourage an increased level of skill and risk. As Russell (2017, p. 13) notes: 'prepubertal gymnasts around the world commonly perform skills that Olympic champions were incapable of performing only a few years ago!'

In such an environment, gymnasts must learn to trust their own abilities (as well as recognise their limitations) and to trust their coach, whose role as a 'spotter' and hands-on 'supporter' when athletes are learning and practicing new skills is central to athletes' safety. The coach, and the trust invested in him/her, is vital, not only for developing happy, confident, and competent athletes but also for ensuring athlete safety during skill development and execution.

Physical contact in WAG

Coaching is a holistic, social process involving 'a constantly dynamic set of intra- and inter-group interpersonal relationships' (Cushion, 2007, p. 399).

Understanding coaching in this way highlights the importance of coaches developing positive relationships with sport stakeholders. It has been suggested that the relationship between coach and athlete is the most significant for it 'is not an add-on to, or by-product of, the coaching process … instead it is the foundation of coaching' (Jowett, 2005, p. 412). In education, the benefits of a positive teacher-student relationship are well established (Murray & Malmgren, 2005), and similar findings apply to sport. A positive coach-athlete relationship has been found to improve athletes' self-confidence, satisfaction, and enjoyment of sport (Kidman & Lombardo, 2010). Jones (2009) emphasised that caring for athletes is central to both coaches' and athletes' success, while Potrac and colleagues found that coaches consider strong social and personal bonds with athletes as essential to improving coaching practice and athletes' performance and overall development, not just as athletes but as people (Potrac, Jones, & Armour, 2002).

Importantly, touch is crucial to the development of positive social and personal relationships (Field, 2003) and can be an important part of coaching (Lang, 2015; Gleaves & Lang, 2017). Defined as 'a class of nonverbal behavior comprised of deliberate physical contact between two or more individuals' (Kneidinger, Maple, & Tross, 2001, p. 44), touch is one of the most basic and powerful forms of communication. It can communicate feelings of approval, reassurance, and security; reduce stress and anxiety; affirm relationships; and provide physical and psychological support, thus contributing to the fostering of warm, caring, interpersonal cultures (Field, 2003). For these reasons, appropriate forms of touch are a useful and effective pastoral and pedagogic tool for sports coaching (Andrzejewski & Davis, 2008). For example, physical contact can be used to provide gymnasts with psychological support – when preparing to perform a standing back somersault on the beam for the first time, for instance, the feel of the coach's hand on an athlete's back can reduce anxiety, giving the gymnast the confidence to mentally prepare and attempt the skill. Meanwhile, touching or grasping an athlete's shoulder to prevent over-rotation when performing a handspring over the vault, and manipulating an athlete's body so she can feel the correct movement sensation before executing the skill, can be beneficial ways of helping gymnasts learn appropriate (and safe) technique.

As Lang (2015) has noted, touch has multiple different functions and, depending on the context, can be used positively or negatively. Crucially, while there are many benefits of touch, we must also not forget that touch can be used to physically and sexually abuse athletes and to desensitise children to sexual abuse and exploitation as part of the grooming process (Roberts & Vanstone, 2014). In 2013, for example, Rutgers University basketball coach Mike Rice was fired when a video emerged of him physically (and verbally) abusing athletes during practice in the US. Among other behaviors, Rice pushed, shoved, and slapped players and threw basketballs at their heads (Van Natta Jr., 2013). Meanwhile in China, a British Olympian working for the BBC as an undercover reporter filmed young children preparing for the 2008 Olympics being beaten by coaches and crying after being forced to repeat painful manoeuvres (BBC Sport, 2005). More recently, the sexual exploitation and abuse of athletes – adults and children, male and female – has received considerable media attention following a series of high-profile cases and convictions involving well-known sports personalities in professional football in England and Scotland (BBC News, 2018b), in US Swimming (Hobson, 2018), and gymnastics in the USA and Brazil (Associated Press, 2018; BBC News, 2018a). In all cases, the perpetrators used ludic forms of physical contact to desensitise 'victims'[4] to later sexual contact. Chris Unsworth, a former youth footballer who was one of the dozens of boys abused by Barry Bennell, described how the convicted scout and coach introduced games that involved touching young players to normalise the practice:

> 'He would move his hands around your body on the outside of your clothes, tickle you, and you would have to do the same to him'. But, he [Unsworth] said, the game would keep going until his hands were 'inside your shirt or inside your underpants'.
> (quoted in Baker & Tingle, 2018)

Coach-gymnast 'touch' in a risk world society

Touch, then, can be used for positive or nefarious ends, and it is important that we remember this rather than fall into the trap of constructing all touch as inherently 'good' or – as if often the case in the research literature – 'bad'. Equally, we must remember the reasons for and impetus behind the implementation of athlete welfare initiatives in sport: over the past two decades, myriad high-profile cases of (predominantly sexual) abuse, exploitation, and maltreatment of athletes, especially of child athletes, across a range of sports and countries have exposed a darker side of sport (Lang & Hartill, 2015). Exposure of such cases in sport has been one of the most successful radicalising events in recent decades, resulting in increased public awareness of sport as a locus of (child and adult) maltreatment and a ramping-up of moral pressure on sports organisations to be more accountable by implementing safeguarding measures for athletes (Lang, 2020). Over the same period, participation in sport has increasingly come to be recognised as a human right in and of itself as well as a vehicle for promoting other key fundamental rights, such as the rights to health, social inclusion, and leisure, and protection from violence, abuse, and maltreatment (Kidd & Donnelly, 2000; see International Olympic Committee, 2015; United Nations General Assembly, 1948, 1989). Over this period, legally binding instruments such as the United Nations (UN) Convention on the Elimination of All Forms of Discrimination Against Women (UN General Assembly, 1979) and the UN Convention on the Rights of the Child (UN General Assembly, 1989) have done much to advance understandings of human rights in and beyond sport. As Kidd and Donnelly (2000, p. 140) note, in sport such legislation has 'inspired increasing respect for athletes' rights'. These developments have, in tandem, resulted in a growing awareness of and demand for the introduction of measures to safeguard athlete welfare (Lang, 2020).

Alongside these developments, however, there have in recent years been a myriad of claims made in mainstream and social media, academia, and politics that adults in child-related settings are becoming increasingly concerned, even fearful, about touching children. Such concerns have been identified across a variety of settings including schools, care homes, physical education classes, and sports clubs across numerous countries such as the UK, USA, Canada, Sweden, Denmark, Canada, and Australia (see for example, Gove, 2012; Lang, 2010; Öhman & Quennerstedt, 2015; Pépin-Gagné & Parent, 2016; Piper, 2014; Piper & Stronach, 2008; Sawer, 2012).

Young people have long been the focus of a range of moral panics – anxiety surrounding risks to children such as obesity, falling educational standards, anti-social behaviour, and child abuse, to name but a few (Ungar, 2001). According to Pain (2006), this epitomises Beck's (1992) 'risk society', a new age of insecurity characterised by risk consciousness and risk avoidance. In particular, concern about the risk of child abuse, especially child sexual abuse and its unpredictable, invisible nature, has become a central fear of parents and legislators (Pain, 2006) and, according to scholars, has escalated in Western societies to the status of a 'moral panic'. Faced with such an intangible threat, active trust (Beck, 1992) between individuals has gradually eroded, resulting in a lack of trust between adults when it comes to child safety. As a result, some coaches, driven by a desire for self-protection, adopt a worst-case scenario and 'defensive' coaching practices such as the avoidance or restriction of physical contact with athletes in the (erroneous) belief that this reduces their perceived risk of being accused of abuse (Lang, 2010; 2015a; Piper, Garratt, & Taylor, 2013; Piper, Taylor, & Garratt, 2012). This, it is often argued, has led to coaching becoming 'conceptually and performatively unchallenged and [this has begun] to affect our capacities to think, act, feel and connect' (Pearce, 2010, p. 905). Piper, for example, argues that coaches' concerns about being accused of abuse and exploitation as a result of touching athletes is damaging the relationship between coaches and athletes and rendering coaching 'impoverished and dehumanized' (Piper, 2015, p. 12).

Concern regarding adult-child touch may be seen as one manifestation of this perceived threat. In the current risk world society, coaches, like other adults working *in loco parentis*, have become objects of distrust by other adults around them and increasing attention is being paid to adult-child interaction, both within and outside sport. Some argue this climate has created an environment in which safety from abuse defines every act of adult-child touch as suspicious, resulting in adults who work with children being positioned as potential abusers. In a risk world society, coaches recognise themselves as both objects of distrust and of vulnerability, that is as 'risky' subjects (e.g. of risk to children) and, simultaneously, 'at risk' of being accused of abuse. This is despite substantial evidence that such allegations remain rare, and allegations that are later proved to be 'false'[5] even more so (Brackenridge, Bringer, & Bishopp, 2005; Children and Family Select Committee Inquiry, 2009; Lang, 2012). Indeed, what these coaches mean when they say they are concerned about being accused of abuse is that they are concerned about being *wrongly* accused of abuse. As one coach put it:

> You don't ever get in a situation where it's just you and a swimmer and nobody else about because then you're opening yourself up to potential allegations, something being said that you haven't done ... Everyone's got to cover their backs.
> (Swimming coach quoted in Lang, 2010)

However, concern about 'false' allegations is a distortion of the reality of abuse – substantiated and non-reported abuse and maltreatment are likely to be more prevalent than unfounded cases. Such concern also has the potential to raise an element of doubt about *all* allegations, even those that are proven (Lang, 2015), and ignores the fact that touch is often used to abuse children and to desensitise them to sexual abuse as part of the grooming process (Roberts & Vanstone, 2014). After all, athlete welfare regulations were introduced to protect *athletes* not coaches. Much of the research on this topic to date fails to acknowledge these points and is predicated on the impact of such regulations on *coaches* rather than on *athletes*. This risks (re)producing damaging negative constructions of adult-child physical contact, exacerbating the moral panic about unfounded allegations of abuse and maltreatment.

Considering an alternative perspective

Alternatives to this negative, coach-centred perspective are, to date, relatively rare in both the media and the academic literature. In the case of the media, most such stories generally appear in the tabloid press and may be a result of editorial bias that regards articles about how hard-working teachers, nursery nurses, and coaches are feeling threatened by so-called 'false' allegations of abuse and exploitation as more 'newsworthy'. Meanwhile within the academic literature, much of the work on touch in sport has been published by Piper and colleagues, and yet this research has significant limitations. Their study aimed to, among others, 'Establish how sports coaching has responded *to wider concern in relation to touch*' and 'Consider the discourses of (e.g.) professionalism, policy, gender, capability, and media, to *the construction of touch in sports coaching as problematic and sexual*' (Piper & Garratt, 2012, p. 2, our emphasis). As such, the study began by assuming that a) 'concern in relation to touch' would be evident in sport, and that b) touch practices in sport were 'problematic and sexual'. The fact the study found this to be the case, then, is unsurprising as it was assumed from the start. Additionally, the study included a sample of fewer than 10 practitioners;[6] most of the 70+ interviewees were academics and senior managers in sports organisations and professional bodies such as the Association for Physical Education (Piper et al., 2013). In other words, those interviewed were neither coaches nor people who work with or even come into regular contact with athletes in a coaching context. The findings from Piper and colleagues' work, then, are not persuasive.

Meanwhile, Öhman and Quennerstedt (2015, p. 13) have offered an alternative explanation for coaches' concerns about touch practices. They, like sociologists of childhood Kitzinger (1988) and James, Jenks, and Prout (1998), argued that dominant constructions of children as vulnerable result in children's right to protection being privileged over their other rights and, as a consequence, protectionism and the management of risk come to dominate the thinking of those who work *in loco parentis*. Öhman and Quennerstedt (2015, p. 3) argued, therefore, that there is a 'need for alternative perspectives on physical contact in order to achieve a more multifaceted discussion and understanding of "touch" [and] "safety"' in sport.

Beyond this, peer-reviewed research on touch practices in sport is limited. There are only a handful of published studies from a narrow range of sports, there have been no quantitative studies to determine how widespread concerns are among adults in sport environments, and little is known about whether there are differences among the views of adults across the different socio-cultural contexts of specific sports – among coaches of different ages, ethnic backgrounds, or qualification levels; or among coaches working with athletes of different ages, ability levels, sex, ethnic background, or with varying abilities. Equally, to date no studies have investigated children and young people's views of touch practices or explored whether children and young people agree with the oft-made assertion (see for example, Hardman, Bailey, & Lord, 2015; Piper, 2015; Piper et al., 2012; 2013) that the coach-athlete relationship is being damaged by coaches' apparent reluctance to touch children.

There is, however, some research beginning to emerge that contradicts previously published –not to mention heavily promoted in the media – accounts of coaches' concerns about touching child athletes. One study from Australia, for example, found no evidence of concern about touching practices among sport stakeholders, including coaches (Scott, 2013). The study involved interviews with 20 sport stakeholders – four administrators/policymakers, two heads of university sports education programmes, and 14 others involved in junior and amateur sport, including coaches, athletes (including two former elite gymnasts-turned coaches), athletes' parents, and officials from various sports. The findings indicated awareness of concern among stakeholders about touching practices but this did not translate to reluctance from adults to become involved in sport as coaches or officials. No documented cases of allegations relating to 'unacceptable touch' were identified, and athletes and athletes' parents considered certain touching practices, especially when instructing and/or ensuring the safety of an athlete, acceptable and a necessary part of sport. Papaefstathiou (2015) reported similar findings in a study into the understandings of competitive track and field child athletes regarding child protection in Cypriot sport. The study of four coaches, four athletes, and two sport administrators found that coaches and athletes believed touching behaviors were acceptable and necessary for athletes' holistic development. Concern about the potential for misunderstandings to arise from touching child athletes was limited, although coaches recognised the need for ethical boundaries regarding appropriate physical contact.

Gleaves and Lang (2017) reported similar findings from parents of child swimmers in the UK. The study, which involved interviews with six parents of competitive youth swimmers within one English swimming club, explored parents' perspectives of appropriate and inappropriate coach-child athlete physical contact. Child athletes' parents acknowledged coach-athlete touching practices were a necessary part of a coach's job. Parents were critical of coaches who restricted their use of physical contact in order to protect themselves at the expense of the impact on the children with whom they worked, considering this a dereliction of coaches' professional and moral duties. Parents also recognised touching practices are contextually specific and identified three circumstances in which they deemed it legitimate:

1. when physical contact was used to prevent, minimise, or treat physical harm to a child;
2. when physical contact was used to teach a child a sport-specific technique or skill;
3. when physical contact was used for pastoral care or moral support purposes.

These findings mirror those from a Canadian study that found that athletes understand coaching may involve physical contact and that such contact can be a useful pedagogical tool (Pépin-Gagné & Parent, 2016). Indeed, athletes said they consider certain forms of coach-athlete physical contact – using touch to demonstrate an instruction during training, for example – a vital part of good coaching practice and necessary to improve athletic performance (Pépin-Gagné & Parent, 2016). A similar study by Kerr, Stirling, Heron, MacPherson, and Banwell (2015) in Canada found that athletes and coaches recognise the many benefits of touch – for effective instruction, injury prevention/management, to enhance wellbeing and develop sportspersonship, for example – and noted that while individuals differ in their tendency to use contact behaviors and in how they feel about being a recipient of such behaviour, touching behaviors are generally used and accepted across sports.

Published data, then, suggest there is *some* evidence that *some* adults in sport, specifically coaches, are restricting their use of physical contact, especially with children – or at least some coaches *say* they are doing so. Most of the data are based on interviews with adult coaches and few lengthy observational studies have been conducted to confirm coaches' behaviours in practice (Lang, 2015 is an exception). The evidence is not conclusive.

Concluding thoughts and future directions

Coach-athlete touch is a common part of sport and is essential to coaching WAG. When used appropriately, touch can help coaches to effectively support the teaching of new skills and, by manipulating body shapes, athletes may be assisted in the development of the kinesthetic awareness needed to perform complex skills. Touch may also be beneficial in preventing, minimising, and managing injury and other types of accidental harm (i.e. grabbing a child to prevent them from crossing over the vault runway while others are training). Further, touch can be useful in the pastoral care of athletes, communicating reassurance and security, and providing psychological (as well as physical) support (Field, 2003; Lang, 2015). Additionally, athletes, and especially children, who do not experience positive, appropriate forms of physical contact may well be less likely to be able to recognise inappropriate contact should it occur (Lang, 2015). For these reasons, coaches who avoid or even restrict their use of physical contact with athletes to protect themselves at the expense of the impact on the athletes with whom they work, may, at best, be less effective coaches (Lang, 2015; Pépin-Gagné & Parent, 2016) and at worst, be neglecting their professional and moral duties as a coach (Gleaves & Lang, 2017; Öhman & Quennerstedt, 2015).

To avoid exacerbating concerns about touching athletes and instead encourage coaches to have confidence in the use of appropriate touch, researchers, the media, coaches, and coach educators must avoid (re)producing the negative constructions that have, thus far, tended to dominate this field. Similarly, it is vital that sports organisations allay concerns and confusion about touching practices in sport and about 'false' allegations of abuse and exploitation. For example, as the socio-cultural context of each sport (and indeed, each club) is different, different sports will have different cultural norms. Equally, as the skills, movements, and requirements of each sport are different, the need to touch athletes to be an effective pedagogue will also vary significantly. To clarify acceptable behaviour, sports organisations should issue clear guidelines on appropriate and inappropriate forms of physical contact within their sport. In terms of research, much more empirical work, particularly longitudinal studies of coaches' practices and perceptions of touching practices, are also sorely needed, as is research that explores and theorises the boundaries of coaches' and athletes' touch practices across a range of sports, and studies that investigate athletes' perspectives on positive (and negative) touching practices and best practice when using touch in coaching.

It is also vital that coaches and all other sport stakeholders (officials, athletes, athletes' parents, coach educators, and academics working in this area) remember that touch can also be used to cause physical and sexual harm. Equally, it is crucial that those involved in sport are educated to understand that not all sexual abuse is predicated on the use of coercion, and that although perpetrators often claim that their offences 'just happen', research suggests that extensive planning and grooming of 'victims' is common (McAlinden, 2006). Coaches and others must understand the role of touch in sexual grooming and the fact that grooming, which is a criminal offence in many (though not all) countries, involves subtle but deliberate behaviors, often enacted over weeks, months, or even years (Brackenridge & Fasting, 2005), many of which are not, in and of themselves, illegal, such as certain touching practices. It is this that so often allows grooming to go undetected. If coaches are to play an effective role in preventing and managing abuse and exploitation, it is vital they recognise the role of touch in this process.

All athletes – whether children or adults, in WAG or other sports – are entitled to bodily autonomy. Coaches and other sport stakeholders need to recognise athletes (adults and children) as active agents in the coaching process and prioritise the best interests of the individual when coaching (Lang, 2015). To this end, athletes should be informed about and asked for their consent for physical contact (Lang, 2015). They need to be taught what is and isn't appropriate physical contact in their sport, that they have a voice in how and when they are touched, and that they have the right to refuse such contact[7] and, equally, be reminded that they may ask for additional physical support if they feel they need it (for example when attempting a new skill). Coaches need to garner and listen to athletes' views and, if touch is neither warranted nor welcome, to find alternative ways of coaching.

WAG clubs and national/international federations should also urgently develop and implement mandatory gymnastics-specific policies and codes of conduct on appropriate forms of coach-gymnast physical contact and the mechanisms for seeking clarification on such contact as well as for reporting concerns. Such policies should be developed with input from gymnasts themselves. To complement these, clubs and federations should develop mandatory education courses for coaches, athletes, athletes' parents, and other sport stakeholders to inform them of the diverse (positive and negative) functions of touch in gymnastics; its usefulness as a pedagogical, pastoral, and safety tool; and the cultural norms for physical contact within the sport. These courses should encourage stakeholders to problematise dominant constructions of coach-athlete physical contact as inherently negative and 'dangerous' for coaches and highlight the rarity of so-called 'false' allegations. They should also teach all gymnastics stakeholders about the fundamental principles of human and children's rights, and specifically *athlete-centred* approaches to coaching gymnastics. For example, courses should educate coaches and other sport stakeholders to ask for and respect the views of athletes on the physical contact they are happy/unhappy with and suggest ways of developing open lines of communication and trusting relationships with gymnasts to ensure that if/when physical contact is used it is mutually consensual, expected, and individualised to the needs of the athlete (i.e. so that athletes who are comfortable with touch when it is used for pastoral care or moral support purposes can receive this and those who are not do not). Meanwhile, athletes should also be educated about when touch may be used and for what purpose in gymnastics, about the socio-cultural norms of touch in their sport as well as their right to bodily autonomy, and where they can go to seek advice or report concerns.

Clubs should also implement codes of conduct for coaches that make clear when physical contact with gymnasts is acceptable/unacceptable and the consequences for failing to follow accepted standards of behaviour. Finally, to encourage open, non-confrontational discussion around touch and other welfare issues, within clubs, designated welfare officers need to proactively and regularly connect with gymnasts (and, where these are children, their parents) to avoid assuming a predominantly reactive role of stepping in when a concern has been raised.

Everyone in sport from the coaches 'on the ground' to organisational heads have a responsibility to do all they can to prevent all forms of abuse and exploitation. While much of the research and media articles on touching practices in (and beyond) sport to date has focused (negatively) on the issue from the perspective of *coaches*, sport authorities must now show leadership in challenging adult-centric views and in promoting athlete-centred practices and perspectives if they are to truly prioritise the welfare and wellbeing of all athletes.

Notes

1 At least for male participants: gymnastics for men was included in the programme at the first modern Olympics in 1896. WAG was introduced in 1928 (FIG, 2016).
2 A 'serious or catastrophic injury' is defined by the NCCSIR and studies conducted under its auspices as 'fatalities, permanent disability injuries, serious injuries (fractured neck or serious head injury)' (NCCSIR, no date).
3 Skiing topped the list for female athletes. Figures were not broken down by gymnastics discipline.
4 We use the term 'victim' here for simplicity but use speech marks to acknowledge the negative connotations associated with the term (for more on this see Hunter, 2010).

5   This term is often used in the vernacular to indicate an allegation that is fictitious, often intentionally so (sometimes also referred to as 'wrongful' allegations). However, at the point of referral/investigation, there is no such thing as a 'false' allegation; all allegations are just that - allegations - and, as such, require investigating to determine the likelihood of their veracity. Additionally, not all allegations result in a conviction (or even a prosecution), and this does not necessarily (or even likely) mean the allegation was fictitious, intentionally or otherwise. As a minimum, a distinction must be made between *unproven* allegations and *unfounded* allegations. Unproven allegations are those where there is insufficient evidence uncovered during an investigation to establish that the maltreatment either occurred or did not occur. Unfounded or unsubstantiated allegations are those that are investigated and proven to be without basis; this could be due to misunderstanding or error on the part of the accuser or other reasons beyond the allegation being intentionally fictitious.
6   These comprised football, swimming, and paddle sports coaches plus PE teachers; the actual sample of sports coaches (as opposed to PE teachers) interviewed is unknown (figures for the number of coaches vs. PE teachers in this sample are not provided in the published material) but must logically be even smaller than 10.
7   With the exception of when such contact is essential for safety/injury management.

References

Andrzejewski, C. E., & Davis, H. A. (2008). Human contact in the classroom: Exploring how teachers talk about and negotiate touching students. *Teaching and Teacher Education*, 24, 779–794.

Associated Press. (2018, April 30). Report: Ex-Brazil gymnastics coach accused of sexual abuse. *ESPN*. Retrieved from http://www.espn.com/olympics/gymnastics/story/_/id/23368732/ex-brazilian-national-gymnastics-team-coach-fernando-de-carvalho-lopes-accused-sexual-abuse.

Baker, K., & Tingle, R. (2018, February 13). Convicted paedophile Barry Bennell who was 'abuser on an industrial scale' of young footballers is found guilty of 36 further child sex offences against 10 victims. *The Mail Online*. Retrieved from http://www.dailymail.co.uk/news/article-5380925/How-football-coach-Barry-Bennell-groomed-abused-boys.html.

BBC Sport. (2005, November 17). Pinsent shocked by China training. *BBC Sport*. Retrieved from http://news.bbc.co.uk/sport1/hi/other_sports/gymnastics/4445506.stm.

BBC News. (2018a, January 25). Larry Nassar: Disgraced US Olympics doctor jailed for 175 years. *BBC News*. Retrieved from https://www.bbc.co.uk/news/world-us-canada-42811304.

BBC News. (2018b, February 19). 'Devil incarnate' Barry Bennell sentenced to 31 years. *BBC News*. Retrieved from https://www.bbc.co.uk/news/uk-43118069.

Beck, U. (1992). *Risk society: Towards a new modernity*. London: Sage.

Brackenridge, C., Bringer, J. D., & Bishopp, D. (2005). Managing cases of abuse in sport. *Child Abuse Review*, 14, 259–274.

Brackenridge, C. H., & Fasting, K. (2005). The grooming process in sport: Case studies of sexual harassment and abuse. *Auto/Biography*, 13(1), 1–20.

Caine, D. J., & Harringe, M. L. (2013). Epidemiology of injury in gymnastics. In D. J. Caine, K. Russell, & L. Lim (Eds.), *Gymnastics handbook of sports medicine and science* (pp. 111–124). Hoboken, NJ: Wiley-Blackwell.

Children, Families and Schools Select Committee Inquiry. (2009). *Allegations against school staff*. London: Her Majesty's Stationary Office.

Cushion, C. (2007). Modelling the complexity of the coaching process: A response to commentaries. *International Journal of Sports Science and Coaching*, 2, 427–433.

Duarte, L. H., Nunomura, M., & Carbinato, M. V. (2015). Artistic gymnastics and fear: Reflections on its causes. *Science of Gymnastics Journal*, 7(3), 7–21.

Edouard, P., Steffen, K., Junge, A., Leglise, M., Soligard, T., & Engebretsen, L. (2017). Gymnastics injury incidence during the 2008, 2012 and 2016 Olympic Games: Analysis of prospectively collected surveillance data from 963 registered gymnasts during Olympic Games. *British Journal of Sports Medicine*, 52(7), 475–481.

Fédération Internationale de Gymnastique (FIG). (2016). About *women's artistic gymnastics*. Retrieved from http://www.fig-gymnastics.com/site/page/view?id=253.

Field, T. (2003). *Touch*. Cambridge, MA: MIT Press.

Fink, H., Hofmann, D., & Ortiz López, L. (2015). Age group development and competition program for *women's artistic gymnastics*. Retrieved from http://www.fig-docs.com/website/agegroup/manuals/Agegroup-wag-manual-e.pdf.

Gleaves, T., & Lang, M. (2017). Kicking 'no touch' discourses into touch: Athletes' parents' constructions of appropriate (adult) coach-(child) athlete physical contact. *Journal of Sport and Social Issues*, 41(3), 191–211.

Gove, M. (2012, November 16). The failure of child protection and the need for a fresh start. Speech at the Institute of Public Policy Research. Transcript retrieved from https://www.gov.uk/government/speeches/the-failure-of-child-protection-and-the-need-for-a-fresh-start.

Hardman, A., Bailey, J., & Lord, R. (2015). Care and touch in trampoline gymnastics: Reflections and analysis from the UK. In H. Piper (Ed.), *Touch in sports coaching and physical education: Fear, risk and moral panic* (pp. 151–166). London: Routledge.

Hobson, W. (2018, February 8). Ariana Kukors, Olympic swimmer, accuses coach Sean Hutchison of sexual abuse. *The Washington Post*. Retrieved from https://www.washingtonpost.com/sports/ariana-kukors-olympic-swimmer-accuses-coach-sean-hutchison-of-sexual-abuse/2018/02/08/446a3fc6-0cd2-11e8-8b0d-891602206fb7_story.html?noredirect=on&utm_term=.69659828746e.

Hunter, S. V. (2010). Evolving narratives about childhood sexual abuse: Challenging the dominance of the victim and survivor paradigm. *The Australian and New Zealand Journal of Family Therapy*, 31(2), 176–190.

International Olympic Committee. (2015). Olympic Charter. Retrieved from https://stillmed.olympic.org/Documents/olympic_charter_en.pdf.

James, A., Jenks, C., & Prout, A. (1998). *Theorising childhood*. Oxford: Polity Press.

Jones, R. L. (2009). Coaching as caring (the smiling gallery): Accessing hidden knowledge. *Physical Education and Sport Pedagogy*, 14, 377–390.

Jowett, S. (2005). The coach-athlete partnership. *The Psychologist*, 18, 412–415.

Kerr, G. A., Stirling, A. E., Heron, A., MacPherson, E. A., & Banwell, J. M. (2015). The importance of touch in sport: Athletes' and coaches' reflections. *International Journal of Social Science Studies*, 3(4), 56–68.

Kerr, Z. Y., Hayden, R., Barr, M., Klossner, D. A., & Dompier, T. P. (2015). Epidemiology of National Collegiate Athletic Association women's gymnastics injuries 2009–2010 through 2013–2014. *Journal of Athletic Training*, 50, 870–878.

Kidd, B., & Donnelly, P. (2000). Human rights in sports. *International Review for the Sociology of Sport*, 35(2), 131–148.

Kidman, L., & Lombardo, B. J. (Eds.) (2010). *Athlete-centred coaching: Developing decision makers*. Worcester: IPC.

Kitzinger, J. (1988). Defending innocence: Ideologies of childhood. *Feminist Review*, 28, 77–88.

Kneidinger, L. M., Maple, T. L., & Tross, S. A. (2001). Touching behaviour in sport: Functional components, analysis of sex differences and ethiological considerations. *Journal of Non-Verbal Behaviour*, 25, 43–62.

Lang, M. (2010). Surveillance and conformity in competitive youth swimming. *Sport, Education and Society*, 15(1), 19–37.

Lang, M. (2012). The extent of coaches' concern about being accused of abuse: A quantitative study. Paper presented at the International Convention on Science, Education and Medicine in Sport pre-Olympic Congress, Glasgow, Scotland, 22 July.

Lang, M. (2015). Touchy subject: A Foucauldian analysis of coaches' perceptions of adult-child touch in youth swimming. *Sociology of Sport Journal*, 32(1), 4–21.

Lang, M. (2020). An introduction to athlete welfare. In M. Lang (Ed.), *Routledge handbook of athlete welfare*. London: Routledge.

Lang, M., & Hartill, M. (Eds.) (2015). *Safeguarding, child protection and abuse in sport: International perspectives in research, policy and practice*. London: Routledge.

Lyons, K. (2014). She'll be right? An Australian perspective on caring for young people in physical education and sport. In H. Piper (Ed.), *Touch in sports coaching and physical education: Fear, risk and moral panic* (pp. 137–153). London: Routledge.

McAlinden, A.-M. (2006). 'Setting 'em up': Personal, familial and institutional grooming in the sexual abuse of children. *Social and Legal Studies*, 15(3), 339–362.

Mueller, F. O., & Cantu, R. C. (2009). Catastrophic sports injury research twenty-sixth annual report: Fall 1982-spring 2008. Retrieved from http://www.unc.edu/depts/nccsi/AllSport.pdf.

Murray, C., & Malmgren, K. (2005). Implementing a teacher-student relationship programme in a high-poverty urban school: Effects on social, emotional and academic adjustment and lessons learned. *Journal of School Psychology*, 43, 137–152.

National Center for Catastrophic Sports Injury Research (NCCSIR). (2017). 1982/83–2015/16 all sport report: Table appendix. Retrieved from https://nccsir.unc.edu/files/2013/10/NCCSIR-34th-Annual-All-Sport-Report-1982_2016_Table-Appendix.pdf.

NCCSIR. (no date). Catastrophic sport injury definition. Retrieved from http://nccsir.unc.edu/definition-of-injury/.

Öhman, M., & Quennerstedt, A. (2015). Questioning the no-touch discourse in physical education from a children's rights perspective. *Sport, Education and Society*, 22(3), 305–320.

Pain, R. (2006). Paranoid parenting? Rematerializing risk and fear for children. *Social and Cultural Geography*, 7, 221–243.

Papaefstathiou, M. (2015). 'It's not what you say, it's how it feels': Touch in the tactile context of Cypriot track and field sport. In H. Piper (Ed.), *Touch in sports coaching and Physical Education: Fear, risk and moral panic* (pp. 85–100). London: Routledge.

Pearce, C. (2010). The life of suggestions. *Qualitative Inquiry*, 16, 902–908.

Pépin-Gagné, J., & Parent, S. (2016). Coaching, touching and false allegations of sexual abuse in Canada. *Journal of Sport and Social Issues*, 40(2), 162–172.

Piper, H. (Ed.) (2014). *Touch in sports coaching and physical education: Fear, risk and moral panic*. London: Routledge.

Piper, H., & Garratt, D. (2012). *Hands-off sports' coaching: The politics of touch. ESRC end of award report. Report No. RES-000-22-4156*. Swindon: Economic and Social Research Council. Retrieved from http://www.esrc.ac.uk/my-esrc/grants/RES-000-22-4156/read.

Piper, H., & Stronach, I. (2008). *Don't touch! The educational story of a panic*. London: Routledge.

Piper, H., Garratt, D., & Taylor, B. (2013). Child abuse, child protection and defensive 'touch' in PE teaching and sports coaching. *Sport, Education and Society*, 18, 583–598.

Piper, H., Taylor, B., & Garratt, D. (2012). Sports coaching in a risk society: No touch, no trust! *Sport, Education and Society*, 17, 1–15.

Potrac, P., Jones, R., & Armour, K. (2002). 'It's all about getting respect': The coaching behaviours of an expert English soccer coach. *Sport, Education and Society*, 7, 183–202.

Roberts, S., & Vanstone, M. (2014). A child sexual abuse research project: A brief endnote. *Journal of Child Sexual Abuse*, 23, 745–754.

Russell, K. (2017). The evolution of gymnastics. In D. J. Caine, L. Lim, & K. Russell (Eds.), *Handbook of sports medicine and science: Gymnastics* (pp. 3–14). Chichester: International Olympic Committee Medical Commission/Wiley-Blackwell.

Sawer, P. (2012). Climate of fear surrounds children's sports coaches. *The Telegraph*. Retrieved from https://www.telegraph.co.uk/news/uknews/9417560/Climate-of-fear-surrounds-childrens-sports-coaches.html.

Scott, C. (2013). The Australian situation: Not so touchy? *Sport, Education and Society*, 18(5), 599–614.

Ungar, S. (2001). Moral panic versus the risk society: The implications of the changing sites of social anxiety. *British Journal of Sociology*, 52, 271–291.

United Nations General Assembly. (1948). *Universal declaration of human rights*. Retrieved from https://www.ohchr.org/EN/UDHR/Documents/UDHR_Translations/eng.pdf.

United Nations General Assembly. (1979). *Convention on the elimination of all forms of discrimination against women*. Retrieved from https://www.un.org/womenwatch/daw/cedaw/text/econvention.htm.

United Nations General Assembly. (1989). *The convention on the rights of the child*. Retrieved from www.ohchr.org/Documents/ProfessionalInterest/crc.pdf.

Van Natta Jr, D. (2013, 3 April). Video shows Mike Rice's ire. *ESPN*. Retrieved from http://www.espn.com/espn/otl/story/_/id/9125796/practice-video-shows-rutgers-basketball-coach-mike-rice-berated-pushed-used-slurs-players.

Part IV

The multiple actors involved in creating an elite gymnast

Jenny's story Part IV: Enough's enough

James Pope

I was amazingly excited about Edinburgh. A big national competition with the potential for internationals ahead if I did well. We were going to be away for four days in all, and as my parents wouldn't be coming along I felt really grown up.

Frank was overseeing the other coaches, and of course, working closely with me. He was the top guy, and despite all the moments we'd had, I was proud to be 'his'. Everyone knew how well he'd done in the past and I was puffed up.

The team coach on the journey up was brilliant fun – so much buzz and energy and joking and just being a kid, in a way. I mean, we all competed against each other and there's no doubt sometimes it was bitchy – but for those few hours on the coach we were just kids on a school outing. The coaches didn't seem to mind, in fact they were joking and chatting and laughing. We never used to see them like that, as a rule. So it felt great. And I was confident. I had been working hard. I'd lost more weight too, to get into that small leotard!

The hotel was pretty smooth, I seem to remember. It was probably only a Premier Inn or something, but to me it felt like we were royalty!

On the first night before the competition began, we all went down for dinner together, not that anyone ate much! The hotel had other guests, of course, and they were all eating their way through soup, and chicken and chips and knickerbocker glories, but of course we were all on diets and we didn't really make much use of any of the menu! The pressure you're always under to keep your weight down … sometimes it's too much to handle, and that night I felt like all I wanted was to have a burger and fries and chocolate milkshake. Frank was watching us, and the other coaches would be saying things like, 'No pigging out!' Caz had come up with a little plan, so we ate little and winked at each other.

The whole food thing was a real pressure, to me anyway. It wasn't like we ever got much real information about what exactly to eat or not, but there was always the awareness that we should be keeping our weight down. I used to skip meals, especially at school where it would be easy to just bin the sandwiches my mum gave me; at home I'd pick and pretend I wasn't hungry – I actually often *was* hungry! Some of the girls I knew would take pills to keep their weight down.

And some coaches seemed to contradict others – like one would say drink plenty of water because that keeps your appetite down, but another would say don't drink too much because you'll get bloated. So we girls would just implicitly be eating as little as possible. I think things have improved, maybe there's proper nutritional support nowadays, but when I was competing, it was random.

After 'dinner', we were allowed to watch some TV, and then it was up to bed for an early start next day. We were all so excited. I shared a room with Caz, which was brilliant.

The coaches came round, knocking on the doors and calling lights out, and I was lying in bed whispering with Caz, waiting for the corridor to go quiet. She'd smuggled some chocolate and crisps in! If Frank had ever caught us he'd have gone ballistic, but we just had to let off some steam. We were giggling and poking each other in the ribs, trying not to make any noise, while shoving down chocolates and crisps in the same mouthful. It was hilarious. I think it's the only time I really broke the rules like that! In a way, my friendship with Caz saved my sanity, but it also made me begin to feel discontented, because she would challenge the status quo. You can't challenge the status quo, not if you want to get anywhere. I had never repeated my mistake of defying Frank in the gym.

Anyway, we were happily enjoying our little secret rebellion, when there was a knock at the door and Frank's voice: 'Jenny? Can I see you?'

'What does *he* want?' Caz whispered.

'Maybe he knows we've got food,' I said.

'Don't answer.' Caz was a bit of a stroppy one and didn't like Frank – but she also wasn't as good as me, and her coach didn't have the same reputation as Frank, so I used to ignore her jibes and remarks about 'Frank the Freak'. We both sat there silent. Maybe he'd think we were asleep.

'Jenny?'

'Yes, Frank?' I had to answer. My heart was thumping. I tried to sound sleepy or something.

'Could you come to my room for a moment, please?'

I looked at Caz, who was giving me an absolutely rude gesture. I throw a sweatshirt on top of my pyjamas and went with Frank, to his room, which was along the corridor. They had a coach on each landing, so there'd always be someone if anything was needed. I was nervous. Again, I keep saying, I see more now I'm looking back: I can feel now how much stress I'd collected into myself. Frank's moods, his anger, the coldness if I didn't perform, the sort-of affection that felt like punishment, the pressure to keep weight down, the photos ... even being away from my parents ... As I walked along the corridor with him a bit ahead of me, I suddenly felt really scared.

We went to his room, and he showed me the photos on his laptop. 'You see this?' he said, showing me a photo he'd taken of me in a floor routine. 'You see that angle of your leg there?' I did see the angle of my leg, and it looked fine to me. 'We need to work on that. That's why these photos are so helpful. Are you wearing knickers?'

'Umm, yes,' I said.

'Can you take your pyjama bottoms off – we'll see your shape better. We'll try to get that leg right.'

This doesn't sound good, does it? And it didn't sound good then either. I'd never heard of anyone practising routines in a hotel room before! But I STILL didn't question it – I knew I felt frightened and odd, but I couldn't challenge it. I felt uncomfortable, but I pulled off my pyjama bottoms, and held the positions he asked for.

'There you go, that's better,' he'd be saying as I stretched a leg up. He'd be coming up and taking photos close to me, from different angles. 'See what I mean?' he said, showing me a picture in the camera screen – 'Better.'

Then he said, 'Here, let me position you.' He touched my calf and pulled my leg to a stretch, then he held my thigh and gently squeezed. 'Feel that muscle? You're amazing,' he said, holding my leg, quite gently. I was no longer stretching, I was just suddenly terrified. 'You know that, don't you? You're going to be great.'

'Thanks,' I said.

'These legs are going to win you a big medal one day.'

He looked at me, and he fixed his eyes on mine, in a way that made me feel really strange. He smiled. I remember the smile. It made my whole body shiver.

I bolted.

I don't know ... Something about his eyes fixed on mine, more than the hand on my thigh. I don't really know what happened in my head.

I rushed back to my room. Caz was awake, waiting for me. 'What the hell?' she said as I threw myself on the bed face down. I hadn't realised but I was crying.

Was it Frank, was it hunger, was it stress, fear, anxiety?

'What's the matter?' She came and hugged me. 'Where are your PJs?'

'I don't know,' I said. 'I want to go home.'

'Go home?! We've been looking forward to this for months.'

'I know! I can't handle it anymore.' I wailed and she held me tight.

'Give me your phone, I'm calling your mum,' Caz said. I loved her for that. I still love her, stroppy Caz. We're still friends.

Mum and Dad drove up and got me in the morning. Frank was stunned, you could see that. But he hadn't come after me when I fled, so he must have known he'd crossed a line. He barely said a word when they knocked on his door and told him they were taking me home and that I wouldn't be competing. He just looked at me, like a puppy looking at its owner. What was he saying? I don't know. But, I felt bad. I actually felt bad for him!

That was the end of the road really. I joined a different club and I worked hard for a while, but my time had ended with the sport. I think I wanted to grow up. I'd been getting hips, no boobs really, the dieting stops the boobs coming, but I did get hips and I wanted to be a teenager, I think. And I was not going to see Frank again. I don't know what he did with those photos of me in his laptop, and I don't know where my pyjama bottoms went, and I don't want to know.

I'm not sure even now I've fully made the transition out of the sport to be honest: it's really hard to give up something that has so shaped your life for a lot of years. I was quite lucky in that I had Caz – she was always going to give up, and when I did she followed me, and we used to talk to each other about all the s*** that we'd experienced and seen. But some girls when they retire do seriously struggle – I've read about girls becoming mentally ill. Something happens to your brain and body when you work as hard and intensely as you do in gymnastics. And when you stop, you go into some kind of shock. You've had that structure to your life for so long, the routine, the support system, the purpose to your life. It took me a long time to find other things to do. I had no good friendships outside of the sport, so I found it hard joining in social activities – what were you supposed to do at a party?

He's still working, as far as I know. My parents didn't cause a fuss. Mum said it was obvious my heart hadn't been in it for a while, and she didn't want me being unhappy. Dad was just Dad – a few hugs and a few jokey words like, 'Well, you'll have to take up football now!' Did they know anything? Maybe I'll ask them one day. Of course, I've read all the news stories, and I've often wondered what would have happened if I hadn't run that night. But it's in the past now. I don't blame them for anything that I went through, but I do sometimes wonder how come they were so 'hands off', so unaware of the extremes. One day I might ask them what they thought was going on that night.

I cried in Mum's arms when they arrived, and Dad was stroking my hair. Must have been hell of a round trip for them. I wonder if they suspected Frank. They never said a word about him, just Mum saying, 'If you've had enough, let's go home.'

I needed to hear that.

Chapter 11

The sorting of gymnasts
An Actor-Network Theory approach to examining talent identification and development in women's artistic gymnastics

Roslyn Kerr

Introduction

There are numerous theoretical approaches that acknowledge the range of actors that influence and contribute to sporting practice. In the context of women's artistic gymnastics (WAG), the role of gymnasts, coaches, parents, managers, judges, medical personnel, and other administrators have all been identified as potential influences on individual gymnasts. However, a type of influence that has received far less acknowledgement in the social science literature is the role played by non-human actors, such as technology and equipment.

One theoretical approach that deliberately highlights the role of non-human actors is Actor-Network Theory (ANT) as developed by Bruno Latour, Michel Callon, and John Law, originally as a method for studying scientific practice (see for example, Callon, 1986; Callon & Law, 1982; Latour & Woolgar, 1979). For ANT, a central argument is that action always occurs through humans and non-humans working together, or, put another way, that there is no social, only the socio-technical (Latour, 2005).

In this chapter, I examine two significant and common gymnastics occurrences: physical ability testing, and the selection of gymnasts into a team, and deliberately highlight the role of various technologies in facilitating these processes. The goal is to demonstrate that although technologies may seem mundane and insignificant compared with the influence of humans, they are in fact crucial to WAG taking place. They hold central roles in ensuring that information can be accurately collected and transferred in order to facilitate significant decision-making as part of the process of creating scientific knowledge.

This chapter draws on ethnographic data collected in New Zealand throughout 2005–2010. In what follows, I first outline the ANT approach, before describing the data collection methods. I then analyse the two contexts of a physical ability test and selection to a national team, with the goal of highlighting the work done by various non-humans in order to facilitate these processes. In essence, I outline the network containing both humans and technologies that produced these selection processes in New Zealand.

Actor-network theory

In a theoretical sense, the core of the ANT approach is to understand how a range of humans and non-humans assemble together to ensure action takes place. For example, a gymnastics routine can be viewed as the result of a human body assembling with a piece of gymnastics apparatus, sometimes facilitated by other components such as hand guards or chalk (Kerr, 2014; 2016). In some ways, this assembling resembles the notion of the creation of a figuration as developed by Norbert Elias (see chapter 13), but where Elias was focused only on humans, ANT emphasises the role(s) played by non-humans.

The non-humans in the assemblage can take on a number of different roles. One is to assist with holding the assemblage together, which Latour (2005) refers to as an intermediary. In the example of a gymnastics routine, a hand guard that assists the gymnast with assembling effectively with the apparatus would be an intermediary. But if the hand guard were to break apart, or be too slippery, and therefore play a role in preventing the completion of the routine, it would be playing the role of a mediator: an actor that prevents a particular action from occurring (Kerr, 2014). These concepts emphasise the way non-humans can be crucial for facilitating or preventing action from taking place.

Latour (1992) argued that often it is humans who can be more fallible than non-humans. He emphasised how humans can be forgetful and unreliable, whereas technology is able to repeat the same action consistently without getting tired, forgetful, bored, hungry, or needing to sleep. Additionally, owing to these qualities, some non-humans are able to hold information in a stable form, which Latour (1999) referred to as an inscription. For example, a piece of paper is able to hold some information written upon it in a stable form, while a computer is able to hold far more information. The significance of these items being able to hold information is that they then allow the information to be moved from one person or place to another, or, in Latour's terms, to be circulated. In sport, the technologies of the video camera and the television were significant because they allowed the circulation of sporting performances. Where previously it was necessary to physically travel to a sports competition to see the action, it is now possible for the action to be stabilised in video form, and circulated globally (Kerr, 2016). The term Latour (1992) uses to describe a non-human able to transfer information in a stable fashion is 'immutable mobile'.

The creation of immutable mobiles is also crucial for the production of science, including sport science. As Gibson (2018) points out, the sports science laboratory works through the creation of inscriptions, which are generally also immutable mobiles, such as VO2max and blood testing equipment. But these types of equipment are also co-participants in the creation of scientific knowledge, in that they act to constitute knowledge in a particular way. As Gibson (2018, p. 9) describes: 'Calibration, for sports scientists, reliably translates abstract inscriptions into the phenomena thereby reifying functioning of human bodies: the wave on the electrocardiogram is the electrical activity of the heat, for example.' As this quote emphasises, the inscriptions produced by the machines become representations of human capacity. The human element becomes invisible, with the inscriptions coming to fully represent the body's make-up and/or ability in a process Gibson (2018) describes as 'dehumanization'. At the same time, in what Gibson (2018) calls 'dehumanization', scientists also ascribe high levels of agency to individuals in a reflection of the neoliberal agenda that places individuals as the central units responsible for their own destiny.

Methods

This chapter is concerned with the initial selection of gymnasts into what is referred to as either 'elite', 'international', or 'high performance'. In New Zealand during the time of this study, there were two competitive options for gymnasts. They could either compete in the 'levels' or 'national' competitions where the goal was only to compete within New Zealand, or they could compete in the 'elite' stream where the goal was to represent New Zealand internationally at the Senior International level, particularly at World Championships, Commonwealth Games, or the Olympic Games. My focus in this chapter is on the processes used to select gymnasts for the latter type of competition. Usually, gymnasts were around eight or nine years of age when they were first eligible to compete in the elite stream, and within elite at the time, they were then required to compete in several age-group 'Stages'[1] until they reached the age when they were eligible to compete in Junior or Senior International.

In the context of New Zealand sport, the National Sporting Organisation (NSO) for gymnastics held significant power in determining selecting processes. New Zealand has a crown entity, Sport New Zealand,[2] which is responsible for all government sporting policy (Collins, 2007; Sam & Macris, 2014). Sport NZ works together with the NSOs such as New Zealand Gymnastics (NZG) in implementing appropriate systems; however NZG does not employ any coaching staff, instead relying on clubs to deliver gymnastics in New Zealand. At the elite level, and at the community sport level, the relationship between Sport NZ and the NSOs has been contractual, where NSOs are funded based on their level of performance (Sam & Macris, 2014). However in the case of gymnastics over this time period, the gymnasts training in elite programmes were not successful enough to receive Sport NZ funding, meaning that NZG was free to design the elite programmes, or delegate to the clubs to design them, without any input from Sport NZ (Barker-Ruchti et al., 2018; Kerr, 2012).

In line with the Latourian approach adopted for this chapter, I aimed to 'follow the actors' involved in the selection processes, which incorporated an ethnographic approach where attention was paid to both human and non-human actors (Latour, 2005). The ethnography incorporated three main facets: participant observation, documentary analysis, and semi-structured interviews, throughout the period 2005–2010.

Participant observations took place at a wide range of gymnastics events. In line with the focus of this study, physical ability testing was observed whenever possible. I also held a role as a volunteer helper at gymnastics competitions which allowed me to observe a large number of elite and pre-elite events and be part of informal discussions with judges, coaches, and administrators about the occurrences and outcomes of the competitions.

A range of documents were collected and analysed. These included strategic documents, such as NZG high performance plans, minutes of meetings, and selection criteria for both entry into the elite stream and for particular competitions, and letters or notices sent to clubs describing or discussing selection procedures and outcomes.

Semi-structured interviews also took place. The process of interviewing involved seeking out participants who appeared to be informed and competent. Finding informed participants is a key aspect of all sociological research that Latour equally argues to be significant and necessary in ANT (Farnsworth & Austrin, 2005; Latour, 2005; Simpson, 2007). A total of 15 semi-structured interviews were undertaken, audio recorded, and fully transcribed. Interviewees included five gymnasts who had undertaken the testing process, three coaches, four sport scientists, two judges, and one representative from NZG. The interview questions were tailored to each type of participant. The gymnasts were asked how they were selected to compete in the elite stream and about their experiences of being elite or pre-elite athletes. The coaches were asked to describe how they identified talent, their views on talent identification and about the systems used in New Zealand for talent identification. The representative from NZG and the sport scientists were asked to discuss their role in talent identification in gymnastics, any testing they had been involved in, and their understanding of why it was undertaken the way that it was.

During the data analysis phase, the data was freely coded at the latent level (Braun and Clarke, 2006) to build up an understanding of the actors involved in the various selection processes. The data was then triangulated to confirm the way actors worked together to produce selection, which allowed the creation of narratives describing the selection processes, which are now presented.

Results

For the period under examination in this study, the dominant mechanism used to identify gymnasts talented enough to compete in high performance programmes was the PAT (Physical Ability Test). As Lidor, Côté and Hackfort (2009) confirm, testing mechanisms of this nature are extremely common across a wide range of sports. Gymnasts wishing to compete in elite or pre-elite grades were required to participate in and pass an annual PAT. Molly, from NZG, described how when gymnasts were young, the rationale for the PAT was to find 'that initial raw talent'. She went on to explain: 'They are tested on strength and flexibility. Those are the 2 core things. Within that there's a broad range of tests.'

Observations of the tests, and the PAT manual, showed they were carried out in a gymnasium where there were 10–15 'stations'. For example, these included a start and finish line for a 20m sprint, a high bar for chin ups, and wall bars for leg lifts. In a demonstration of how WAG cannot be considered as purely a network of human actors, the role of the gymnastics equipment in facilitating the testing was strongly evident. For example, one of the exercises tested the number of 'tricep dips' each gymnast could perform on the parallel bars, an exercise that simply was unable to be performed without parallel bars. This illustrates the ANT argument that although non-humans like equipment may be considered mundane and insignificant, they form vital roles in ensuring gymnastics can take place. In this context, the pieces of equipment acted as intermediaries (Kerr, 2014; Latour, 2005), in working smoothly with the gymnasts to facilitate the testing.

Extending the argument, the equipment was also part of the construction of the scientific knowledge created by the testing. As Latour and Woolgar (1979) argued, in all scientific work, equipment is not merely a tool that uncovers knowledge, it is part of the creation of that knowledge. This point is also made in the talent identification literature, where 'talent' is argued to be a social construction. Csikszentmihalyi and colleagues (1997, p. 23) argue that talent is socially constructed, meaning that talent 'is a label of approval we place on traits that have a positive value in a particular context in which we live'. Similarly, Sommerlund and Strandvad (2012) argue that talent entails much more than giftedness and is not only socially constructed, but constituted by those that evaluate performance, embodied by those recognised as talented and literally materialised through a range of non-human actors. In the case of the WAG PAT testing, labels of approval were placed on very particular movements performed on carefully chosen equipment (usually gymnastics apparatus), which was then understood to be an indication of 'talent'.

For WAG in New Zealand, a decision was made early on in the 2000s that the best people to evaluate the presence of 'talent' were sport scientists. One of the sport scientists in the study described how scientists were incorporated into the testing process owing to the belief that in comparison with coaches, scientists would be objective:

> coaches and parents complained about the objectivity. The coaches who used to do the tests were very biased. Sports scientists were brought in because they could be objective.
>
> (Penny, sports scientist involved in the testing)

In this quote, Penny evokes the notion that decision-making through objective and rational means is preferable and ideal, and reflects a logic that Lidor, Côté and Hackfort (2009) argue stems from the historic influence of the Soviet Union in sport. They describe how the Soviet talent identification model focused on the importance of scientific tools and data in the talent detection processes. Indeed, other interviewees emphasised that it was not merely the scientists themselves who were providing the objectivity, but the increased use of scientific equipment:

> We're using a lot more equipment, photographs and electronic devices to do all the tests.
>
> (Molly, from NZG)

> the other difference here was the introduction of more digital cameras and video camera stuff, which does take away a lot of the subjective thing. They used a camera for the splits positions, all the hyper splits positions … they could measure angles whereas before it's always been someone's assessment of, well, that's a 3 or that's a 4. Now it's like, that's 183 degrees.
>
> (Tricia, coach)

These quotes indicate that where it was the gymnastics equipment that allowed the necessary movements to be performed, it was scientific equipment that was crucial for the processes of measuring and evaluating. Therefore, the network that creates gymnastics performance also includes both sports scientists and their equipment. Further, in terms of the desired objectivity, in line with Latour's (1992) argument that non-humans can be more reliable than humans, it is the combination of the equipment and the scientists that provides this objectivity, not merely the scientists. For example, when a photograph is taken of a gymnast sitting in splits and the angle of the split measured by a computer program, and written into a spreadsheet, there is no need for an objective scientist. Instead, there is a need for a person who can work the computer program. Thus, the scientists were introduced not because they were objective, but because they possess and use the cameras, tape measures, and software program which were considered to provide objectivity. This is an example of what Gibson (2018) refers to as the assembly-line nature of laboratory work, where scientists may be reduced to merely those-who-work-the-instruments.

In terms of analysing the results, the various inscriptions that recorded the results of the testing, such as spreadsheets, performed a vital role in allowing the results to be circulated and shared. In finalising and analysing the results, the sharing occurred both between NZG and the scientists. In short, the cameras, tape measures and software rendered the performances of the gymnasts mobile. Prior to the introduction of these tools, the performances were immobile, forcing a coach to be the mobile actor who travelled the country and evaluated the gymnasts. Whereas these inscriptions allowed the gymnasts' performances to be translated into numbers and video data which could be gathered together in one place, compared, and evaluated, a process the gymnasts' parents agreed to as part of the testing process. Once translated, the performances could be stored on paper or on camera and sent to one place for evaluation. The software program's ability to translate the visual data to numbers allowed final results to be tabulated. Due to their stable form, they were later able to be circulated and shared with coaches, parents, and gymnasts.

Molly, from NZG, raised the importance of international circulation and comparability at the Senior International level. At this level, she described how the testing took on a different form from the PAT, and became about screening the gymnasts for comparative reasons, as opposed to detecting talent:

> At a Senior International level when there's funding available we enhance the testing because the shape of the gymnasts and size of the gymnasts are so important. We do a full anthropometry test as well with all their measurements, not just fat testing, all their bones and everything. Because we have international data to actually compare that against. So the international federation has a development program which has guidelines for us to compare ... with artistic we do have a benchmark and we have to adapt that to NZ conditions.

Given the goal of elite sport is for athletes to compete comparatively against those from other nations, it follows that testing mechanisms that allow direct comparison regarding size and shape could also be useful. However, the usefulness of such mechanisms has been challenged in the academic literature, which notes that these sorts of tests are not always believed to be effective in predicting future success (Anshel & Lidor, 2012; Baker, Cobley, & Fraser-Thomas, 2009; Güllich, 2014; Vaeyens et al., 2009). Indeed, studies of highly successful coaches' understandings of athlete selection have found that at the Senior International level, the majority of the athletes are physically capable and consequently coaches argue that other factors, such as 'feel for the game', are more significant (see for example, Christensen, 2009; Lund & Söderström, 2017).

Further, in this study, there was one scientist who questioned whether the inscriptions produced by the tests were reliable. Judy, a sports scientist who was at one stage contracted by NZG to evaluate the PAT test, described how the scientists awarded the gymnasts the actual scores for the tests, such as how many chin ups performed, then converted these scores to an overall figure. This figure was then given a percentage weighting, and sent to NZG, who calculated a final score and made the final decisions about selection, before sending these results to the coaches.

Judy felt, however, that the data provided from the tests was insufficient for the decisions being made: 'It is really tough making decisions based on these scores. Really tough.' She described how in many cases, the scores were not reliable enough and did not reflect the different ranges and abilities:

> For example, in some tests there was not a lot of difference, such as sit ups in 10 seconds where almost everyone got between 7–9; it's too small a range to be significant enough. Similarly, in the sprint test, only a few girls actually got on the scale, and in other tests, everyone was really high. They didn't show up all the different ranges.
>
> (Judy)

Consequently, Judy felt that making decisions based on the data collected was not producing reliable results.

In another critique, one coach argued that although the results received from the Senior International testing were circulated effectively, there was not enough interpretation of the data to make it useful:

> And you get that data back, but at no time do they sit down with the coaches and/or athletes and say this is what all the data means. What do we need to be looking for improvement wise? It's just, well, this is the data and you get a big wad of paper with it on. Like I say, I think it could be quite useful, but it needs to go a further step.
>
> (Mike, coach)

Mike's comment echoes Gibson's (2018) argument about the way sport science data is treated. Gibson (2018) observed how the process of testing athletes and producing inscriptions dehumanised the athletes, as it converted their physical abilities into purely numerical data. This process links with what has been termed the 'scientisation' of sport, which emphasises the increasing use of numerical data for coaching and athlete development (see Svensson, 2016). Gibson (2018) then noted how, in his study, the data was rehumanised when the numbers were reconnected with the individual athletes and used to demonstrate particular types of talent or ability. However in this case, Mike's comments suggest that although the dehumanisation process had been undertaken very effectively, with the athletes' performances reduced to a numeric form, there had been no rehumanisation process which meant he was unable to use these results in any meaningful manner.

Athlete selection for the national team

While the circulation of inscriptions as immutable mobiles was important for talent identification and other testing processes, it was of even greater importance for processes of selecting athletes for national teams. National team selection can be an immensely fraught process owing to it, by necessity, being exclusive. In this section, I include a comparison of the team selection processes for WAG and men's artistic gymnastics (MAG) that occurred for the 2006 Commonwealth Games, which was a particularly interesting scenario and highlights the importance of inscriptions being able to circulate globally.

The first step in selecting the gymnasts for Commonwealth Games was to create a qualifying mark that the gymnasts must achieve. In both MAG and WAG, the Commonwealth Games includes a team competition, an individual competition, and individual apparatus competitions. Kevin, a judge, described how the team was the most important consideration and that the qualifying mark was set based on what other competing teams were achieving:

> We first and foremost want to select a team. We would tend to put the team score of say Australia and Canada to one side because they're another level. We try and target ourselves around Malaysia, South Africa and probably England, from a team point of view. We go out in the year of competition and establish what the team score would be from those countries.
>
> (Kevin)

The process of establishing the scores of the other countries was where inscriptions that can circulate globally became crucial. To definitively determine the rankings of the countries, it was necessary to find the results of all the relevant countries, preferably at the same competitions. However, with the exception of World Championships, there were very few competitions that all the national teams attended, making it very difficult to make comparisons. The situation was exacerbated by the structure of Commonwealth Games, where nation states such as the UK compete as Great Britain at many competitions, but as England, Scotland, and Wales at Commonwealth Games. Consequently, technologies such as the internet, search engines, email, and excel spreadsheets were all used to generate a spreadsheet that allowed the ranking of different national teams. These kinds of technologies are not generally considered a significant part of sporting practice, but this example shows how they are in fact a vital component of the gymnastics network. This confirms Latour and Woolgar's (1979) argument that social processes between people are often considered separately from technical work, when in fact both work together at all times through the sociotechnical. Here, while individuals were responsible for locating the results of other countries, it was the combination of the individuals together with nonhumans such as computers and software that made the collection of this data possible.

Nonetheless, despite these technologies, it proved difficult for the selection committee to determine the mark that the gymnasts needed to achieve, which was a frustration for one coach:

> Where we had, for example, the guys were initially coming 5th team or better, they changed it to getting in the top 50%. I didn't agree on that totally. Well, I didn't agree on it at all because when it comes to the time, how do we know how many teams there will be? We don't know if there's going to be 6 teams in it or 16 teams. So my argument is that I know that 5th is at a certain standard, round Scotland, Wales, those sorts of countries and I think that's the sort of standard we should be in amongst. So it would have made more sense to say that, rather than have a mark where you don't know what it is till very close to the date.
>
> (Mike)

The 'they' that Mike refers to as making the decision he disagreed with was the New Zealand Olympic Committee (NZOC). As a judge, Kevin, described, the system consisted of NZG creating the criteria for gymnastics, choosing their selected gymnasts, and then making a case to the NZOC for their selection:

> The team for Commonwealth Games, because it's a multi-sport event, you have to put forward a case for your team to NZOC. Now that group of four selectors will sit there and they know nothing about gymnastics, they know nothing about cycling, they know nothing about equestrian! They might have their pet passions, but they know nothing. So you've got to go to them with a really solid case for why you want to submit these five people as a team. So we say this is how we picked them, this is where we believe they will sit at the moment, as a team. We have picked these individuals because, and then you move on to the all around and the individual apparatus and their expectations of medalists. It's got to be all transparent and up front. They've got to be convinced that you haven't just juggled.[3]
>
> (Kevin)

However, for 2006, Mike described how the NZOC was responsible for making the change to requiring proof that the team would finish in the top 50% of the field. This case highlights how people without any knowledge of gymnastics can also be a significant part of the gymnastics network. Indeed, their influence can be extremely strong. For women's gymnastics in 2006, the NZOC agreed with NZG's recommendation of a team of five gymnasts. At the time, there were only five gymnasts competing in women's gymnastics at the senior elite level and they were all selected into the team.

By contrast, their decision in MAG had a different outcome, even though there were similarly only five eligible gymnasts. After looking at the scores the gymnasts had achieved, the NZOC decided that only four gymnasts were required in the team. A member of NZG at the time argued that the NZOC did not understand the 5–4–3 format described above and therefore considered it only necessary to send three gymnasts. NZG had tried to explain that in gymnastics there are a great number of variables and they needed more than three gymnasts. The NZOC eventually decided to send four gymnasts, leaving NZG to make the extremely tough decision to choose four out of five athletes. The athlete who was not chosen quit the sport on the day the decision was announced, with his coach and parents both believing that an injustice had been done.

Conclusion

This chapter has examined the way a range of different actors assembled together to identify gymnasts as talented, and later selected into the national team. While the majority of literature on talent identification focuses on the people and processes involved in selection, particularly the views of coaches, this chapter deliberately highlighted the roles played by non-humans, specifically gymnastics apparatus and scientific equipment. The apparatus were necessary for the completion of many of the movements deemed necessary for the physical ability testing, and the scientific equipment produced the inscriptions which allowed gymnasts to be designated as talented. The latter point is particularly significant in acknowledging Latour and Woolgar's (1979) argument that scientific knowledge is produced through scientific practice. In this case, talent was produced through the particular network of gymnasts, apparatus, scientists, and equipment all working together. While a popular conception of talent is that it is something inherent that is discovered by scientists and their equipment, following Latour and Woolgar (1979), I suggest that it is the exact network and particularly the scientific instruments that created a very distinct understanding of gymnastics talent that allowed gymnasts to be selected (or not) into the high performance programme.

While the process of selecting gymnasts into the national team may appear at the outset to be a purely social processes in not using any particular scientific technologies, I argue that, instead, the process required a strongly connected international network in order to determine the team. Owing to the need to identify where the New Zealand team would be likely to finish in comparison with other teams, it was necessary for NZG to build a case to the NZOC. To do so, they required the collection of results data from a wide range of competitions which was only possible to obtain through the international network of the internet, and through the existence of inscriptions in the form of results spreadsheets.

This chapter highlights that while it may be tempting to consider sport as a purely social practice, and to focus on the role of actors such as gymnasts, coaches, judges, administrators, scientists, and parents, much of the work that these people achieve is facilitated in some way by non-human actors. As Latour (1992) noted, non-humans can often be more reliable than humans, and, more importantly, allow the circulation of data that is crucial for decision-making in sport.

Notes

1 The 'Stages' required gymnasts to perform a range of set elements in their routines, designed to provide the preparation necessary for learning the more difficult skills expected at Junior or Senior International.
2 Previously SPARC (Sport and Recreation New Zealand).
3 By 'juggled' Kevin refers to the potential for sports' committees to provide misleading data to the NZOC which would allow scores to be set lower and potentially allow more athletes from their sport to attend.

References

Anshel, M. H., & Lidor, R. (2012). Talent detection programs in sport: The questionable use of psychological measures. *Journal of Sport Behavior*, 35(3), 239.

Baker, J., Cobley, S., & Fraser-Thomas, J. (2009). What do we know about early sport specialization? Not much! *High Ability Studies*, 20(1), 77–89.

Barker-Ruchti, N., Schubring, A., Aarresola, O., Kerr, R., Grahn, K., & McMahon, J. (2018). Producing success: A critical analysis of athlete development governance in six countries. *International Journal of Sport Policy and Politics*, 10(2), 215–234.

Braun, V., & Clarke, V. (2006). Using thematic analysis in psychology. *Qualitative Research in Psychology*, 3(2), 77–101.

Callon, M. (1986). Some elements of a sociology of translation: Domestication of the scallops and the fishermen of Saint Brieuc Bay. In J. Law (Ed.), *Power, action and belief: A new sociology of knowledge? Sociological review monograph* (pp. 196–233). Boston, MA: Routledge Kegan Paul.

Callon, M., & Law, J. (1982). On interests and their transformation: Enrolment and counterenrolment. *Social Studies of Science*, 12, 615–625.

Christensen, M. K. (2009). An eye for talent: Talent identification and the 'practical sense' of top-level soccer coaches. *Sociology of Sport Journal*, 26(3), 365–382.

Collins, C. (2007). Politics, government and sport in Aotearoa/New Zealand. In C. Collins & S. Jackson (Eds.), *Sport in Aotearoa/New Zealand society* (2nd edn). Melbourne: Thomson.

Csikszentmihalyi, M., Rathunde, K., & Whalen, S. (1997). *Talented teenagers: The roots of success and failure*. Cambridge: Cambridge University Press.

Farnsworth, J., & Austrin, T. (2005). Assembling portable talk and mobile worlds: Sound technologies and mobile social networks. *Convergence: The International Journal of Research into New Media Technologies*, 11, 14–22.

Gibson, K. (2018). Laboratory production of health and performance: an ethnographic investigation of an exercise physiology laboratory. *Sport in Society*, 1–19.

Güllich, A. (2014). Selection, de-selection and progression in German football talent promotion. *European Journal of Sport Science*, 14(6), 530–537. doi:10.1080/17461391.2013.858371.

Kerr, R. (2012). Integrating scientists into the sports environment: A case study of gymnastics in New Zealand. *Journal of Sport and Social Issues*, 36, 3–24.

Kerr, R. (2014). From Foucault to Latour: Gymnastics training as a socio-technical network. *Sociology of Sport Journal* 31(1): 85–101.

Kerr, R. (2016). *Sport and technology: An actor-network theory perspective.* Manchester: Manchester University Press.

Latour, B. (1992). Where are the missing masses? Sociology of a door. In J. Law & J. Bijker (Eds.), *Shaping technology-building society: Studies in sociotechnical change.* Cambridge, MA: MIT Press.

Latour, B. (1999). *Pandora's hope: Essays on the reality of science studies.* Cambridge, MA: Harvard University Press.

Latour, B. (2005). *Reassembling the social: An introduction to actor-network-theory.* Oxford: Oxford University Press.

Latour, B., & Woolgar, S. (1979). *Laboratory life: The social construction of scientific facts.* London: Sage.

Law, J. (2004). *After method: Mess in social science research.* London: Routledge.

Lidor, R., Côté, J., & Hackfort, D. (2009). ISSP position stand: To test or not to test? The use of physical skill tests in talent detection and in early phases of sport development. *International Journal of Sport and Exercise Psychology*, 7(2), 131–146.

Lund, S., & Söderström, T. (2017). To see or not to see: Talent identification in the Swedish Football Association. *Sociology of Sport Journal*, 1–27.

Sam, M. P., & Macris, L. I. (2014). Performance regimes in sport policy: Exploring consequences, vulnerabilities and politics. *International Journal of Sport Policy and Politics*, 6(3), 513–532.

Simpson, T. (2007). Following the action: Using actor-network theory and conversation analysis. *New Zealand Sociology*, 22(1), 28–47.

Sommerlund, J., & Strandvad, S. M. (2012). The promises of talent: Performing potentiality. *Theory and Psychology*, 22(2), 179–195.

Svensson, D. (2016). *Scientizing performance in endurance sports: The emergence of 'rational training' in cross-country skiing, 1930–1980.* Doctoral dissertation, KTH Royal Institute of Technology.

Vaeyens, R., Güllich, A., Warr, C. R., & Philippaerts, R. (2009). Talent identification and promotion programmes of Olympic athletes. *Journal of Sports Sciences*, 27(13), 1367–1380.

Chapter 12

Using a multilevel model to critically examine the grooming process of emotional abusive practices in women's artistic gymnastics

Froukje Smits, Frank Jacobs and Annelies Knoppers

Introduction

The existence and promotion of youth sport has often been based on various assumptions about its value and role in society. Youth sport is assumed to be a site where pleasure/enjoyment, physical and social development, and learning to perform and win are emphasised (Coakley & Pike, 2014; Singer, 2004). Fun and pleasure are assumed to form the basic values underlying youth sport. This fun and pleasure is enhanced when children learn valued physical and social skills that contribute in a positive manner to their social and physical wellbeing and development as adults-to-be (Fraser-Thomas, Côté, & Deakin, 2005). Learning to win and performing well under pressure are assumed to be necessary for this development to occur (e.g. Claringbould, Knoppers, & Jacobs 2015; Fraser-Thomas & Strachan, 2014; Ryan, 1995). The importance of winning and achievement increases when a child engages in elite youth sport, especially sports that involve young athletes such as competitive gymnastics and swimming. This emphasis on winning is known as the discourse of performance/achievement. As we explain further on, discourses are ways of thinking about certain ideas, objects, and things.

Another newer discourse has been circulating in elite youth sport as well. In the last decade, the issue of physical, psychological, and sexual abuse of athletes by coaches has received a great deal of attention (e.g. Brackenridge & Fasting, 2005; Fasting & Brackenridge, 2009; Gervis & Dunn, 2004; Grahn, 2014; Johns & Johns, 2000; Owusu-Sekyere & Gervis, 2014; Pinheiro et al., 2014; Raakman, Dorsch, & Rhind, 2010; Ryan, 1995; Stirling & Kerr, 2008, 2013; Vertommen, Schipper van Veldhoven, Harthill, & Van Den Eede, 2015). This has led to a discourse of child protection and safeguarding that assumes that adults need to ensure that children and youth play in an environment in which they are safe and are not abused by coaches. The circulation of this discourse in youth sport has not, however, eradicated abusive coach-athlete relationships

Athletes who are in an abusive coach-athlete relationship often learn to adapt to and/or accept the occurrence of abusive coaching behaviours through a process called grooming. Grooming is the term applied to the gradual preparation of a child by the abuser through the normalisation of harassment and, sometimes, sexual abuse (Cense & Brackenridge, 2001; Montserrat, 2011). Scholars have shown how the process of grooming enables coaches to sexually abuse athletes, often for many years, without resistance from athletes (Cense & Brackenridge, 2001; Moget, Weber, & Van Veldhoven, 2012). Leberg (1997, p. 26) suggests that there are three types of grooming involved in this process: 1) physical grooming that may lead to and include inappropriate touching of the athletes' bodies; 2) psychological grooming of the athlete and family, that may occur for example when a coach constantly tells an athlete and her parents that she needs to spend more time with him for practice, and 3) grooming of the social environment or the community, for example a coach building such a good reputation for competitive success that s/he becomes an unquestioned authority in the sport domain.

Stirling and Kerr (2008) have argued that grooming does not only lead to sexual abuse but also to emotional abuse. The focus of this chapter is on the occurrence of emotional abusive behaviours by coaches of elite women gymnasts. Stirling and Kerr employed the following definition: 'Emotional abuse refers to a pattern of non-contact deliberate behaviors by a person within a critical relationship role that have the potential to be harmful to an individual's [emotional] well-being' (p. 178). Our study focuses on the grooming process of Dutch elite women gymnasts so that they (seemingly) tolerate and normalise systematic emotional abuse.

Theoretical framework

Frameworks that have been used to examine the grooming process as well as the abuse of athletes often focus primarily on interactions between coach and athlete at the micro level (e.g. D'Arripe-Longueville, Fournier, & Dubois, 1998; Gervis & Dunn, 2004; Maitland, 2012; McMahon & Zehntner, 2014; Stirling & Kerr, 2009; 2013). The solution then seems to be to create rules and procedures that restrict touch and define illegitimate coach-athlete interactions (Piper, Taylor, & Garratt, 2012). Such research does not explain, however, how abuse may be sustained by individuals, social ideologies embedded in discourses and institutions. The results of our work with elite gymnasts suggests, for example, that a grooming process at the individual or micro level does not occur in isolation from other processes that take place at club/local organisational level (meso) and at the national and international (macro) level (Knoppers, Smits, & Jacobs, 2015). In this chapter therefore, we focus on the primary actors, specifically parents, coaches, and directors of sport clubs/organisations that are involved in producing elite women's gymnasts. We identified several dynamics that enabled coaches to engage in grooming processes that resulted in the emotional abuse of young female gymnasts. The elite child athlete is therefore not the only focus of our study, but also parents, coaches, and directors. We used a multilevel model to examine practices that played out in the grooming process of emotional abuse at macro, meso, and micro level of elite women gymnasts.

Multilevel model

A multilevel model can be used as a relational framework that bridges the divide between macro-(inter)national, meso-local organisational, and micro-individual levels of analyses to achieve a more comprehensive framing of the grooming process in elite youth sport (see also Syed & Ozbilgin, 2009). Figure 12.1 presents an illustrative summary of the multilevel model for the Dutch elite gymnastics sports context we used in our study.

Young women elite gymnasts participate in a sport that is organised in institutional contexts. The International Gymnastics Federation (FIG) and the National Gymnastics Federation (NGF) in the Netherlands comprise the macro level. These federations are responsible for the rules of the sport, organising international and national competitions, determining who can participate, scoring systems, selection of judges, competition formats, etc.

Micro level: individual level

Meso level: organizational club level

Macro level: organizationl national and international level

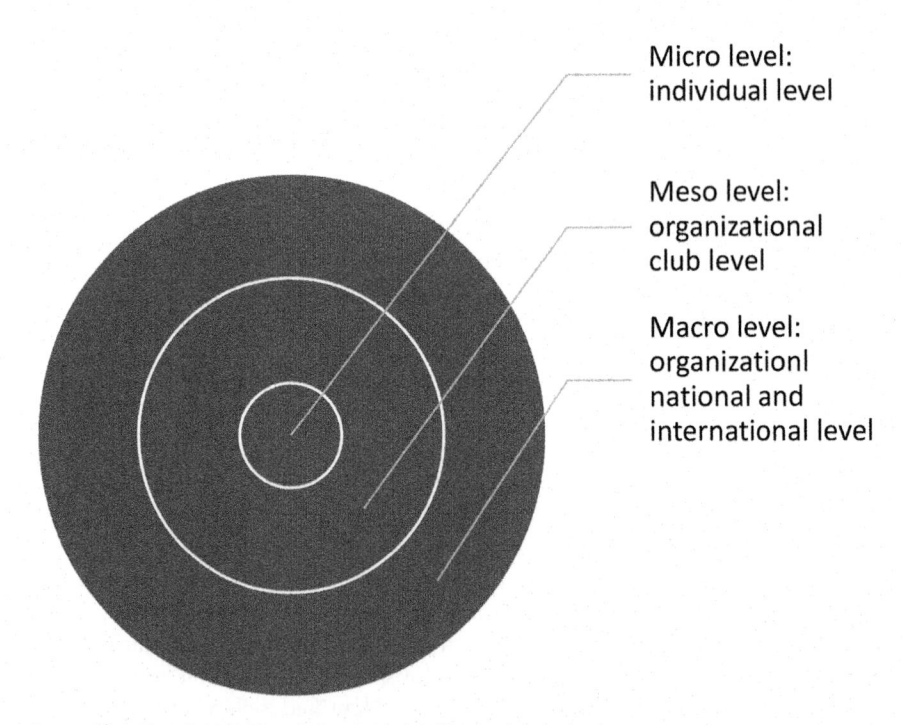

Figure 12.1 Dutch WAG multilevel model (drawn by author)

The local organisational or meso level consists of sport associations or clubs that are responsible for their own organisational policies, the focus of their club (recreational, competitive, and/or elite), job descriptions, professional practices, and use of space. These clubs are locally based and participation is voluntary for athletes. The clubs are structurally autonomous. Local clubs, therefore, are responsible for the development of elite women gymnasts. Parents often support and encourage their children to participate in (elite) youth sports. We therefore also included parents as being part of the meso and individual level that contributed to the occurrence of grooming of the young gymnasts. The individual/intrapersonal level (called the micro level) includes personal factors such as interactions, emotions, beliefs, values, and social-relational influences in the athlete-coach relationship. These levels do not work as separate components but interact and inform the other levels. For example, the board of directors of a sport club (meso level) tends to be held responsible for the wellbeing of their athletes and other members of the club (micro level).

Discourses and discursive practices

We draw on the notions of discourses and discursive practices to explore how athletes, parents, coaches, and directors legitimate their ways of thinking and doing about elite gymnastics. This results process of legitimisation creates 'regimes of truth' that normalise abusive practices (Foucault, 1977). A regime of truth is a way of thinking about something that has become common sense or seen as 'fact'. Discourses are embodied and enacted through discursive practices, that is, we assume that all practices are situated within discourses.

Foucault (1977) argued that individuals and organisations position themselves with respect to discursive practices; they may accept, resist, or negotiate their use of these discursive practices. Foucault (1977) also assumed that power/knowledge is always present because discourses act on individuals but the degree of that enactment varies by individuals and the context in which they live and perform. Therefore, power is always productive as it gives meaning to everyday practices (Foucault, 1977). Discursive practices produce ways of doing and of thinking and create regimes of truth about what is considered normal and abnormal. Normalisation is a disciplinary technique of power that functions as a system of control over individuals. We use the term 'normalisation' to refer to a web of normalising practices that disciplines people to follow a discursive regime. For example, gymnasts and their parents may learn and accept that practising 30 hours a week at a very young age is 'normal' and desirable. Figure 12.2 shows how we used Foucault's notions of regime of truth, disciplinary power, and normalisation to examine how primary actors situated in these three levels positioned themselves in their ways of doing and thinking with

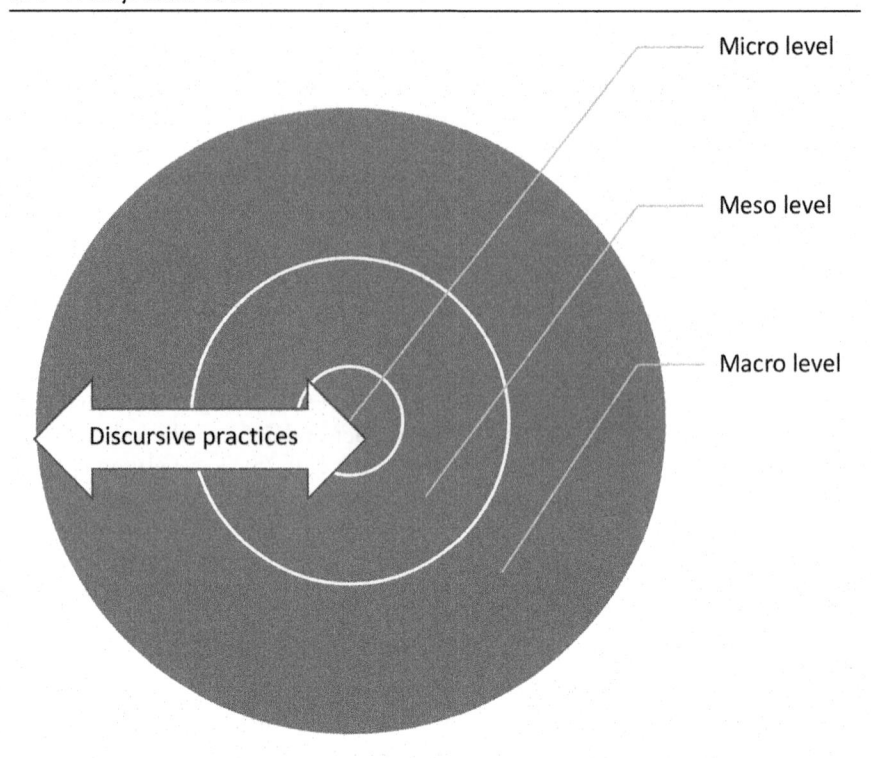

Figure 12.2 Discourses and discursive practices in Dutch WAG multilevel model (drawn by author)

respect to the dominant discursive practices outlined in the beginning of this chapter that may enforce grooming.

Multilevel theorising assumes that discursive practices at the micro level are embedded at and emerge from the macro level and that discursive practices at macro level often develop through the interaction and dynamics of meso and micro level elements (Cunningham, 2012). For example, directors of local clubs at the meso level may hire coaches to produce winners in elite youth sport and may also expect them to engage in discursive practices that encourage pleasure and positive development at the individual micro level. We used this model to analyse how primary actors in Dutch elite women's gymnastics (athletes, parents, coaches, and directors of sport federations and sport clubs) positioned themselves in relationship to the discursive practices of elite youth sport and how these dynamics interacted to create situations that facilitated the grooming processes of emotional abuse. The purpose of this study, therefore, is to use a multilevel model to critically explore the complexity of the grooming process of emotional abuse. In so doing, we attempt to understand how emotionally abusive practices may be sustained and/or challenged in elite women's gymnastics.

Methodology

We conducted semi-structured interviews to discover how 14 elite women gymnasts (ages 14–30 years) experienced elite gymnastics. The study involved eight currently active gymnasts and six former gymnasts from nine different elite clubs whose gymnasts perform at the highest national and international levels. These are the athletes who were selected by the NGF for international competitions. We also held 12 interviews with parents (ages 36–51 years) of these athletes. These interviews supplied data for a micro level analysis. In addition, we conducted semi-structured interviews to explore the discourses and discursive practices used by five coaches (ages 36–53 years) and five members (ages 42–61) of boards of directors of the NGF (macro) and of local sport clubs (meso) that produce elite female gymnasts. We analysed the data by identifying the behaviours/practices of the primary actors and the possible discourses that produced them. We then looked at the ways the actors drew upon these discourses to legitimate the ways in which elite gymnastics was conducted by these coaches and regulated by directors. (For further detail see Jacobs, Smits, & Knoppers, 2017 and Smits, Jacobs, & Knoppers, 2017.)

Results

Although initially we tried to present the results per level, we found this was a difficult task since the multilevel approach assumes interaction between the levels. The analysis showed that the dominant norm for coaching behaviours at the micro level involved literally and metaphorically belittling female gymnasts. The interviewed athletes had learned that their opinions were not important, that the coach is the person in charge who polices and regulates their behaviour, and that s/he is to be trusted because s/he has their best interests at heart. 'Coaches are always angry at women gymnasts anyway, that's just normal, that's the way is has to be' (female gymnast).

Former and current female gymnasts regularly used similar words to describe the intimidating grooming actions taken by coaches such as: 'very mean', 'ignoring', 'humiliating', 'swearing', and 'blaming'. They and their parents did not necessarily like these behaviours but accepted these behaviours as being part of the development of elite athletes (Smits, Jacobs, & Knoppers, 2017). These quotes reflect how grooming processes normalise emotional abuse in coach-athlete interactions (micro level). This faith and trust of the female gymnasts in the coach was one of the pillars that reinforced a coach-athlete relationship of dependency. They were groomed to accept this behaviour of belittlement as 'normal' and as required for their development. Such findings are similar to those reported elsewhere (Gervis & Dunn, 2004; Stirling & Kerr, 2007; 2009).

We however also analysed how these micro level processes were part of and supported by discursive practices that transcended them. In the following paragraphs we give examples of discursive practices of elite youth sport that occurred in grooming processes and normalised emotionally abusive behaviours. We first present how the discourse of pleasure played out at all three levels.

Discursive practices of pleasure

All actors (athletes, parents, coaches, directors) used the discourse of pleasure or enjoyment as the primary driver for athletes to begin in gymnastics and stay involved. A female gymnast remembered how enjoyment was the reason for her to continue to stay active in gymnastics from an early age: 'When I practised gymnastics at younger age as a pupil, I was always last in the competitions. I didn't mind at that time, it was just about having fun and enjoying [the sport], that's what it was all about.' An elite coach explained that pleasure is a fundamental aspect for every training:

> The foremost thing is that the athlete should always have fun in the sport, that however, does not mean that they sometimes think: 'this was a tough and difficult practice'. But, [that they also think] we worked well together, I am tired and satisfied.

Parents who encountered abusive coaching behaviours later on in the careers of their daughters explained the importance of the discourse of pleasure: 'People ask me sometimes: "why did you allow her to practice at the elite level?" My child enjoyed gymnastics so much, it went so well, it was just the fun she experienced while involved in gymnastics.' A director involved in the organisation of elite gymnastics at the local level (meso level) agreed with the important role of the discourse of pleasure, including at the elite level:

> All in all, practices are set up and organised in a way that we hope that every practice is fun and a special moment. Anyway, if they do not make it in elite sport, they can take it [those moments of pleasure] with them in their sport career elsewhere at a lower level.
> (Director of local elite gymnastics club)

The board of directors used macro level discursive practices to describe pleasure as a main component in gymnastics: 'Safety, pleasure and positivity are more important than winning. The purpose of gymnastics may never begin with winning.' Club directors (meso) and those working at the national level for the NGF (macro) level additionally emphasised that they did what they could to ensure that pleasure and positive development predominated in elite women's gymnastics. They backed this up by pointing to their requirement that coaches consent to the use of child friendly policies and that coaches did agree to do so. The directors assumed this meant coaches prioritised pleasure and positive development and used positive pedagogies (Jacobs, Smits, & Knoppers, 2017). Paradoxically, although directors at the meso and macro levels governed sport with an emphasis on discursive practices of pleasure, at the same time they created a context that emphasised high performance or achievement that informed coaching behaviour in other (unintended) ways.

Discursive practices of winning and toughness

All actors affirmed the discursive practices of pleasure, performance, and positive development as being important. However, an additional discursive practice, the discursive practice of winning, emerged from the interviews as a factor that contributed greatly to grooming. It was the use of this discursive practice that normalised toughness and the assumption that abusive behaviours were needed to develop this. Two directors, one at the national level and the other at the club level, explained:

> Elite sport is primarily about winning. That characterises elite sport. The moment you say that is not so, then there is nothing left to talk about. If you say to your coach that winning is unimportant and that pleasure or development are more important, then that elite coach will leave your club.
> (Director of local elite gymnastics club)

> Parents do not come because you promise a child friendly or child focused programmes. No, people who want elite sport do not come for that; they come because they want to win.
> (NGF director)

Parents agreed: 'If an athlete or parent complains too much, you're out. They have to work hard.' This agreement supported the grooming process of athletes as evidenced in remarks athletes made: 'I was a practice animal, that made it easy for the coaches, I didn't complain and did what the coaches demanded, even when I was in pain' (female gymnast).

The coaches themselves however, were not free from the power of various discourses about sport either. They were disciplined by the discursive practices of expertise and achievement. A coach explained how this worked:

> We are so afraid that athletes will lose their elite mentality, that they see things in life that may be more attractive and make them want to quit. That is the big fear and that is why the doors of the gym are closed and athletes are not allowed to participate in anything else.
> (Coach)

By claiming expert knowledge, coaches became the guardians of a grooming process that shaped the behaviours and skills of the athletes at micro level and directors within sport clubs at meso level who were silent about the practices they observed.

Discursive practices of silence

A code of silence was another of the discursive practices that occurred at all three levels and encouraged the continuation of emotional abusive coaching behaviours. A director of a sport club described how these discursive practices became part of the grooming process as follows:

> If parents complain then their daughter will be told the next morning at practice, 'You do not tell your parents those kinds of things. What we do and say, stays here and you do not share that with your mother.' She [the gymnast] gets yelled at and is shamed in front of the others and/or is isolated during practice. You know that this girl will never say anything at home anymore. That is what I call total control.

Parents became part of the normalisation process of grooming and as a parent realised when reflecting on the daughter's involvement: 'Looking back, she kept quiet about a lot of things.' Athletes confirmed that this is how they become part of the grooming process, led by the discourse silence at the micro level:

> Previously when I told [my parents] what happened and they complained, I was treated 1000 times more harshly in the gym. Others said; 'Did you have to complain again to your daddy and mommy?!!!' So, at one point you do not tell them anything anymore. And as you get older, you also do not want to burden your parents with your problems.
> (Female gymnast)

In other words, all actors at three levels created a regime of truth at all three levels, based on their normalising judgement with assertions of rationality and validity that seemed to legitimise the discourse of silence as a grooming factor that contributed to emotional abusive practices.

Discursive practices of disciplining the body (weight)

Finally, the discursive practices of disciplining the body for weight management goals also contributed to the grooming process that enabled abusive coaching behaviours to occur. Weight management discursive practices used in the clubs were unquestioned by all actors at the three levels. A coach described his/her view of the relationship between weight and performance:

'It's a shame if you are an athlete who has talent and skills, but you are too heavy.' Gymnasts have internalised this regime of truth about their bodies:

> Of course, the NGF is unhappy if you do not have a skinny body. They can't really let you take part in an international match [because] then they'd see a chubby kid walking around on TV, if you get my meaning ... It [weight control] is really tough for me. I find it very difficult but I really do my best to stay at the desirable weight.
>
> (Female gymnast)

A director of an elite sport club described how athletes reacted to such practices such as weight:

> There are some coaches who weigh an athlete regularly, often once or twice per week. The athletes know this and go to the toilet to induce vomiting. They are forced to think it [elite gymnastics] is primarily about their weight.

Directors who were aware of such weight control management did nothing however to stop such practices, assuming this was part of elite gymnastics. Similarly, although parents were concerned about how elite gymnastics practices influenced their daughters' self-image and embodiment, they normalised this management. A parent explained for example the regime of truth about weight and body development: 'That development of becoming a woman, it's all forbidden, because then you become too heavy. And that's true, because when you weigh more, things work differently.' This disciplining of the body was the opposite of the discursive practices of pleasure.

Conclusion

These data from those involved at macro, meso, and micro levels of sport suggest that the power of discursive practices of pleasure was secondary to the disciplinary power of the discursive practices of achievement and child protection and safeguarding. These discursive practices are part of the grooming factors that enabled emotional abusive practices in elite women's gymnastics. The results of our research on these elite gymnasts, their parents, and directors at local and national levels suggest that a grooming process at the micro level does not occur in isolation from other processes that take place at the meso and macro level. In other words, grooming at the micro level by the coach is not an isolated practice, but is part of a complex dynamic of discursive practices that extends beyond the coach-athlete relationship. This includes discursive practices used at the meso level such as the goals of a sport club where a programme is housed, available pedagogical models, role of management, and directors of sport clubs, etc. In addition, the use of discursive practices by those at the macro level include the governance of the sport at the national and international levels, the attention paid to sport in the public imagination and the images used by the media. Discourses and their accompanying discursive practices about pleasure, the persistence of a code of silence, the emphasis on winning and toughness and 'proper' body weight support ways in which institutions are shaped. These discursive practices used by those at both at macro and meso levels informed coach-athlete interactions at the micro level in this study. Similarly, these interactions reproduced dominant discursive practices about elite women's gymnastics. The use of discursive practices that facilitated emotionally abusive behaviour by coaches was therefore not confined to one level but occurred at all levels and transcended them. Together these discursive practices acted on the primary actors involved in our research to normalise emotional abusive behaviour by coaches and allowed it to continue. We assume our results are not unique and that similar processes occur in other elite (gymnastics/sport) contexts.

Although policies have been created to eradicate all types of abuse in youth sport, research shows that the discourse of achievement/winning/performance is often used worldwide to justify coaching behaviours that continue to normalise emotional abuse, including that of young athletes (Owusu-Sekyere & Gervis, 2014). This institutional context makes change difficult. Although powerful (autocratic) coaches may shape the directions of norms in the contextual micro level, they themselves are constrained by the discursive practices that flow from the meso and macro levels and, at the same time, the discourses used by coaches to legitimate their behaviours may in turn shape the regimes of truth that predominate at the meso and macro levels. Change, therefore, may only be possible if the discursive practices that drive or shape the institutional context are completely transformed; this includes the primacy accorded to discourses of winning and performance. Compliance with the discourse of safe guarding and protection therefore requires the involvement of all actors. They all need to think critically about their ways of thinking about and practising sports and especially about the notion of developing mental toughness. If not, changes in rules will have little impact on coaching behaviour. This critical approach needs to become an essential or cornerstone of coach education, of support networks for directors and of athlete education. For example, Denison and Avner (2011) argued for a Foucauldian based approach to coaching in elite sport. Such an approach could be used by all actors involved to critically reflect on everyday coaching practices and the history and source of such practices as a step toward an understanding and practising of ethical coaching (see also Denison, 2007; Denison, Mills, & Konoval, 2015; Jacobs, Claringbould, & Knoppers, 2014). Since our study focused on women gymnastics, such an approach could have implications for women in gymnastics as well for elite women athletes in general.

References

Brackenridge, C. H., & Fasting, K. (2005). The grooming process in sport: Case studies of sexual harassment and abuse. *Auto/Biography*, 13, 33–52.

Cense, M., & Brackenridge, C. (2001). Temporal and developmental risk factors for sexual harassment and abuse in sport. *European Physical Education Review*, 7, 61–79.

Claringbould, I., Knoppers, A., & Jacobs, F. (2015). Young athletes and their coaches: disciplinary processes and habitus development. *Leisure Studies*, 34(3), 319–334.

Coakley, J., & Pike, E. (2014). *Sports in society: Issues and controversies* (2nd edn). London: McGraw Hill/OU Press.

Cunningham, G. (2012). A multilevel model for understanding the experiences of LGBT sport participants. *Journal for the Study of Sports and Athletes in Education*, 6(1), 5–20.

D'Arripe-Longueville, F., Fournier, J. F., & Dubois, A. (1998). The perceived effectiveness of interactions between expert French judo coaches and elite female athletes. *Sport Psychologist*, 12: 317–332.

Denison, J. (2007). Social theory for coaches: A Foucauldian reading of one athlete's poor performance. *International Journal of Sports Science and Coaching*, 2(4), 369–383.

Denison, J., & Avner, Z. (2011). Positive coaching: Ethical practices for athlete development. *Quest*, 63(2), 209–227.

Denison, J., Mills, J. P., & Konoval, T. (2017). Sports' disciplinary legacy and the challenge of 'coaching differently'. *Sport, Education and Society*, 22(6), 772–783.

Fasting, K., & Brackenridge, C. (2009). Coaches, sexual harassment and education. *Sport, Education and Society*, 14(1), 21–35.

Fraser-Thomas, J., Côté, J., & Deakin, J. (2005). Youth sport programs: An avenue to foster positive youth development. *Physical Education and Sport Pedagogy*, 10(1), 19–40.

Fraser-Thomas, J., & Strachan, L. (2014). Personal development and performance? In J. Baker, P. Safai, & J. Fraser-Thomas (Eds.), *Health and elite sport: Is high performance sport a healthy pursuit?* (pp. 15–32). London: Routledge.

Foucault, M. (1977). *Discipline and punish: The birth of a prison*. New York: Pantheon Books.

Gervis, M., & Dunn, N. (2004). The emotional abuse of elite child athletes by their coaches. *Child Abuse Review*, 13(3), 215–223.

Grahn, K. (2014). Alternative discourses in the coaching of high performance youth sport: Exploring language of sustainability. *Reflective Practice*, 15(1), 40–52.

Jacobs, F., Claringbould, I., & Knoppers, A. (2014). Becoming a 'good coach'. *Sport, Education and Society*, 21(3), 411–430.

Jacobs, F., Smits, F., & Knoppers, A. (2017). 'You don't realize what you see!': the institutional context of emotional abuse in elite youth sport. *Sport in Society*, 20(1), 126–143.

Johns, D. P., & Johns, J. (2000). Surveillance, subjectivism and technologies of power. An analysis of the discursive practice of high-performance sport. *International Review for the Sociology of Sport*, 35(2), 219–234.

Knoppers, A., Smits, F., & Jacobs, F. (2015). 'Turnonkruid: gemaaid maar niet gewied'. *Onderzoek naar het dames (sub)turntopsportklimaat* [*The weeds in gymnastics: Cut but not eliminated: A study of women's elite gymnastics*]. Utrecht: University Utrecht/Utrecht University of Applied Sciences/The Hague University of Applied Sciences.

Leberg, E. (1997). *Understanding child molesters: Taking charge*. London: Sage.

Maitland, A. (2012). *Organisational culture and coach–athlete relationships: An ethnographic study of an elite rowing club.* PhD dissertation, UK: Brunel University School of Sport and Education.

Montserrat, M. (2011). Don't be mistaken – this does concern you! *Qualitative Inquiry,* 17(9), 864–874.

McMahon, J., & Zehntner, C. (2014). Shifting perspectives: Transitioning from coach centered to athlete centered. *Journal of Athlete Centered Coaching,* 1(2), 1–19.

Moget, P., Weber, M., & Van Veldhoven, N. (2012). Sexual harassment and abuse in Dutch sports: A short review of early research and policy by the NOC*NSF. In C. Brackenridge, T. Kay, & D. Rhind (Eds.), *Sport, children's right and violence prevention: A sourcebook on global issues and local programmes* (pp. 123–128). Uxbridge: Brunel University Press.

Owusu-Sekyere, F., & Gervis, M. (2014). Is creating mentally tough players a masquerade for emotional abuse? In D. Rhind, & C. Brackenridge (Eds.), *Researching and enhancing athlete welfare* (pp. 44–48). London: Brunel University.

Pinheiro, M. C., Pimenta, N., Resende, R., & Malcolm, D. (2014). Gymnastics and child abuse: An analysis of former international Portuguese female artistic gymnasts. *Sport, Education and Society,* 19(4), 435–450.

Piper, H., Taylor, B., & Garratt, D. (2012). Sports coaching in risk society: No touch! No trust! *Sport, Education and Society,* 17(3), 331–345.

Raakman, E., Dorsch, K., & Rhind, D. (2010). The development of a typology of abusive coaching behaviours within youth sport. *International Journal of Sports Science and Coaching,* 5(4), 503–515.

Smits, F., Jacobs, F., & Knoppers, A. (2017). 'Everything revolves around gymnastics': Athletes and parents make sense of elite youth sport. *Sport in Society,* 20(1), 66–83.

Stirling, A. E., & Kerr, G. A. (2007). Elite female swimmers' experiences of emotional abuse across time. *Journal of Emotional Abuse,* 7, 89–113.

Stirling, A. E., & Kerr, G. A. (2008). Defining and categorizing emotional abuse in sport. *European Journal of Sport Science,* 8(4), 173–181.

Stirling, A. E., & Kerr, G. A. (2009). Abused athletes' perceptions of the coach-athlete relationship. *Sport in Society,* 12, 227–239.

Stirling, A. E., & Kerr, G. A. (2013). The perceived effects of elite athletes' experiences of emotional abuse in the coach-athlete relationship. *International Journal of Sport and Exercise Psychology,* 11, 87–100.

Syed, J., & Özbilgin, M. (2009). A relational framework for international transfer of diversity management practices. *The International Journal of Human Resource Management,* 20(12), 2435–2453.

Ryan, J. (1995). *Little girls in pretty boxes: The making and breaking of elite gymnasts and figure skaters.* New York: Warner.

Singer, R. (2004). Are we having fun yet? In P. Pufall and R. Unsworth (Eds.), *Rethinking childhood* (pp. 207–225). Piscataway, NJ: Rutgers University Press.

Vertommen, T., Schipper-van Veldhoven, N. H., Hartill, M. J., & Den Eede, F. V. (2015). Sexual harassment and abuse in sport: The NOC*NSF helpline. *International Review for the Sociology of Sport,* 50(7), 822–839.

Chapter 13

A figurational approach to women's artistic gymnastics

Claudia Pinheiro and Nuno Pimenta

Introduction

Athletes or any other sport members cannot be conceived as isolated individuals, but as individuals who have relationships with, and are dependent on, other actors, which means that they not only influence others, but they are also influenced by many others. Women's artistic gymnastics (WAG), like all sports, can be considered a complex social context, that involves not only the gymnasts and coaches, but also many other actors that have an important impact upon participants' experiences, behaviours, perceptions, and careers. In this context, WAG can be seen as a sport figuration where multiple networks of 'mutually orientated and dependent people' are at work (Elias, 1978, p. 261).

Therefore, in order to fully understand WAG's figuration, it is crucial to think about the interdependent relationships between people, the established positions they occupy within the figuration, as well as the relationships across the multiple figurations that people hold (Elias, 2001). This means that besides the gymnasts and coaches, one should look and study also the medical staff, supporters, sports club administrators, the national sport federation, media, parents, school, peers, and so on. Although not acknowledging or being aware of the impact they might have on others, all these actors are mutually interdependent and, intentionally/non-intentionally and consciously/non-consciously, influence and are influenced by others.

In this chapter, we will outline some of the core principles of figurational sociology and then enlighten how this approach can help to better understand WAG social networks. In order to achieve these purposes, we will draw on a range of already existing studies.

Figurational sociology: some principles

Figurational sociology, developed by Norbert Elias, has the concept of figuration as its main idea. With this concept, Elias sought to avoid unhelpful dualisms such as individual/society, individual/object, or cause/effect as if they could exist independently from each other. In fact, from a figurational perspective, society and individuals are not separate but, as Elias (1980, p. 141) puts it, 'they are two different but inseparable levels of the human world'. Elias emphasised the idea that people maintain different relationships with others for many reasons and at many levels, thus forming interdependency chains, which he referred to as figurations. The concept of figuration thus refers to the 'interdependency ties and power balances of mutually orientated and dependent people' (Elias, 1989, p. 45), which acknowledges the way individuals may share goals and influence each other.

For Elias (1980), the relations may be direct or indirect and while they cannot be precisely measured, they can be felt by individuals who constitute multiple and co-existing figurations. Humans are always and everywhere part of figurations, which may increase in size and complexity as societies change.

The concept of figuration can be applied to small groups as well as to societies composed of large numbers of interdependent individuals. While small figurations, such as teachers and students in a classroom, are relatively easy to observe and study, figurations such as societies are more difficult to comprehend. The latter are more difficult to identify because the interdependency chains are not only larger but also more differentiated and thus more complex. Therefore, when one plans to study the structure and dynamics of a figuration one cannot take into account solely their individual components and properties. It is important to 'explore the (processual) way in which these individual components are bonded to each other in order to form a complex and fluid unit' (Pimenta, 2015, p. 77). Since a figuration is not the sum of individuals but a web of interacting people, in order to understand any figuration it is crucial to think about the interdependent relationships between individuals, the established positions they occupy within the figuration, as well as the relationships across multiple figurations that people hold (Elias, 2001). This becomes even more important when referring to complex figurations, that is, figurations that are more differentiated and have larger interdependency chains.

Elias also warned against conceiving the pressures and influences upon individuals as if they emerged from social structures that exist apart from individuals. That is, as if social structures were above individuals, abstract social forces exerted upon them and intentionally leading people to adopt some behaviours and attitudes and to accept certain values and norms. In other words, the *habitus* seems to be moulded by external forces or non-human entities.[1] However, Elias emphasises that such social pressures do not derive from abstract non-human entities. In fact, other individuals, who are also elements of figurations, exert such pressures.

These dynamic networks of interdependency ties are not simply face-to-face relationships. While we are more aware of the influence of people physically or emotionally close to us, we also have relationships with and are dependent on people we have never met. Therefore, people not only influence but are also influenced by many humans.

Since figurations are 'complex networks of social relationships' (Dopson, 1994, p. 146), they cannot be explained solely in terms of the actions or interests of just one individual or group of individuals. Although individuals' actions, interests, and motives play a part in those processes, they have their own dynamics and can lead to unplanned and unintended outcomes. As Roderick (1998, p. 77) mentions 'the purposive actions of interdependent people often interweave to produce trends which no one has planned or intended and which constitute and constrain the perceptions, goals and actions of people'.

A central dimension of figurations or dynamic interdependency ties is power, conceptualised not as an element or property possessed only by particular individuals and groups, but as a characteristic of all human relationships and a central aspect of the concept of interdependency (Elias, 1978). Figurational sociology focuses on the understanding of the structures that mutually dependent human beings establish and the transformations they undergo, both individually and in groups, in part due to the increase or decrease of their interdependencies and degree of power. Power is always a question of relative balances, never of absolute possession or absolute deprivation, for no one is ever absolutely powerful or absolutely powerless. Power is not static because the chains that link us to other members of the figuration are dynamic and always in a constant flux. Every member of any figuration has some kind of power and influence over other members. Thus, it seems more adequate to speak of power differentials, balances of power, or power ratios.

Involvement and detachment are two other important concepts of figurational sociology. According to Elias (1987), in order to develop a more object-adequate analysis of any social process, individuals should be relatively detached, more precisely, they need an appropriate balance between involvement and detachment. Elias does not say that individuals have to be completely detached. In fact, no one can be wholly detached, since individuals are always members of many social groups that influence them, which constrain them. As already mentioned, individuals are not isolated and separate from others. Others affect their thinking and actions. In this sense, individuals cannot be wholly detached. They are always involved either emotionally or physically, though to a higher or lower level. The concepts of involvement and detachment do not refer, then, to two separate and different categories but to two concepts that are related or interdependent (Elias, 1987).

It is possible to say that a person is highly emotionally involved when a statement tells us more about the beliefs and concerns of that person than of the process under analysis. But a strong involvement can decrease, and when that happens, the balance between involvement/detachment begins to decrease towards detachment.

Individuals who are highly involved 'can only look at whatever happens to them from their narrow location within the system' (Elias, 1987, p. 10). That is, individuals who are highly emotionally involved in a process tend to see themselves as 'the central frame of reference for everything they experience' (Elias, 1987, p. xxxvii). These individuals have great difficulty in standing back and looking at themselves as if they were outside, that is, in a more detached manner. For them, it is hard to distance themselves from their own concerns and values. As a consequence of such strong emotional involvement, their understandings of social processes become distorted, since their convictions, their cherished beliefs interfere with their analyses. It should be added that whenever the pressure of tensions to which their groups are exposed increase, their level of involvement gets higher and it becomes more difficult for them to approach such situations in a more detached way.

Thus, when analysing processes, individuals should not try to be wholly detached – since it is not possible – but should try to obtain the highest level of detachment possible. Individuals should try to put aside their personal convictions and concerns in order to be able to study the relevant processes in a more detached manner. Only a relatively detached analysis will result in a more realistic or reality-congruent analysis of the processes one is seeking to understand.

Another aspect of Elias's work is his analysis of established-outsider relations. His theory is about power relations and the social dynamics between dominant and subordinate groups. The established groups (for example, males) are generally characterised by strong social cohesion, long standing integrated social networks, and great power. Exclusion and stigmatisation of the outsiders by the established group can be powerful weapons used by the latter to maintain their identity and to assert superiority. Individuals that tend to deviate from the established standards are depicted as the 'minority of the worst', while leading outsiders, with characteristics or group cohesion more similar to the established group, are the 'minority of the best' (Liston, 2005). The social dynamics of stigmatisation seek to maintain the established (e.g. males) groups through control of the outsider group (e.g. females). According to Mennell (1998, p. 135) 'it is a general characteristic of established-outsider relations that the outsiders identify with and "understand" the established better than the established do the outsiders'. In this regard, 'feelings of superiority on the part of males and inferiority on the part of females reflect the increasing interdependence between males and females' (Liston, 2005, p. 27). Furthermore, an 'established group tends to attribute to its outsider group as a whole the "bad" characteristics of that group's worst section' and, on the other hand, 'the established group tends to be modelled on its exemplary section' (Elias & Scotson, 1994, p. xix). This struggle between males and females is a characteristic of all figurations, including sport. The increasing female empowerment movements have been responded to with male driven power struggles. This has resulted in continuous changes in the gender power balance.

WAG: a figurational approach

As discussed in earlier chapters of this book, during the last three decades of the twentieth century, WAG underwent significant changes that resulted in increased complexity of skills and demanding training regimes that have been regarded as problematic for young gymnasts (see, for example, Pinheiro et al., 2014).

WAG can be regarded as a complex social context, involving gymnasts and coaches, as well as many other direct and indirect actors, which influence participants' experiences, behaviours, perceptions, and careers. In this context, WAG can be considered as a sport figuration where multiple networks of 'mutually orientated and dependent people' are at work (Elias, 1978, p. 261).

By belonging to the gymnastics figuration, gymnasts are invariably influenced by the thoughts and actions of many other members. Due to their involvement in this figuration, in some cases athletes may not be fully aware of the influences other members may have on their behaviour. In some cases, gymnasts are so involved in the figuration that they may not be able to see the possible dangers of, for example, neglecting an injury or not questioning and reporting different kinds of abuse. It can be said that, as gymnasts become more enmeshed in this gymnastics figuration, they are not only likely to be more influenced by their interdependencies with other members of the figuration, but it also becomes more difficult for them to challenge or resist, for example, unethical practices or less adequate behaviours. Hughes and Coakley (1991) argue that athletes learn, from an early age, a sports ethic that becomes normalised and taken for granted by the gymnasts. Some of the key features of this sports ethic are 'a willingness to make sacrifices … and a tacit acceptance that there is no limit to the pursuit of the ultimate performance' (Maguire, 2002, p. 3). According to Pinheiro, Pimenta, Resende, and Malcolm (2014, p. 438), gymnasts' early involvement in the gymnastics figuration may lead them 'to incorporate the norms, values, beliefs, dispositions and behaviour patterns of the broader gymnastics group'. Therefore, as noted by Roderick (1998, p. 78), 'particular notions, attitudes and beliefs connected to sports participation become embedded subconsciously by athletes, that is, come to be an aspect of these athletes' "second nature"'.

Gymnasts' early socialisation into the sport, together with their ambition for competitive success, makes it difficult for many of them to question or even resist 'behaviors which are often presented as the "only way" to achieve sporting goals' (Pinheiro et al., 2014, p. 438). It is possible to say that these athletes are so strongly involved emotionally that it is difficult for them to stand back and examine their personal experiences in a more detached manner.

In order to fully understand the WAG figuration, besides the interdependencies between gymnasts and coaches, it is, also, crucial to look at the interdependent relationships between many other actors within this figuration, such as parents, sports club administrators, national federations, school, peers, and medical staff. All these actors, though not being aware of the impact they might have on each other, influence and are influenced by others.

Gymnasts and other significant actors

Gymnasts and coaches

According to Gervis and Dunn (2004), athletes' results are determinants for the careers and reputation of coaches. In other words, it is through their athletes' results and successes that coaches are rewarded with recognition and success. This means that coaches have a lot to lose if their athletes are not successful (Pinheiro et al., 2014). Gymnasts also need coaches with specialised knowledge and specific skills in order to attain success. If their performances are good and they achieve success, not only do the gymnasts achieve recognition but also their coaches obtain credit and increase their influence within the sport. While coaches need athletes' success, for many athletes, coaches are regarded as the ones who control the access to their desired goals. This means that gymnasts and coaches are mutually interdependent. Nevertheless, in a performance context, coaches find themselves in a privileged position since they claim to have the knowledge, experience, wisdom, and resources that will allow athletes to achieve success (Pinheiro et al., 2014).

Many coaches, besides their own personal expectations, are subjected to external pressures from many other actors who also expect good results from them. Such pressures may lead them to view their athletes as machines: as productive bodies that exist and are shaped to achieve victories (Heikkala, 1993). Thus, in their relationship with gymnasts, many coaches, although believing they are working in the best interests of gymnasts' well-being, place a great emphasis on performances and results. Such pressures and expectations may lead to coaches' disciplinary practices and less appropriate behaviours. Many coaches attempt to justify these practices and behaviours as the only way to achieve results.

On the other hand, gymnasts have a tendency to accept, without challenging and questioning, these practices and behaviours, thus legitimising coaches' authority and disciplinary practices. Although gymnasts may be aware of the deviant nature of the acts they sometimes experience, their commitment to the sport ethic, and their sense of dependence on the coaches and other members of the gymnastics figuration, may lead them to develop a heightened level of tolerance towards less appropriate behaviours. Additionally, the coaches' opinion and how they act when, for example, an athlete is injured has a strong impact on the athletes' behaviours. They are a part of the gymnastics figuration and their acts and beliefs affect or even constrain athletes' perceptions and actions. According to Stirling and Kerr (2009), the lack of the necessary psychological maturity to think critically about these aspects (this lack of maturity is often present in WAG, a sport where an early specialisation occurs), may help to explain young gymnasts' acceptance of these practices and behaviors.

Between coaches and gymnasts, exists, then, a mutual dependency that helps to shape the *habitus* of gymnasts in harmony with the norms of the sport. In this context, gymnasts that reflect the prominent culture of the gymnastics figuration, in other words, that exhibit a 'good attitude' are used as 'role models for imitation' (Loland, 2011, p. 18). Those gymnasts that are not prepared to make sacrifices in order to attain success 'are likely to be stigmatized as not having the right attitude' (Roderick, Waddington, & Parker, 2000, p. 169).

As previously mentioned, as athletes become more enmeshed in the gymnastics figuration, they are likely to be more influenced by their interdependence with other members of the figuration. Female gymnasts' early involvement in the gymnastics figuration may lead them to perceive themselves as being in a less influential position, thus being particularly susceptible to coaches' practices.

A research project conducted with the male and female gymnastics national teams in Portugal (Pimenta, 2015) revealed that female gymnasts are more likely to accept coaches' authority and less appropriate behaviours (verbal and emotional abuses) than male gymnasts. This research showed that coaches of female gymnasts are in a relatively more powerful position when compared with the relationship between male athletes. Different types of abuse, besides serving to confirm female gymnasts as more submissive, also help coaches to perpetuate their stronger position.

Hargreaves (1994) notes that women are constrained to believe in, and to acknowledge, their inferiority to a point that prevents them rejecting the ideology of male hegemony. Following Elias and Scotson's (1994) theory of established-outsiders, the dominant (male) group may assert its superiority to a point that it is hardly questioned by the outsiders (females). This may help to legitimise, in the mind of female gymnasts, gender social differences in sport.

According to research, females tend to have lower levels of self-confidence and express this in sporting activities (Bowker, Gadbois, & Cornock, 2003). This might relate to what Connell (1987) has called a 'gender order'. Messner and Sabo (1990, p. 107) contend that 'the gender order is a dynamic process that is constantly in a state of play'. In fact, the interrelationships between varying forms and strategies of gender domination and subordination are in constant flux (Dunning, 1999; Kane & Snyder, 1989; Weidman, 2010). In other words, Annandale and Hunt (2000) refer to it as the fluid social relations of gender. In spite of females' lower self-confidence, they can be empowered. According to Maguire and Mansfield (1998) such female empowerment can be achieved by acquiring skills and physical characteristics of 'established women'. Female athletes' tendency to have lower levels of confidence in their athletic skills, may help to rationalise the gendered power differences between coaches and athletes. Maguire and Mansfield (1998, p. 122) associated female competitiveness with a 'double-blind' process: 'some women are arguably empowered at the expense of other women'. Thus, winning or achieving good results may be one of the few strategies female athletes have to achieve a greater power position inside the sport figuration. Moreover, according to Maguire and Mansfield (1998), winning female athletes may create an 'established' group and look to 'outsiders' with a 'they' image.

Parents

As mentioned above, when analysing WAG, there are other interdependencies that cannot be ignored, such as the interdependencies between gymnasts and parents. For many parents, their child's involvement in gymnastics signifies a considerable investment not only financially but also in time and energy. As parents become progressively more involved in the gymnastics figuration, they began to expect certain types of behaviours and attitudes, as well as results, from their children. They want to see some return for their personal and financial investment. Moreover, for many parents, being a parent of a high performance athlete 'becomes a significant part of their identity' (Donnelly, 1997, p. 399). Therefore, they start to exercise various kinds of pressure upon their own children. Through the way they act they consciously/non-consciously pressure their own child, who 'recognizes that his/her desire to change goals, or to retire, poses a threat to the identity of at least one of his/her parents' (Donnelly, 1997, p. 399). On one side there are the parents placing pressure on their own children, on the other side, there are the gymnasts who do not want to disappoint their parents. Gymnasts may feel constrained to continue practising intensively, through pain and injury, and even to tolerate disciplinary practices and less appropriate behaviours.

Coaches, parents, sports club administrators, and national federations

Many parents tend, also, to place considerable trust in the coach, since he/she is the one with the knowledge and the resources to help their children achieve success. According to Pinheiro et al. (2014, p. 439), 'this may be due to a lack of knowledge about the sport in which their child is involved, a lack of knowledge of the training techniques or an inability to understand the complex set of interdependencies involved in elite sport'. This goes hand in hand with national federations and club administrators' expectations.

They also seek results to help them justify annual investments (Pinheiro et al., 2014).

It is important to mention that not only gymnasts maintain a mutual dependency with their parents. Coaches, in their daily practice, also maintain a strong interdependency with parents; that sometimes may constrain their actions. Although it is important to maintain a close relationship with parents, sometimes that relationship becomes problematic. Many parents place additional pressure on coaches because they wish to see results. While many coaches may feel pressured to act in ways they are not expected to act, others try to maintain a certain distance (Pinheiro et al., 2014; Pinheiro & Pimenta, 2015). In the search for results, many sports club administrators and national federations may intervene, directly/indirectly, intentionally/unintentionally, on the coaches' actions constraining them to act in ways they 'would not act except under compulsion' (Elias, 1978, p. 84).

Many coaches, besides their own expectations, feel pressured to adhere to the expectations of the organisations that employ them. This may lead them, as previously mentioned, to act and make decisions that might go against the well-being of the athletes (Donnelly, 1997).

Gymnasts, coaches, and medical staff

Research has shown that the athlete-coach-clinician relationship is a crucial one especially if one is thinking about healthcare provision in sport. The medical staff tend to become intentionally or unintentionally enmeshed in the culture of risk that prevails in sport, committed to strive for better performances and higher risks. They are active agents in this process and are often pressured to try to find faster rehabilitation processes. However, the contrast between this pressure, and their training as healthcare professionals, requires them to often assume two opposite roles. Sometimes they support the culture of risk, other times they contribute to a culture of precaution, shielding athletes from pressure from coaches and enabling athletes to take 'sensible risks' (Safai, 2003).

According to Malcolm (2006, p. 377) 'a central characteristic of the interaction between clinicians and athletes is a process of negotiation, exchange, and trust building'. While a parallel exists between these pressures and those that a 'normal' patient attempts to exert, these bargaining processes may differ in degree (Pimenta, 2015). Therefore, in order to better understand this difference, sociologists should take into account the balance of power between the respective parties. As Malcolm (2006, p. 377) mentions, 'while sociologists of medicine have traditionally argued that medicine constitutes perhaps the most powerful profession in Western societies, sociologists of sport have argued that sports physicians often occupy a relatively weak or subordinate role'. Data gathered during a research project conducted with the male and female gymnastics national teams in Portugal (Pimenta, 2015) showed that these power relationships are in constant flux, influenced by factors such as the seriousness of the injury and the athlete's age. According to this research, it was not possible to find a single format for medical treatment decision-making. Athletes reported different experiences, with some mentioning that it is the gymnast who decides if he/she was able to compete; others noted that such decisions were primarily negotiated between the coach and the athlete (Pimenta, 2015). The coaches also reported different perspectives. While some described it as the coach who decides if the gymnast is able to continue practising, others argued that the coach has the responsibility to help athletes to gather informed data. This research revealed that, 'at least in face of what gymnasts consider as a normal or recurrent injury, the medical perspective is not what usually influences a decision about whether or not an athlete should continue competing' (Pimenta, 2015, p. 198). In fact, sometimes athletes tend to disregard doctors' and physiotherapists' medical advice.

The same research has revealed that athletes, and in this particular case gymnasts, are prepared to take risks with their health and especially to continue training and competing while injured or in pain. In this context, coaches, and other members of the gymnastics figuration, desire that the injured gymnast returns to train and competition as soon as possible. The gymnast's predisposition to continue training and competing while injured or in pain goes in line with the desires and demands of other members of the gymnastics figuration, such as parents and coaches (Brackenridge, Bringer, & Bishopp, 2005; Donnelly, 1997; Roderick et al., 2000; Waddington, 2000). As Pike (2005, p. 207) notes, 'to achieve the end of maintaining an athletic identity, the means were those expected by others in the organization, regardless of the consequences for their health'. This may lead athletes to sometimes ignore, reject, or even joke with certain medical advice. Frequently, athletes and coaches, when choosing and evaluating treatments, tend to prefer one that enables them to continue practising and competing.

In the gymnastics figuration, it is possible to argue that medical provision tends to be relatively limited and largely directed by coaches. Thus, the medical staff tend to have diminished practice autonomy. The consequences of this are that while interpersonal relations influence specific cases, the overall pattern is one in which coaches control, shape, and guide both medical treatment and decisions about whether gymnasts should continue training and competing.

Conclusion

From all that has been discussed, it is possible to observe the existence of a power imbalance in the gymnastics figuration. Gymnasts tend to be in a relatively weak position in relation to other adult members of the gymnastics figuration. Individuals learn from very early ages to follow adults' instructions. For many young individuals it is difficult to resist and question the authority of adults. This also applies to the adult/coach-gymnasts relationship. In the gymnastics figuration, gymnasts, and especially young gymnasts, are expected to follow coaches' instructions because they are adults. Due to their social position, it is difficult for many gymnasts to resist adult power. Moreover, since gymnasts have less knowledge and skills when compared to adults, and mainly to their coaches, gymnasts' lower status and relative dependence is constantly reinforced (Cense & Brackenridge, 2001).

Although being in a relatively weak and dependent position in relation to adults, gymnasts are not powerless, since their actions also impact the actions of others. In fact, the various actors discussed above are highly dependent on the gymnasts' actions and performances for the realisation of their own goals (Pinheiro et al., 2014). The more deeply gymnasts are involved in the gymnastics figuration the more likely they are to be influenced by other members of the figuration and therefore increasingly conform with the gymnastics culture (Pinheiro et al., 2014). In this context, gymnasts' efforts to deal with pain, injuries, risk, intensive training, weight control, coaches' disciplinary practices, and abusive behaviours are likely to reflect beliefs that prevail in the culture of the gymnastics figuration.

To sum up, female gymnasts are so deeply enmeshed in a culture of risk that makes it difficult for them to stand back and examine their relationship with other actors of the WAG figuration in a more detached manner.

Note

1 In an Elisian sense *habitus* means a 'second nature'. For example, individuals learn from very early ages to exercise a great control of their emotions. Firstly it is an external control, but then such constraint is internalised by the individual who begins to exercise it almost in an autonomous manner. That is, such constraint turns into a 'second nature'. In other words, it becomes part of his/her *habitus*.

References

Annandale, E., & Hunt, K. (2000). Gender inequalities in health: Research at the crossroads. In E. Annandale & H. Kate (Eds.), *Gender inequalities in health* (pp. 1–35). Buckingham: Open University Press.

Benn, T., & Benn, B. (2004). After Olga: Developments in women's artistic gymnastics following the 1972 'Olga Korbut phenomenon'. In E. Dunning, D. Malcolm, & I. Waddington (Eds.), *Sport histories: Figurational studies of the development of modern sport* (pp. 172–190). Abingdon: Routledge.

Bowker, A., Gadbois, S., & Cornock, B. (2003). Sports participation and self-esteem: Variations as a function of gender and gender role orientation. *Sex Roles*, 49(1–2), 47–58.

Brackenridge, C., Bringer, J. D., & Bishopp, D. (2005). Managing cases of abuse in sport. *Child Abuse Review*, 14(4), 259–274. doi:10.1002/car.900.

Cense, M., & Brackenridge, C. (2001). Temporal and developmental risk factors for sexual harassment and abuse in sport. *European Physical Education Review*, 7(1), 61–79.

Connell, R. (1987). *Gender and power: Society, the person and sexual politics*. Stanford, CA: Stanford University Press.

Donnelly, P. (1997). Child labour: applying child labour laws to sport. *International Review for the Sociology of Sport*, 32(4), 389–406.

Dopson, S. (1994). *Managing ambiguity: A study of the introduction of general management in the National Health Service*. PhD, University of Leicester, England.

Dunning, E. (1999). *Sport matters: Sociological studies of sport, violence and civilisation*. London and New York: Routledge.

Elias, N. (1978). *What is sociology?* London: Hutchinson.

Elias, N. (1980). *Introdução à sociologia*. Lisbon: Edições 70.

Elias, N. (1987). *Involvement and detachment* (E. Jephcott, Trans.). Oxford: Basil Blackwell.

Elias, N. (1989). *OProcesso civilizacional* (1st edn, vol. 1). Lisbon: Publicações Dom Quixote.

Elias, N. (2001). *The society of individuals* (E. Jephcott, Trans.). New York and London: Continuum.

Elias, N., & Scotson, J. (1994). *The established and the outsiders* (2nd edn). London: Sage.

Gervis, M., & Dunn, N. (2004). The emotional abuse of elite child athletes by their coaches. *Child Abuse Review*, 13, 215–223.

Hargreaves, J. (1994). *Sporting females: Critical issues in the history and sociology of women's sports*. London and New York: Routledge.

Heikkala, J. (1993). Discipline and excel: techniques of the self and body and the logic of competing. *Sociology of Sport Journal*, 10, 397–412.

Hughes, R., & Coakley, J. (1991). Positive deviance among athletes: The implications of overconformity to the sport ethic. *Sociology of Sport Journal*, 8, 307–325.

Kane, M. J., & Snyder, E. (1989). Sport typing: The social 'containment' of women in sport. *Arena Review*, 13(2), 77–96.

Liston, K. (2005). Established-outsider relations between males and females in male associated sport in Ireland. *European Journal for Sport and Society*, 2(1), 25–33.

Loland, S. (2011). The normative aims of coaching – the good coach as an enlightened generalist. In A. Hardman & C. Jones (Eds.), *The ethics of sports coaching* (pp. 15–22). New York: Routledge.

Maguire, J. (2002). *Performance efficiency or human development? Reconfiguring sports science*. Paper presented at the Idrett, Samfunn og Frivillig Organisering Conference, Oslo.

Maguire, J., & Mansfield, L. (1998). 'No-body's perfect': Women, aerobics, and the body beautiful. *Sociology of Sport*, 15(2), 109–137.

Malcolm, D. (2006). Unprofessional practice? The status and power of sport physicians. *Sociology of Sport Journal*, 23(4), 376–395.

Mennell, S. (1998). *Norbert Elias – an introduction*. Dublin: University College Dublin Press.

Messner, M., & Sabo, D. (1990). *Sport, men, and the gender order: Critical feminist perspectives*. Illinois: Human Kinetics.

Pike, E. C. J. (2005). 'Doctors just say "Rest and take Ibuprofen"': A critical examination of the role of 'non-orthodox' health care in women's sport. *International Review for the Sociology of Sport*, 40(2), 201–219.

Pimenta, N. (2015). *Experiences of pain and injury in male and female artistic gymnastics: A figurational sociological study*. Doctor of Philosophy PhD, University of Loughborough.

Pinheiro, M. C., & Pimenta, N. (2015). Sociologia e treino desportivo: Implicações para a formação do treinador. In R. Resende, A. Albuquerque, & R. Gomes (Eds.), *Formação e saberes em desporto, educação física e lazer* (pp. 159–173). Lisbon: Visão e Contextos, Edições e Representações, Lda.

Pinheiro, M. C., Pimenta, N., Resende, R., & Malcolm, D. (2014). Gymnastics and child abuse: an analysis of former international Portuguese artistic gymnasts. *Sport Education and Society*, 19(4), 435–450.

Roderick, M. (1998). The sociology of risk, pain and injury: A comment on the work of Howard L. Nixon II. *Sociology of Sport Journal*, 15, 64–79.

Roderick, M., Waddington, I., & Parker, G. (2000). Playing hurt: Managing injuries in English professional football. *International Review for the Sociology of Sport*, 35(2), 165–180.

Safai, P. (2003). Healing the body in the 'culture of risk': Examining the negotiation of treatment between sport medicine clinicians and injured athletes in Canadian intercollegiate sport. *Sociology of Sport Journal*, 20(2), 127–146.

Stirling, A., & Kerr, G. (2009). Abused athletes' perceptions of the coach-athlete relationship. *Sport in Society*, 12(2), 227–239.

Waddington, I. (2000). *Sport, health and drugs*. London and New York: E & FN Sport.

Weidman, L. (2010). Homophobia, heterosexism, and ambivalence in the premier issue of Sports Illustrated Woman/Sport. In L. Fuller (Ed.), *Sexual sports rhetoric: Global and universal contexts* (pp. 147–158). New York: Peter Lang.

Chapter 14

Navigating sports medical practice in women's artistic gymnastics
A socio-cultural analysis

Astrid Schubring and Natalie Barker-Ruchti

Introduction

Elite level women's artistic gymnastics (WAG) is a high risk sport. According to the International Federation of Gymnastics (FIG) Medical Commission, WAG's particular risk factors are landing impact, aerial difficulty, intense year-round training, age, and developmental status of gymnasts (Leglise & Binder, 2019), which research has shown to cause chronic overuse syndromes and injury rates up to 22.7 per 1000h of exposure (Sands, Shultz, & Newman, 1993). Beyond physical health risks, problematic coaching practices and body ideals are found to impact gymnasts' psycho-social welfare (Barker-Ruchti & Schubring, 2015; Kerr, Berman, & Souza, 2006; Pinheiro, Pimenta, Resende, & Malcolm, 2014). Body dissatisfaction, disordered eating, and eating disorders are also common (Kerr et al., 2006; Neves et al., 2017). In response to these issues, national WAG organisations have established sports medical support services for national WAG teams, which are concerned with ensuring athlete health. Today, such services play an integral part of many high-performance sport systems (e.g., Anderson & Jackson, 2012; Malcolm, 2017; Safai, 2007; Theberge, 2008).

The progressive institutionalisation of sports medical services has led to a body of critical research on the role of health care professionals, their organisation, and working practices (for an overview, see Malcolm & Safai, 2012). There is, however, a paucity of such research on WAG. To address this gap, this chapter undertakes a case study to examine the working realities of two health care professionals in one European WAG team. More specifically, we aim to (a) outline the scope of duty the two professionals face on a day-to-day basis in WAG; (b) describe the ways they negotiate their professional practice with gymnasts and coaches; and (c) demonstrate the cultural and organisational limitations that influence their health care work.

A socio-cultural conception of sport medical provision in elite sport

To understand the role and practice of sports medical professionals in elite gymnastics, we draw on the sociology of pain and injury in sport (Young,

2004), and conclude that sports medicine constitutes a 'social practice' (Bourdieu, 1984) constrained and enabled by the respective elite sport context it is situated in.

Situating medical professionals in elite sport

Since the 1990s, scholars have repeatedly described elite sport as a cultural setting, which normalises pain and injury, and numerous studies exist in which female and male athletes, coaches, and officials justify or even glorify taking health risks in the quest of sporting success (e.g., Howe, 2001; Nixon, 1992; Pike & Maguire, 2003; Schubring, Bub, & Thiel, 2014). To explain the broad acceptance of health hazards, sport sociologists have introduced a number of concepts that help to understand the socio-cultural dynamics at work – first and foremost for athletes, but as Waddington (2012) demonstrates, even for sports medical professionals.

According to Hughes & Coakley (1991), many elite sport contexts constitute a 'sports ethic' that encourages striving for distinction, making sacrifices, and accepting few limits in order to reach selection or success. In WAG, this culture includes striving for perfection (Cervin, chapter 2). Further, athletes are often situated in rather closed, institutionalised networks within which they depend on coaches, teammates, and managers. Implicit or explicit pressures from these so-called 'sportsnets' (Nixon, 1992), career insecurities (Roderick, 2006), and shortcomings in coaching or management (Anderson & Jackson, 2012; Huizenga, 1995) are found to contribute to a 'culture of risk' (Nixon, 1992) that easily coerces athletes to 'over-conform' (Hughes & Coakley, 1991) to the above described ethic. Thus, athletes may 'choose' to train despite pain, compete when injured or sick, neglect recovery, or eat too little, practices widespread in elite WAG (e.g., Barker-Ruchti & Schubring, 2015; Kerr et al., 2006; Schubring & Thiel, 2014; Tynan & McEvilly, 2017).

Like athletes, medical professionals may be subject to the socio-cultural dynamics of risk and risk-taking in sports. Yet, in contrast to athletes, these professionals must follow the same ethical code of conduct[1] as medical professionals in other work fields (FIMS, 2020).[2] Various studies have illustrated, however, that 'sports ethics' may compromise medical practice (Malcolm & Safai, 2012). Research has shown that as sports medical staff are practising 'within an organization in which the key values are not professional values relating to health, but lay values relating to sport success' (Waddington, 2012, p. 219), they may experience role conflict, loss of autonomy, ethical challenges, and compromised practice (Anderson & Jackson, 2012; Scott, 2012). For example, clinicians may experience pressure from sportsnets to clear athletes for competition despite medical indication (Huizenga, 1995). The latter becomes possible because sports medical professionals are assigned the role of service providers 'whose job it is to look after the "stars"' (Waddington, 2012, p. 219). This loss in status often goes along with low remuneration or even voluntary engagement (Malcolm, 2006). The reasons why sport medical professionals may accept relatively poor working conditions are often non-professional, such as a love for a sport, or desire to give something back to the sport they had practised earlier (Malcolm, 2017; Waddington, 2012). These constellations, coupled with the earlier described socio-cultural dynamics in elite sports, create affordances for health care professionals to 'over-conform' with the sports ethic (Waddington, 2012).

The negotiation of medical practices in elite sport

Although there is ample evidence of sports medical practitioners buying-into the ethic of elite sport and breaching professional standards (Howe, 2001; McMahon & McGannon, 2018; Roderick & Waddington, 2000), some researchers argue that sport medical practice constitutes a negotiation between medical standards of care and performance premises of elite sport (Safai, 2003; Scott, 2012). This scholarship draws attention to the ways health care providers counter or at least temper the dominant culture of risk, indicating that the negotiation is enabled (or limited) by the contextual features of the sports settings under study (Kotarba, 2001; Waddington, 2012). For example, Safai's (2003) work on medical treatment of student-athletes at a Canadian university illustrates how the institutional context and its student welfare policy enabled clinicians to establish a 'culture of precaution' and negotiate risk-taking, health, and safety with the injured student-athletes. The role sports contexts play in diversifying the quality, complexity, and even style of health care delivery to athletes has further been explained by structural and cultural similarities between the two (Kotarba, 2012; Waddington, 2012).

Following, we will draw on the outlined scholarship to examine sport medical practice in WAG in one European country. Besides Kerr's (2012) work, no prior research on WAG medical support staff exists, but we hypothesise that medical professionals commissioned to care for elite gymnasts experience similar challenges as medical professionals in other competitive sports. Elite WAG can be characterised as dominated by a culture of risk that values striving for perfectionism; normalises and even silences physical, social, and emotional health hazards; and coaches who maintain an authoritarian position in a closed sportsnet. However, recent research highlights changes in WAG culture (Kerr, Barker-Ruchti, Schubring, Cervin, & Nunomura, 2017) and we estimate that contextual features will shape the experience of the sports medical professionals allowing for more or less negotiation of a medical 'culture of care' within the elite WAG setting under study.

Methodology

To investigate sports medical practice in WAG, we draw on a small-scale qualitative study on health care provision in one European country's WAG team. In the interests of preserving study participants' anonymity, we use a fictional name for the country under study (Sorana), and retain further details on the professionals and the project. For contextualisation of the findings, we briefly characterise the status of WAG in Sorana, before reporting on data collection and analysis.

WAG context under study

Artistic gymnastics has a long tradition in Sorana, both as a sport for all and as a high-performance sport for girls/women and boys/men. Over the last decades, Sorana has regularly qualified a national team and/or individual gymnasts for major international WAG competitions. Gymnasts have won medals at World Championship and the Olympic Games. Like in other European countries, the national governing body and general funding of (elite) sport are the main funders of a number of training centres spread throughout the country, coaching staff, and support services (e.g., medical care; career guidance; nutritional advice). To access elite training and support services for free – or for minor fees – gymnasts have to be part of the junior or senior national team, a status allocated based on performance. Sorana elite gymnasts are mostly amateurs, who only receive minor sponsorship contracts, prize money, or national funding. Accordingly, most WAG elite gymnasts pursue an educational or professional career besides their sport. Health care for Sorana national team gymnasts encompasses sports medical services not included in the public health insurance programme, such as sports medical examinations and access to physiotherapists and nutritionists.

Data collection and analysis

The first author conducted semi-structured interviews with health care providers of the WAG national team. She informed participants about the aim of the study, ethics, and the voluntary nature of their participation. Herein, we focus on the interviews conducted with the team's long-standing physician (Lena)[3] and a physiotherapist (Simon). Both had the necessary professional qualifications and national certificates to care for Olympic athletes. The tape-recorded interviews lasted 45 and 110 minutes. Astrid read the interview transcripts repeatedly to inductively identify central themes in the data before more deductively (Sparkes & Smith, 2014) carving out three themes that resonated with the earlier outlined questions: a) health problems sports medical professionals faced; b) sport medical professionals' role understanding and negotiation of care; c) cultural and organisational limitations to medical care in WAG. Lastly, the authors critically reviewed the identified themes, interview passages, and interpretations to agree on meaning, consistency, and appropriateness.

Results

In what follows, we present our findings along the three identified themes. We first outline the health problems identified by the sports medical professional and their scope of duty in gymnast health care. This description allows better understanding of the reality of medical practice in WAG. Second, we present how the interviewees understood their role and how the actual treatment was negotiated with gymnasts and stakeholders. We close by providing insights into the cultural and organisational limitations the professionals experienced in medical practice.

The sports medical professionals' scope of duty in gymnast health care

The sports physician Lena and the sports physiotherapist Simon described being primarily commissioned to ensure the provision of health and injury care at national team training camps and competitions (e.g. immediate care of injury, recovery massages, taping). Additionally, Lena was responsible for regular medical check-ups in order to identify and remedy possible health problems early, but also to test gymnasts' fitness for competition. The medical problems the professionals encountered most commonly in the junior and senior national team gymnasts were pain and injuries, and issues relating to weight control.

More specifically, Lena, who was very familiar with the gymnasts' medical history, listed overuse and injury conditions such as 'acute sport damages like problems at the growth plates', 'hyperlordosis', but also 'interarticular injuries' of the spine as typical. Simon described 'problems with the tail bone',[4] 'problems with the ankle', and 'heel problems' due to osteophytes as commonly causing long lay-off times. In addition, both narrated incidences where gymnasts had incurred traumatic injuries, such as a whiplash injury or an elbow fracture. Besides injuries, Simon, who spent several weeks per year with the team, described treating a range of pains 'in the ankle, shin splint, and lumbar spine'.

Beside pain and injury, Lena and Simon described weight and food control as another health concern. For example, Lena outlined effects of low body fat on the gymnasts' hormone balance: 'We have quite a number of girls who with eighteen do not yet have their periods or they have lost it again because they are keeping themselves so slim.'

Closely connected to this concern, the physician described gymnasts' eating behaviour as the area where she saw 'the greatest need for improvement'. The physiotherapist Simon also acknowledged disordered eating, stating 'I know that there are problems or were also with regard to bulimia mostly or anorexia'. Like Lena, Simon considered eating disorders a clear indication 'to take someone immediately out of training' or to 'intervene psychologically'.

Negotiating care in a culture of pain and weight control

Practising health care in elite sport constitutes a challenging endeavour. As we earlier established, medical professionals are obliged to negotiate their professional practice and ethical norms with contextual ideals, culture, and relational networks (Scott, 2012; Waddington, 2012). In the following, we first outline how the interviewees themselves defined their professional role, before describing how Lena and Simon navigated their work in Sorana elite WAG.

Definition of professional role

Lena and Simon shared a personal interest in elite sports and enjoyed their 'side-job' as health care providers for the national team. While they were well aware of the short- and long-term health risks of elite WAG, they saw their role primarily in 'helping gymnasts to come out of the thing as healthy as possible' (Simon) or 'if at all possible without negative effects' (Lena). Outlining his underlying reasoning, the physiotherapist Simon explained: 'High-performance sport is definitely not healthy. We can try to make it as healthy as possibly but with the loading in gymnastics, although it's versatile it still has one-sided loading. It's for sure not healthy.'

Simon starkly distinguished between 'sport for health' and 'elite sport'. Based on this distinction, he reasoned that his role was not to question the premises of elite sport and its costs in terms of time, effort, and health, yet reconciled possible contradictions in his role as health care provider by establishing two different paradigms to guide his work outside and inside of elite sport:

> As a physio, I have to always make some distinction between what I see in my clinic and what I see in sport where I have to say okay I have to fix it in a way that is tolerable for health and beneficial to the athlete. And those are two different things for me.

The formula 'tolerable for health and beneficial to the athlete' was a pragmatic way to reconcile the medical logic of health care with the logic of performance sports. This was also a reasoning that Lena adopted to guide her work in WAG. Taken together, the health care professionals described their role in WAG as a mix of 'damage control', 'fixing' of problems, and 'protecting gymnasts from greater harm'. Their understanding was of course shaped by the expectations of the gymnasts and coaches in the sportsnet – as exemplified in Lena's description of a typical consultation situation:

> The [gymnasts] come to you and tell you I have this and that problem because they all want to be able to perform and they want to quickly get rid of the problem that hinders them from performing. So they come to you and say 'doc I have this problem. Can you help me?'

Navigating medical care in WAG

Simon and Lena described various situations in which they had to navigate between sport's paradigm of performance and obligations towards gymnasts' health care. Notably in or prior to competitions, they experienced the necessity of making compromises for the sake of performance. Simon, for example, believed in the principle 'that the body knows best what it needs and with medication one must be particularly cautious'. He further explained that he believed that:

> From a health perspective and this is where we come in and where I try to influence, it's no good to [medically] kill pain and then continue to train. If [a gymnast should continue to train], then the pain should have gone away so that its cause is no longer there. That is actually the key mission of physiotherapy.

While Simon clearly aimed to properly take care of pain, he conceded to medication 'in extreme situations but then it's the job of the doctor'. One such situation occurred when a gymnast a few days prior to an international competition presumably had torn a ligament, and the gymnast and coach consulted Simon to see 'if one could do something'. Together, the physician and the physiotherapist ' agreed to still before puncturing the ankle, which was swollen, to use taping and for the competition, give her a Voltaren pill'.

While the decision to treat the gymnast so that she could compete is easily justified from an elite sport perspective, it is less justified from the care perspective Simon outlined when he talked about remedying the cause of pain instead of suppressing it. The incident also illustrates how sports medical staff may be prone to 'overconforming' to the sports ethic (Waddington, 2012) even if they in principle aim to moderate it through medical intervention. Another challenge that comes with 'medical risk-taking' is the question of responsibility in case further injury had occurred in the competition.

In contrast to examples where Simon and Lena made compromises in their professional practice and used medical expertise to help gymnasts to perform, the interviewees also reported setting limits of medical care. For example, Lena described how she repeatedly addressed coaches and even pressured them to take action against the disordered eating behaviour she saw:

> I've been to many competitions where I told the coach that if your gymnast continues with such disordered eating, then I will not provide fitness of competition. Ok? Either you take her to a nutrition specialist, or psychologist, you talk about it and try to solve or if you don't do it, then I'm not the consulting doctor anymore.

Lena knew that some gymnasts' weight problems were nothing she could 'fix' at a competition, but she tried to use the power of her role and medical mandate to put pressure on the coach. Her status as long-standing physician in WAG gave Lena a degree of independency that allowed her to correct the coaches and speak on behalf of gymnasts' health. Taken together, interviewees navigated professional practice between medical risk-taking and care, with situational factors (e.g. competition versus training) and professionals' status, power, and degree of independence influencing the extent of compromises made to medical standards.

Cultural limitations to medical care in WAG

When traveling with the national team, Simon was available to offer recovery massage or treatment of e.g. blockages, tensions, pains, and injuries to the gymnasts. Treatment was commonly arranged on the day by him asking gymnasts during or at the end of training: 'Who would like or still needs something today? Who else has problems?' Although Simon, like medical professionals in other sports (Malcolm, 2006), adopted the role of a service-provider who offered 'treatment on demand', he experienced that gymnasts reluctantly reporting health problems:

> They say much later if something is wrong so that on many occasions, I'm only the fire extinguisher. So things that in principle already are a problem weeks before, I see them if it goes bad in the second or third or sometimes even last day before a camp ends. Then they say I have – but for weeks – this and that problem. Because there is always something more acute. Well, if I compare it with [athletes in another sport] who much more easily listen inside the body, the gymnasts are mostly the exact opposite. Small injuries don't count. Bruises are irrelevant. For them, real injuries start only when others for sure would have already quit the sport.

The quote describes that a strong culture of risk permeated the national WAG team under study. Additionally, it suggests that the culture and organisation of the sport supported and possibly even enforced the systematic silencing of pain in WAG (Tynan & McEvilly, 2017). For one, the national team gymnasts often struggled with a variety of problems at a time, which led them to ignore or not consider a good deal of pain and injuries as irrelevant. This situation resulted in gymnasts silencing pain and injury as long as training was not seriously constrained. One junior team gymnast treated by Lena explained the practice of normalising pain and postponing treatment: 'I hurt very often somewhere. If I were to run to the doctor each time, then I would have a permanent consultation.'

Another factor that is likely to increase injury risk is the intensity and extent of year-round elite gymnastics training, which can leave little time for gymnasts to engage in adequate recovery and therapeutic treatment (for similar findings see Kerr, 2012). Simon suspected that at the end of training, the wish for some spare time led teenaged gymnasts to reason 'I don't want therapy. I don't feel like it and I just need peace'.

A third, crucial variable in the gymnasts' decision to silence pain and injury or not to use the health care offered, was, according to Lena, gymnasts' coaches, who want gymnasts in training, and the competition between the gymnasts in the national team. Lena described: 'The coach says that when you now say that you have something serious on your back, always back pain, then they will not take you to whatever competition is on. That also happens.'

As a consequence, gymnasts may choose to or be coerced to conceal pain and injury from team colleagues and the national team coach. This dilemma may go as far as for gymnasts taking pain-killers without prior consultation with the medical professionals. Simon recalled one such case, with a gymnast who experienced considerably limited range of movement, but 'suddenly in competition, everything went well'. Concerned, he decided to follow up with the gymnast who revealed to him that she had taken pain-killers in order to perform. Well aware that it was likely an adult parent, coach, or clinician in her close sportsnet who had provided the medication, this incident led Simon to talk to the national team coach and 'to agree that we in principle don't want this [self-medication with pain-killers]'. Consequently, a variety of socio-cultural factors can complicate gymnasts' reporting and the early/adequate treatment of their health problems despite the medical care being made readily available to them.

Organisational limitations to medical care in WAG

While research found medical care for female athletes to be lower in quality and availability compared to services provided to male athletes (Kotarba, 2012), differences may be less pronounced in Olympic sports (Scott, 2012; Theberge, 2008) and based on our interviewees' accounts the availability of health care services was described as good for female gymnasts. For example,

Simon applauded that national team training camps were always accompanied by a licensed sports physiotherapist and Lena considered the medical check-ups as an asset for athlete care. However, the way WAG health care was organised and funded in Sorana set limits to the quality of care. These limitations became apparent in Lena and Simon's descriptions of their work conditions. Both pursued regular jobs as medical professionals and worked only intermittently as sports medical professionals for the Sorana WAG teams. 'No federation could afford to pay a permanent clinician who is obviously present in training, who is always there', explained Lena. Consequently, Lena rarely came along on training camps in contrast to Simon, who spent several weeks with the team doing most of the 'ground work':

> Of course, from time to time it would be nice to have a clinician present during the training camp, but no time, no money. It simply doesn't work. Although the clinicians are also paid badly, but for the money anyhow no one comes, no one closes their clinic.

The fact that the daily allowance paid by the federation to health care professionals did not equate with their regular salaries lowered the status of sports medical care provision to a benevolent service. Nevertheless, the mandate of care for the national teams was taxing and Simon and Lena talked about conflicts with their regular work and private lives:

> The care always requires a great deal of manpower and a lot of clinicians like me nowadays don't have the time you would actually need to do all of it. You can't really do it on your own.
>
> (Lena)

> We have taken in another colleague because it simply got too much in scope. My boss doesn't allow this too often [me] taking unpaid leave. My family would also like to spend their holidays with me every now and then so that's why at some point it is a problem of time.
>
> (Simon)

To remedy the problem, the federation had extended the medical team, which allowed Lena and Simon to 'outsource' parts of their work, or to alternate participation in national team events with others. While this turn-taking does not constitute a problem per se, but can, as Lena argued, protect health care providers and gymnasts from 'wear off effects' as 'a third person who comes on board can better spot some things', the interviewees acknowledged negative side effects. For example, Simon assessed that collaboration within the medical team was 'in practice non-existent' as they rarely met or operated together. From a therapeutic perspective, Lena mentioned that the follow-up of individual gymnasts was inconsistent, given that 'a lot of clinicians work together on the athlete'. The physiotherapist Simon added shortcomings in the documentation and transmission of information within the medical team explaining:

> I would prefer if I could have a patient portfolio for one or the other gymnast. So that I simply know something about the progress of what has happened (-) maybe in a written form. It was always no problem. But I think this could be optimised. I had everything via the national coach, s/he held all the strings in her hand.

In summary, the sharing of the work in a larger team of medical professionals diffused the tension the team physician and physiotherapist described with regard to the time demands of medical care in WAG and its limited financial resources. While the extension of the medical team may strengthen the quality of care, the interviewees described problematic side effects. Namely, that information on gymnast-patients' medical histories was lost or passed on via/stored with the national team coach, instead of within the medical team. Given the influence WAG coaches are reported to have on gymnasts' readiness to utilise the health care actually available to them, the implicit inclusion of the national team coach into the medical team involves risks for the autonomy of sports medical services in WAG and may further discourage the gymnasts from using the medical care provided.

Conclusions

The results demonstrate that the medical professionals were under pressure to adjust to a performance-focused and training-intense WAG culture, while being given limited power and semi-professional work conditions. This complicated professional practice and resulted in a pragmatic work ethic of 'tolerable for health and beneficial to the athlete'. When navigating professional practice with coaches and gymnasts in WAG, the interviewees shared cases of enforcing health protective measurements and making compromises that would not be acceptable in non-sporting contexts. Taken together, the findings stress the importance of sport medical interventions in WAG, but also highlight the need for further improvement. To address the identified socio-cultural underpinnings of compromised medical practice in WAG and to ensure appropriate health care for gymnasts, we propose the following:

- *Elite WAG health standards.* Our case study demonstrates that a deep-seated culture of risk and alignment with the sport ethic govern WAG and WAG health care. In response, the health professionals modified the health standards they adhered to outside of elite sport to damage control and medical tolerability. For the gymnasts, such compromised health care can negatively impact performance, career longevity, and short- and long-term health and wellbeing. We propose that national WAG organisations lead the development of WAG-specific health standards in close collaboration with sport medical organisations (e.g., FIMS) and experienced WAG medical personnel. Such standards should identify sports specific injuries and health conditions that require excluding gymnasts from training/competition, detail adequate medical treatment, and prescribe return-to-training protocols (for a similar standard, see McCrory et al., 2013).

- *Effective medical care.* We found that organisational limitations compromised the two medical professionals' care practices. Employment conditions, insufficient staff, and shortcomings in documentation procedures and communication were reported as particularly impeding. We propose that national WAG organisations consider, in collaboration with health care practitioners, how effective medical care can be financed and implemented. The employment of permanent medical teams, relevant, ethically appropriate, and efficient care systems, and regular and clear communication between medical professionals, coaches, gymnasts, and parents, would significantly improve medical care, and benefit athlete performance, health, and wellbeing, and reduce health costs. As a result, national governments' elite sport investments would be more effective.
- *Inclusion of health care in daily training schedule.* Our case study, as other research, demonstrate that elite athletes' health care in all its forms is practised outside of daily training schedules. In WAG, where daily training hours are long and gymnasts are often still at school or other education, health care can be cumbersome and neglected. Yet, recovery from training and (pre-)rehabilitation exercises are vital for best performance. We propose that WAG organisations and stakeholders integrate this form of health care in gymnasts' daily training schedules. This would (a) signal that health care is important; (b) assure that it is performed regularly; and (c) free up time for gymnasts for other areas of life (e.g., socialising; schooling; sleep). Taken together, integrated health care has potential to reduce stress an over-committed schedule may cause.

Notes

1 This code includes the premises to care for and protect athlete-patients' health and well-being; act in best interest of the patient; respect medical confidentiality; and fully inform on potential harm of treatment or athlete-patients' own risky behaviour (Holm & McNamee, 2009; FIMS, 2020).
2 For the complete vision statement see 'International Federation for Sports Medicine' (FIMS): http://www.fims.org/.
3 All names given are pseudonyms.
4 Lena also talked about these problems, explaining them to be caused by 'repeated microtraumata', which led to inflammation or damage of the growth plate.

References

Anderson, L., & Jackson, S. (2012). Competing loyalties in sports medicine: Threats to medical professionalism in elite, commercial sport. *International Review for the Sociology of Sport*, 48(2), 238–256. doi:10.1177/1012690211435031.

Barker-Ruchti, N., & Schubring, A. (2015). Moving into and out of high-performance sport: The cultural learning of an artistic gymnast. *Physical Education and Sport Pedagogy*, 21(01), 69–80. doi:10.1080/17408989.2014.990371.

Bourdieu, P. (1984). *Distinction: A social critique of the judgement of taste* (R. Nice, Trans. 7th edn). Cambridge, MA: Harvard University Press.

Fédération Internationale de Médecine du Sport (FIMS). (2020). *Code of ethics*. Retrieved 15 January 2020, from https://www.fims.org/about/code-ethics/.

Holm, S., & McNamee, M. (2009). Ethics in sports medicine. *BMJ*, 339, b3898. doi:10.1136/bmj.b3898.

Howe, P. D. (2001). An ethnography of pain and injury in professional rugby union: the case of Pontypridd RFC. / Une ethnographie de la douleur et des blessures dans l'Association Professionnelle de Rugby: le cas de Pontypridd RFC. *International Review for the Sociology of Sport*, 36(3), 289–303.

Hughes, R., & Coakley, J. (1991). Positive deviance among athletes: The implications of overconformity to the sport ethic. *Sociology of Sport Journal*, 8(4), 307–325.

Huizenga, R. (1995). *You're okay, it's just a bruise: A doctor's sideline secrets about pro football's most outrageous team*. New York: St. Martin's Griffin.

Kerr, G., Berman, E., & Souza, M. J. D. (2006). Disordered eating in women's gymnastics: Perspectives of athletes, coaches, parents, and judges. *Journal of Applied Sport Psychology*, 18(1), 28–43. doi:10.1080/10413200500471301.

Kerr, R. (2012). Integrating scientists into the sports environment. *Journal of Sport and Social Issues*, 36(1), 3–24.

Kerr, R., Barker-Ruchti, N., Schubring, A., Cervin, G., & Nunomura, M. (2017). Coming of age: coaches transforming the pixie-style model of coaching in women's artistic gymnastics. *Sports Coaching Review*, 1–18. doi:10.1080/21640629.2017.1391488.

Kotarba, J. A. (2001). Conceptualizing sports medicine as occupational health care: Illustrations from professional rodeo and wrestling. *Qualitative Health Research*, 11(6), 766–779. doi:10.1177/104973201129119523.

Kotarba, J. A. (2012). Women professional athletes' injury care. In D. Malcolm & P. Safai (Eds.), *The social organization of sports medicine: critical socio-cultural perspectives* (pp. 107–125). Abingdon: Routledge.

Leglise, M., & Binder, M. (2019). *L'accidentologie en gymnastique [gymnastics injuries]*. Retrieved from http://www.fig-gymnastics.com/site/files/page/editor/files/Medical-Doc-Laccidentologie%20en%20gymnastique-f.pdf.

Malcolm, D. (2006). Unprofessional practice? The status and power of sport physicians. *Sociology of Sport Journal*, 23(4), 376–395.

Malcolm, D. (2017). *Sport, medicine, and health: The medicalization of sport*. Abingdon: Routledge.

Malcolm, D., & Safai, P. (2012). Introduction: The social science of sports medicine. In D. Malcom & P. Safai (Eds), *The social organization of sports medicine: Critical socio-cultural perspective* (pp. 1–22). Abingdon: Routledge.

McCrory, P., Meeuwisse, W. H., Aubry, M., Cantu, B., Dvořák, J., Echemendia, R. J., ... Turner, M. (2013). Consensus statement on concussion in sport: the

4th International Conference on Concussion in Sport held in Zurich, November 2012. *British Journal of Sports Medicine,* 47(5), 250. doi:10.1136/bjsports-2013-092313.

McMahon, J., & McGannon, K. R. (2018). The athlete–doctor relationship: power, complicity, resistance and accomplices in recycling dominant sporting ideologies. *Sport, Education and Society,* 1–13. doi:10.1080/13573322.2018.1561434.

Neves, C. M., Filgueiras Meireles, J. F., Berbert de Carvalho, P. H., Schubring, A., Barker-Ruchti, N., & Caputo Ferreira, M. E. (2017). Body dissatisfaction in women's artistic gymnastics: A longitudinal study of psychosocial indicators. *Journal of Sports Sciences,* 35(17), 1745–1751. doi:10.1080/02640414.2016.1235794.

Nixon, H. L. (1992). A social network analysis of influences on athletes to play with pain and injuries. *Journal of Sport and Social Issues,* 16(2), 127–135. doi:10.1177/019372359201600208.

Pike, E. C. J., & Maguire, J. A. (2003). Injury in women's sport: Classifying key elements of 'risk encounters'. *Sociology of Sport Journal,* 20(3), 232–251.

Pinheiro, M. C., Pimenta, N., Resende, R., & Malcolm, D. (2014). Gymnastics and child abuse: an analysis of former international Portuguese female artistic gymnasts. *Sport, Education and Society,* 19(4), 435–450. doi:10.1080/13573322.2012.679730.

Roderick, M. (2006). A very precarious profession: Uncertainty in the working lives of professional footballers. *Work, Employment and Society,* 20(2), 245–265. doi:10.1177/0950017006064113.

Roderick, M., & Waddington, I. (2000). Playing hurt: managing injuries in English professional football. *International Review for the Sociology of Sport,* 35(2), 165–180.

Safai, P. (2003). Healing the body in the 'culture of risk': Examining the negotiation of treatment between sport medicine clinicians and injured athletes in Canadian intercollegiate sport. *Sociology of Sport Journal,* 20(2), 127–146.

Safai, P. (2007). A critical analysis of the development of sport medicine in Canada, 1955–1980. *International Review for the Sociology of Sport,* 42(3), 321–341. doi:10.1177/1012690207088115.

Sands, W. A., Shultz, B. B., & Newman, A. P. (1993). Women's gymnastics injuries. A 5-year study. *American Journal of Sports Medicine,* 21(2), 271–276.

Schubring, A., & Thiel, A. (2014). Coping with growth in adolescent elite sport. *Sociology of Sport Journal,* 31(3), 304–326.

Schubring, A., Bub, E.-M., & Thiel, A. (2014). 'How much is too much?' The social construction of elite youth athlete exercise tolerances from the coaches' perspective. *Journal of Sport and Social Issues,* 39(4), 308–331. doi:10.1177/0193723514557820.

Scott, A. (2012). Making compromises in sports medicine: An examination of the health-performance nexus in British Olympic sports. In D. Malcolm & P. Safai (Eds.), *The social organization of sports medicine: Critical socio-cultural perspectives* (pp. 227–246). London: Routledge.

Sparkes, A. C., & Smith, B. (2014). *Qualitative research methods in sport, exercise and health: from process to product.* New York: Routledge.

Theberge, N. (2008). The integration of chiropractors into healthcare teams: a case study from sport medicine. *Sociology of Health & Illness,* 30(1), 19–34. doi:10.1111/j.1467-9566.2007.01026.x.

Tynan, R., & McEvilly, N. (2017). 'No pain, no gain': former elite female gymnasts' engagements with pain and injury discourses. *Qualitative Research in Sport, Exercise and Health*, 9(4), 469–484. doi:10.1080/2159676X.2017.1323778.

Waddington, I. (2012). Sports medicine, client control and the limits of professional autonomy. In D. Malcolm & P. Safai (Eds.), *The social organization of sports medicine. Critical socio-cultural perspectives* (pp. 204–226). Abingdon: Routledge.

Young, K. (Ed.) (2004). *Sporting bodies, damaged selves: sociological studies of sports-related injury*. Oxford: Elsevier Press.

Conclusion

Roslyn Kerr, Natalie Barker-Ruchti, Carly Stewart and Gretchen Kerr

In 2019, Simone Biles broke the record for the number of World Championships medals won by any gymnast, male or female. Given that men compete on two more apparatus than women, providing them with two greater opportunities to medal, Biles' accomplishment is extraordinary. Her success, as a 22-year-old African American, also highlights the immense changes that the sport of women's artistic gymnastics has experienced, as emphasised throughout this book.

As outlined in the first section, while up until the 1990s, the sport was dominated by an Eastern bloc mentality comprising of centralised training regimes, the last two decades have seen significant change. An increased range of countries are now represented on the podium, along with greater diversity in age, ethnicity, and body type. While there are still gymnasts who resemble the pixie-like appearance of Nadia Comaneci, they are counterbalanced by the maturity of older gymnasts, some of whom have had children, such as Oksana Chusovitina and Aliya Mustafina, and appear 'slight' compared to the muscularity of Simone Biles. But in perhaps the largest contrast to Comaneci, many gymnasts are now breaking their silence.

As the second section of the book demonstrates, the individual stories of gymnasts can have a profound impact on their lives. In research terms, they reveal nuanced experiences and insight into the often-problematic effects of the intense training regime and training culture demanded by the sport. They also reveal the experiential and bodily ways, often not seen, in which gymnasts are impacted in their pursuit of perfection such as the discomfort of a body exposed by the leotard for, often, teenage girls. But these experiential stories also gain power and a life of their own when they are picked up by the media, and due to their explicit content and capacity to shock, meaning that they can be a starting point for challenging unequal power relationships reproduced by coaches, parents, and sport science personnel that have rendered gymnasts silent in the non-digital media past.

A development over the last two years has been the greater appearance of some very prominent gymnasts in the media. Specifically, Aly Raisman's role as a spokesperson against abuse in the Larry Nassar case, and Simone

Biles' tweets challenging first the US Gymnastics Association over their appointment of a new CEO and more recently the Fédération Internationale de Gymnastique (FIG) over the grading of her new skills, are comments from outspoken and successful gymnasts which the sport has rarely seen before. It would be valuable in further research to understand the role of the celebrity gymnast and their potential to inspire cultural change.

Speaking to the underlying causes of the problems experienced by gymnasts, in section three of the book, we see the ways in which women's artistic gymnastics (WAG) is dominated by a coaching dynamic that disempowers gymnasts. While a strong coach-athlete relationship, as expressed by the 3+1Cs model, can provide both gymnasts and coaches with increased wellbeing, paradoxically some of the same qualities that lead to closeness can also leave athletes very vulnerable to various forms of harms including sexual, psychological, and physical abuse, and neglect. As chapter 10 emphasises, coaching policies and practices in WAG need to be designed with awareness of the unique context and embedded cultural norms of the sport in mind.

However, as section four brings home, the problems we may see in WAG culture should not be attributed to coaches alone. Other actors such as parents, managers, Federation officials, and sports scientists all contribute to reinforcing many of the traditional ways that WAG has worked. These actors find themselves in a difficult position, sometimes feeling conflicted by the demands of WAG but feeling the need to align themselves with a strong performance ethic in the name of results. So although centralised regimes are less common than they once were, it has proved difficult to produce any definitive cultural change. Indeed, cultural change remains the most significant area where further research and understanding is needed so that we can move beyond shining a light on individuals' behaviours to questioning the culture itself and the complexity of meanings and constructions that inform those behaviours and norms.

This book has been primarily focused on the elite level of the sport, but as chapter five eludes, there are a range of other high-level non-elite forms of WAG which have drawn little academic attention thus far. For example, Katelyn Ohashi, known as the only gymnast to have ever beaten Biles in an international competition, made headlines in 2018 with her college level Perfect 10, and spoke out against the elite WAG culture in comparison with her college experience. Examination of the way WAG is performed and practised in a range of other non-elite environments that offer a different model, such at university or college as in chapter 5, could provide fruitful areas to explore alternative WAG cultures.

Similarly, as referred to in chapter 13, men's artistic gymnastics (MAG) does not have the same culture of subjugation as WAG. While male gymnasts are unsurprisingly more empowered than female gymnasts owing to patriarchy and the position of men in sport and society (Hargreaves, 1994), they challenge the assumption that a culture of docility is necessary for producing successful gymnasts. The cultural differences of WAG and MAG are highlighted through the way coaches movement between MAG and WAG is not uncommon, causing us to question how coaching norms and values are manipulated by sub-cultural norms and relations of power in the environment. In other sports, there has been progress with female athletes becoming more respected for their athletic prowess as a result of mixed-sex training (see for example, Channon 2014; Fink et al., 2016), so the effects of such a regime in gymnastics would be a controversial but interesting arrangement to explore and may hold hope for reconstructing deeply set gendered arrangements.

WAG, and sport more broadly, are certainly not the only areas currently focused on cultural and behavioural change. Indeed, one of the most prominent areas where behaviour change is of crucial importance at a global level is in the area of sustainability. While this book has primarily drawn on the disciplines of sociology, psychology, and history, a large body of interdisciplinary work is growing in response to climate change, similarly focused on cultural change. For example, the extensive scholarship of Elizabeth Shove (2010; 2012) and others in the practice theory oeuvre who focus specifically on the changing of daily practices with the goal of understanding how more environmentally conscious behaviour can be produced. Authors writing in sport could adopt some of the learnings from these other areas to enact cultural change.

It is hoped too, that this WAG-focused collection may be of benefit to contributing to future change. This book collects together research and researchers from a wide range of nations and backgrounds, yet all writing specifically on the one sport. The book is unique in its very clear focus on the culture of WAG, and thus offers the potential for acting as an education mechanism for those who similarly would like to see change in the sport.

While this book has traced the development of the sport in terms of the changing standards of femininity throughout different time periods, an area that has received very little explicit attention in WAG are the wider gendered dynamics. As a sport that has such a strong female domination, there is surprisingly little work on the governance and management of WAG from a gendered perspective. For example, there has never been a female President of the FIG, and many of the WAG national head coaches are male. The stories and experiences of female coaches, officials, managers and directors are a missing part of WAG's story.

Indeed, one goal of this book has been to strongly emphasise the importance of stories. The inclusion of our fictional story was intended to highlight the power of stories and their effects. Jenny's story enables us to connect to key ideas and to one another as readers interested in this sport, and to learn new and multiple understandings of the complex phenomenon that is WAG. We hope that the significance of the story for the many research stories told in this book has been apparent throughout and that it impacts the reader in a way that inspires change in thought or action. While Jenny's story may have been fiction, it is unfortunately all too common that gymnasts live out any one or many aspects of her story, and we look forward to a time when the stories that pour out from gymnastics have changed for the better.

References

Channon, A. (2014). Towards the 'undoing' of gender in mixed-sex martial arts and combat sports. *Societies*, 4, 587–605.

Fink, J. S., Lavoi, N. M., & Newhall, K. E. (2016). Challenging the gender binary? Male basketball practice players' views of female athletes and women's sports. *Sport in Society*, 19, 1316–1331.

Hargreaves, J. (1994). *Sporting females: Critical issues in the history and sociology of women's sports*. London and New York: Routledge.

Shove, E. (2010). Beyond the ABC: Climate change policy and theories of social change. *Environment and Planning A*, 42(6), 1273–1285.

Shove, E. (2012). Putting practice into policy: Reconfiguring questions of consumption and climate change. *Contemporary Social Science*, 9(4), 415–429.

Index

abuse 2–3, 46–8, 55, 58, 60–1, 82, 84–6, 88–95, 146–50, 161–3, 166, 168, 191, 207, 209; allegations of 55, 60, 163, 166; of athletes 149–50, 160, 191; cases 61; child 30, 47, 82, 144, 147, 162–3; emotional 82, 89–90, 143, 146, 191–2, 194–5, 200, 209; experiences of 59, 94, 147; of Nassar 47–8, 84, 86, 92–5, 151; non-reported 163; physical 82, 86, 143, 232; preventing and managing 167; psychological 88; sexual 86; verbal 87
abusers 85–6, 94, 146, 163, 191
abusive behaviours 87, 89–90, 152, 196–7, 200, 213
abusive practices 47, 99, 193, 199
abusive relationships 91, 154
acrobatics 1, 17–21, 24, 28–33, 72; codifying 20; emerging styles of 20; feats 28; performing routines 2, 17; and 'transgressions of femininity' 29
'acrobatisation' 11, 19, 28–9, 32; appeals to notions of 'domesticated femininity, incestuous sexuality and paedophilia' 29; and the influence of Olga Korbut 1, 16–21, 25–6, 29, 31, 51; phenomena of 11; poses problems for femininity 24; and the role of Americans beginning the trend towards youth 18; and the role of the media in advertising and popularising this new style of WAG 11; and safety measures 21; of women's artistic gymnastics 13, 17, 19
Actor-Network Theory 177–8, 180
Alexandrov, Alexander 43–4, 56
allegations 47, 58, 60, 151, 163, 165, 169; of abuse 55, 60, 163, 166; false 163, 166, 168–9; potential 163; unfounded 163, 169
Amanar, Simona 81
amateurism 18, 35–7, 48, 219
American gymnastics teams 18, 29–30, 38, 46, 48, 83, 88
Anderson, Gwen 30, 92
ANT *see* Actor-Network Theory
Antonini Philippe, Roberta. 121, 123–5, 127
anxiety 90–1, 124–5, 127, 132, 160, 162, 175
apparatus 1, 11, 13, 31, 75, 159, 178, 181, 187, 231; acrobatics on the 18; balance beam 1, 11, 13, 16–18, 20–1, 27, 57, 66, 76, 81, 89, 158, 160; floor 1–2, 13, 16, 18, 20–1, 25, 27, 55, 88, 175; handheld 13; portable 13; uneven bars 1, 20, 81; vault 1, 13, 16, 27, 76, 82, 89, 118, 160, 166
artistic gymnasts 51, 87, 89, 91, 100–1, 159; *see also* gymnasts
asymmetric bars *see also* uneven bars 89, 159
Athens Olympics 2004 40
athlete protection 95; double standard for 95
athlete welfare 3, 46; initiatives 161; regulations 163; safeguarding of 162
athletes 25–7, 29, 35–6, 46–8, 91, 94–5, 121–9, 132–7, 143–54, 158–68, 183–4, 190–1, 193–9, 207–12, 217–18; abuse of 149–50, 160, 191; coaching environment 136; competitive 143, 145; experienced 25, 127; female 2, 81, 86, 89, 125, 127, 159, 168, 210, 224, 233; male 31, 89, 209, 217, 224; maltreatment of 143, 146, 151, 161;

scoring of 27, 36; selection of 183–4; talented 46, 159; young 27–8, 82, 85, 94, 150, 190, 200; *see also* child athletes
Atlanta Olympics 1996 37–8, 82
audiences, appeals and demands of 20, 26, 29, 37, 104, 107
Australia 32, 38, 44–6, 52, 54–5, 57–8, 61, 101, 162, 164, 185; bringing British expert coaches for workshops to 57; implementing state-managed sport policies 57; targeting male Soviet coaches for recruitment 44
Australian Gymnastics Federation 55, 57
Australian Institute of Sport 55, 57–8
authority 18, 83, 87, 94–5, 130, 144, 152, 208–9, 213; of coaches 151–2, 209; positions of 146, 152; and sexual abuse 151; significant 146; unquestioned 125, 191

balance beam 1, 11, 13, 16–18, 20–1, 27, 57, 66, 76, 81, 89, 158, 160
balletic training routines 11
Barcelona Olympics 1992 48
Barker-Ruchti, Natalie 1, 3, 17, 19–21, 29–32, 51, 53, 71, 75, 79, 99, 101, 109, 112
bars 7, 13, 16, 18, 20, 27, 89, 159; asymmetric 89, 159; high 11, 181; parallel 11, 13, 181
beam *see* balance beam
behaviours 11–12, 109–10, 122, 136–7, 147, 149, 166, 168, 195, 198, 200, 203–4, 207–8, 210, 232; anti-social 162; coaching 195, 197–8, 200; criminal 151; eating 220; unacceptable 147, 150
Beijing Olympics 2008 158, 161
Biles, Simone 1, 3, 28, 38, 47–8, 81, 121, 124, 145, 231–2
billet families 57
Bitang, Mariana 56, 58
boards of directors 193, 195–6
bodies 2, 12, 14, 16–18, 30–1, 66, 69–70, 72–4, 76–7, 79, 87–8, 99–113, 117–19, 198–9, 222–3; athlete's 21, 160; broken 82; disciplined 103–4, 106, 108; female 12, 99, 112; governing 46–8, 52–4, 60, 112, 219; human 179; lived 100, 112–13; 'narratives' 100, 102–4, 108, 110, 113

bodily processes 111
body image 88–9, 91
body-self 100, 102–3, 105, 113; alterative gymnastic 105, 110; disruptions 109–11; narratives 99, 101, 103, 105, 107, 109, 111; relationships 75, 102
Bono, Mary 47–8
Boorman, Aimee 121–2, 124, 145
Booth, Elizabeth 35, 51
Brackenridge, Celia H. 85–6, 91, 144–53, 163, 167, 190–1, 212–13
Brazilian coaches 60
Brazilian Gymnastics Confederation 59
Brazilian Olympic Committee 55, 59–60
Brestyan, Mihai 46, 55, 58
British Gymnastics 88, 158
Brixia Brescia 56–7, 60
Brundage, Avery 35
bullying 66
Burke, Michael 70, 125–6, 147–50

calisthenics 12
cameras 20, 26, 118–19, 182–3
Canadian gymnastics programme 40
Carbinatto, Michele 69–70, 72, 74, 76, 78–80
care 4, 18, 31, 67, 70, 82, 88, 124, 137, 145–7, 150, 218–20, 222–3, 225, 227; culture of 218; demonstration of 86; practices 227; quality of 225–6
careers 4, 32, 35, 38, 44, 84, 90, 101–2, 105, 107–9, 148, 150, 196, 203, 207–8; advancements 151, 153; aspirations 150; athlete's 148, 152; female gymnast's 152; gymnastic 44, 102; insecurity 217; international 14; professional 219; short gymnastics 89
caring 133, 146, 160; emotional 123; gymnastics coach 79
Casella, Enrico 56, 60
cases 2, 61, 82, 90, 104, 144, 146, 161, 184, 186–7, 207, 212, 224; abuse 61; documented 165; extreme 82; high-profile 161; reported 3; shared 226; unfounded 163
Caslavska, Vera 14, 15, 16, 19–20
Cavallerio, Francesca 51, 125
Cense, M. 86, 145, 147–51, 191, 213
Cervin, Georgia 1, 13, 18–19, 26–8, 30, 32, 37–8, 109, 217
child abuse 30, 47, 82, 144, 147, 162–3

child athletes 24, 28, 33, 94, 161, 164–5, 192
child gymnasts 18, 30
children 25, 31, 42–3, 45, 161–8, 190, 193, 210, 231; desensitising of 160; filming young 161; investigating 164; rights of 168; touching 162, 164
Children and Family Select Committee Inquiry 2009 163
Chinese Cultural Revolution 54
Chinese gymnastics 53–4
Chisholm, Ann 1, 3, 12, 14, 17, 27, 29
clinicians 211, 217, 224–6
clubs 9, 26, 41–2, 54, 59, 61, 73, 77, 117–18, 165–6, 168, 176, 179–80, 193, 197–8; and coaches 167, 197–8; gymnastic 9; and gymnasts 52, 59, 168, 179; and parents 167; trampoline 105; university gymnastics 72
coach-athlete relationships 2, 117, 121–3, 125–9, 132–7, 143–4, 146, 148–9, 151–2, 154, 164, 193, 195, 199; abusive 147, 190; complicated 1; dyads 134, 136, 145, 149, 153; eradicated abusive 190; established 135; good quality 121, 123; good quality dyadic 137; healthy 151; interactions 126, 195; physical contact 137, 165, 168; positive 145, 147, 160; power in 121–37; quality 123; sharing information 125–6; strong 232; trusting 125
coaches 30–3, 39–41, 43–6, 56–60, 75–7, 79–92, 121–9, 132–7, 143–54, 158–69, 173–4, 180–4, 190–200, 207–13, 222–4; and the aging population 43, 54–5, 61; Brazilian 60; club 41, 58; as educators 166–7; emigrant 46, 52; and emigration 56, 60; female 44, 233; immigrant 46; junior 118, 146; male 2, 30–1, 46, 112, 125; misusing their power 124–5; national 39–40, 56, 60, 226, 233; power of 125–7, 129; relationship with athletes 135; Romanian 44–6; serial winning 128; Soviet 55, 59–60
coaching 18, 28, 30, 32, 106, 121, 126–7, 136–7, 145, 150, 159–60, 162–5, 167, 184, 200; authoritarian styles 33; and coaches 30, 121, 126, 137, 150; education 51, 55, 57–8, 200; full-time 51; gymnastics 31, 39, 91, 168; new techniques 30; of prepubescent girls 2; processes 124, 136, 160, 167; staff 127, 179, 219; styles 46; success 79, 128, 183; sustainable agenda 113
coaching behaviours 195, 197–8, 200; abusive 82, 152, 190; emotional 191, 198, 200; encountering of 196; unacceptable 125
coaching environments 127, 136; impersonal 124; relational 127; safe 136–7
coaching practices 125–6, 137, 216; abusive 89; defensive 162; good 165; improving 160; unrelenting 124
code of silence 198, 200
Cold War 24, 26, 32–3, 51
Comăneci, Nadia 1, 7, 24–32, 41–2, 44, 46, 51, 81, 231; coaches Bela and Marta Károlyi 31; and the Cold War contest between the old order and the new 27; and the obsession with perfection 27; scores a symptom of Cold War rivalries 24; scores limited by the ceiling of the scoring system at 10.0. 24, 27; suicide attempt at the age of 15 years 81
Commonwealth Games 179, 185–6
communication strategies 123
Communists 42, 44–5, 52, 54, 62; coaches 58; gymnasts 51; influence 57
competitions 13, 17–18, 20–1, 25–7, 31, 37, 104, 107, 110, 117–18, 179–80, 185, 187, 220, 222–4; gymnastics 27, 37, 180; individual 185; major 43; national 119, 173, 179, 192; university 72
competitive successes 51–2, 54, 56, 59–61, 191, 207
computer programs 182
conditions and events that have shaped the six countries' WAG development prior to and since 1989 **55**
countries 12, 14, 16, 18, 35, 39–42, 45–6, 52, 54–5, 58–62, 144, 161–2, 183, 185–6, 219; Eastern bloc 26, 30, 35–6, 44, 231; European 218–19; former Communist 52, 59, 61; non-Communist 52, 54, 61–2; post-1989 58; Western 18, 43, 46
cultural changes 232–3
cultural norms (of different sports) 166–7

culture 44, 46–7, 89, 101, 103, 105, 125, 132, 160, 209, 213, 217, 221, 223, 232–3; body in-folds 105; consumer 111; dominant 218; of precaution 211, 218; of risk 211, 213, 217–18; strong 223
'culture of care' 218
Curitiba Training Centre 55, 59
Czechoslovakia 12, 14, 16

Dantzscher, Jamie 88, 90, 92
data collection and analysis 184, 219
Dawes, Dominique 38
decisions 90, 123–4, 129, 133–4, 149, 153, 181, 184, 186–7, 211–12, 222, 224; employment 153; final (about selections) 135, 183; making of 153, 184
Deford, Frank 26, 29
dehumanisation processes 184
depression 90–1, 132
Deva training centre (Romania) 41
directors 40, 123, 191–200, 233; board of 193, 195–6; club 196
disciplined bodies 103–4, 106, 108
disciplines 3, 30, 72, 89, 100–1, 109–10, 112, 158, 193, 198–9, 233
discourses 12, 45, 83, 93, 95, 163, 190–1, 193, 195, 197–8, 200; consistent 91; cultural 104; and discursive practices Dutch WAG multilevel model 193, 195; historical gymnastic 101; and performance-focused worship towards gymnastics 42; subcultural 110; 'no touch' 158–9, 161, 163, 165, 167
discursive practices 193–200; of disciplining the body (weight) 198; dominant 194; of elite youth sport 194, 196; macro level 196; of silence 198; use of 200; of winning and toughness 197
distrust, objects of 126, 162–3
doping, state-funded 40
DPSIM see dyadic power-social influence model
Drewe, Sheryle Bergmann 125–6
Dutch elite women gymnasts 191, 194
Dutch Sports Federation 57
Dutch WAG multilevel model 192
dyadic power-social influence model 103, 129, 132, 134, 136–7
dynamics 191, 194, 204–5; social 128, 206; socio-cultural 217–18

Eastern bloc 26, 30, 35–6, 44, 231; coaches 43; countries 26, 36; gymnasts 18; National Olympic Committees 36; sport 35–6, 42
eating disorders 82, 89–91, 111, 125, 216, 221
education 41–2, 45, 94, 160, 227; coaching 51, 55, 57–8, 200; courses 167; gymnastics 12, 69–80; see also coaching education; see also higher education
Elias, Norbert 178, 203–7, 209, 211
elite 165, 179–80, 193, 200; coaches 196–7; female athletes 81, 101, 195; funding of sport 219; isolated training camps 86; or pre-elite grades 181; programmes 179; training at a younger age 159; training centres 56–7; women gymnasts 29, 191–6, 199–200; youth sports 193
elite gymnastics 4, 54–5, 59, 193, 195–6, 199, 216; clubs 196–7; experiences of 195; practices 199; training 60
elite gymnasts 38, 57, 81, 118, 173, 191, 199, 218
elite sport 18, 52, 57, 59, 183, 196–7, 200, 210, 216–18, 221, 226; between 1989 and 2000 52; investments 59, 227; practising health care in 221; rebuilding of 58; training methods 54; youth 190, 192, 194, 196
emigration of Eastern bloc coaches 43–5
emotional abuse 82, 89–90, 143, 146, 191–2, 194–5, 200, 209; experiences of 91; practices 190–1, 193–5, 197–9; systematic 191
emotional caring 123
employment 18, 52, 60, 153, 227
empowerment 3, 40, 123, 137, 206, 210; female athlete 3, 210; social 40
environment 85, 100–1, 118, 124, 136–7, 159, 162, 190, 233; impersonal 124; non-elite 232; social 132, 134, 136, 191
European Gymnastics Federation 53
experiences 43, 69–70, 83, 92–3, 101–3, 105, 111–12, 124, 133, 137, 147–8, 166, 206, 208, 218; abusive 91; anxiety 124; college 232; gendered-based 95; unhappiness 87
exploitation 82, 151, 160–3, 166–8; allegations of 55, 60, 163, 166; grooming process of 86; online 144; sexual 86, 144, 151, 161; of trust 147

families 40–1, 57, 84, 87, 90, 143, 145, 149–50, 153–4, 191, 225
fear 31, 71, 74–5, 77, 84, 93, 117, 119, 124, 136, 146, 148–9, 158, 175; central 162; co-existing 79; of disfigurement 111; of gymnasts 74; of injuries 159
Fédération Internationale de Gymnastique 13, 18–21, 24, 26–8, 30, 35–8, 48, 54, 99, 158–9, 168, 192, 216, 232–3
Fédération Internationale de Médecine du Sport 217, 227
federations 19, 61, 225; and coaches 82, 167; international sports 36, 56; national sports 28, 203, 208, 210–11; responsible for the rules of sport 192
female athlete empowerment 3, 210
female athletes 2, 81, 86, 89, 125, 127, 159, 168, 210, 224, 233
female bodies 12, 99, 112
female femininity 1–2, 11–14, 17, 19, 24, 29–30, 33, 233
female gymnastics 209, 211
female gymnasts 25, 29–30, 81–2, 89–90, 94, 99–101, 112, 146, 148, 151–3, 192, 195–9, 209, 213, 224
femininity 1–2, 11–14, 17, 19, 24, 29–30, 33, 233
field notes 106–7
FIG *see* Fédération Internationale de Gymnastique
figurations 204–9, 213; co-existing 204; complex 204; creation of 178; and the established positions they occupy within the 203; and figuration sociology 203; multiple 203–4
FIMS *see* Fédération Internationale de Médecine du Sport
financial resources 45, 226
floor 1–2, 13, 16, 18, 20–1, 25, 27, 55, 88, 175
friendships 152–3, 174; based upon each party being advantageous or useful to the other 153; and the building of trust 86; and the different types that exist 153; and the imbalance of power in the relationship between a gymnast and her coach 152; and the notion of utility 153; and the unequal influence and power of the coach-athlete relationship 125

funding 18, 36, 40–1, 48, 56, 58–9, 61, 183, 219; governance 39; governmental 42; insufficient 61; sponsorship 37, 61; state 41–2, 48, 58; systems 61

gender 1, 100, 127, 163, 209–10, 233
Gibson, Kass 178–9, 182, 184
girls 7–9, 29, 40, 66, 75, 93, 95, 110, 117–19, 159, 174, 176, 184, 198, 220; frail 29; pre-pubescent 31; teenage 231; white 3; young 2, 30–1
Giulianotti, Richard. 52–3
GK Elite Sportswear 38
glocalisation 53
goals 70, 92, 122, 132, 136, 143, 150, 177, 179, 183, 199, 204–5, 208, 213, 233; coach's 150; higher level 129; mutual 150; sharing personal 148, 150; weight management 198
gold medals 38, 41, 47
good quality relationships 123
governing bodies 46–8, 52–4, 60, 112, 219
grooming 86, 147, 167, 191, 193–4, 197–9; and emotional abusive practices 190–200; physical 86, 191; psychological 86, 191; sexual 167
'grooming process' 86, 147, 150, 160, 163, 191–2, 194–9
gymnasiums 8, 16, 31, 44, 66–7, 73–4, 81, 84, 87–8, 92, 119, 174, 181, 197–8; and coaches 82, 88, 197; and gymnasts' bodies photographed for faults 117; and positive coach-athlete relationships 145; and training teams 117
gymnastics 1–3, 11–13, 16–21, 26–8, 30–2, 35–7, 39–46, 48, 53–4, 68–75, 77–80, 99–100, 179–81, 186–7, 196; acrobatic 27; adult 75; apparatus 1, 11, 13, 31, 75, 159, 178, 181, 187, 231; bodies 73–4, 100; body-self and identity 102, 105–6, 109–11; camps 84; careers 70; clubs 9, 38; coaches 30–3, 39–41, 43–6, 56–60, 91, 143–54; community 17, 85; competitions 27, 37, 180; culture 69, 99–100, 107, 213; discipline 168; environment 112–13; equipment 181–2; female 209, 211; figuration 207–10, 212–13; networks 185–6; and the performance of Romania at the 1976 Olympic Games

25; rhythmic 13, 41; stories 4, 69–71, 73–5, 77–80; success 16, 24, 32, 38–9, 47–8, 95, 232–3; training programs 4, 31, 69–71, 73–5, 77–80, 224; university 74–5; world 25–6, 70
Gymnastics Australia 58
gymnasts 1–4, 13–14, 26–32, 39–41, 55–60, 69–81, 83–95, 99–113, 133–4, 150–4, 177–83, 185–8, 207–13, 222–7, 231–2; adolescent 101; deferring identity crises 101; elite women 29, 191–6, 199–200; former 43, 69–70, 89, 92, 95, 195; image disorders and eating disorders 58–9, 111; individual 1, 38, 41, 177, 219, 226; international 30; male 31, 93, 100, 209, 232; narratives 83; older 78–9, 104, 231; young 18, 28–30, 43, 81, 92, 105, 159, 193, 207, 209, 213

head coaches 40, 44, 56, 60, 233; Andrei Rodionenko 40, 44; Leonid Arkayev 39; Valentina Rodionenko 43
health 108–9, 121, 143, 146, 148, 152, 154, 161, 212, 217–18, 220–1, 223, 226–7; athlete's 154; enforcing 226; long-term 227; mental 88, 94; problems 3, 220, 223–4; risks 216–17, 221; standards 226–7
health care 221–2, 224, 226–7; delivery 218; integrated 227; professionals 211, 216, 218–19, 221, 225–7; services 224
Heitinga, Simone 57, 60
Helsinki Olympics 1952 13
high performance sport 121, 179–80, 187, 197, 210, 219, 221
high risk sport 146, 158, 216
higher education 69–71, 73, 75, 77–9
Houlihan, Barrie 51, 53, 57
Howe, P. David 217–18
human resources 45

incomes 35, 40; and decreasing interest from both parents and children for gymnastics 45; for individual gymnasts 38; post-competition state rewards and the life pension system 42; and reputations dependent upon athletes' performance results 148, 150; of Soviet and Romanian gymnasts 48; and spectatorship 37

individuals 46, 48, 53, 102, 104, 126–7, 160, 162, 166, 179, 185–6, 191, 193, 203–6, 212; experience 102; interdependent 204; isolated 203; particular 103, 205; young 213
injuries 7, 9, 76, 78, 82, 84–5, 88–90, 92, 101–2, 158–9, 162, 210, 212–13, 216–17, 220–4; interarticular 220; life-changing 102; managing 166; painful hip 85; permanent disability 168; post-retirement 91; psychological 89; rates of 158, 216, 224; recurrent 212; training-induced 89; traumatic 158, 220; whiplash 220
international federations 36–7, 54, 183, 216, 227
International Gymnastics Federation 53, 192
International Olympic Committee 18–19, 28, 35–7, 53, 161
International Sport and Leisure 37
internet 119, 185, 187
interviewees 164, 180, 182, 220–2, 224–6
IOC *see* International Olympic Committee
ISL *see* International Sport and Leisure

Jacobs, Frank 90, 99, 190–1, 195, 197, 200
Jowett, Sophia 121, 123–5, 136–7, 143–5, 147–51, 154, 160

Károlyi, Márta 31, 45–6, 82
Károlyis, Bela 25, 31–2, 43, 45
Kerr, Gretchen 101, 125, 143, 145, 147–9, 151–2, 190–1, 195
Knoppers, Annelies 90, 99, 190
knowledge 61, 126, 136–7, 151–2, 178, 181, 186, 208, 210, 213; expert 54, 198; lack of 210; scientific 177–8, 181, 187; specialised 151, 208; transfer 45
Kotarba, Joseph A. 218, 224

Lang, Melanie 158, 160–8
Larson, Mattie 84–5
Latour, Bruno 177–8, 180–2, 185, 187–8
lay values (relating to sport success) 217
leotards 8, 14, 21, 25–6, 84, 88, 99–101, 103, 105–7, 109–13, 118–19, 173, 231
Lidor, Ronnie 180, 182
London Olympics 2012 41, 158
Lord, Rhiannon 105, 107–8, 110

Maguire, Joseph. 52, 207, 210
major power theories **130**
Malcolm, Dominic. 87, 99, 148, 207, 211, 216, 218, 223
male coaches 2, 30–1, 112, 125
maltreatment 3, 143–4, 151, 161, 163, 169; of athletes 143, 146, 151, 161; experience of 154; literature 152; relational 143
media attention 61, 82, 144, 161
media narratives 81, 83, 85, 87, 89, 91, 93, 95
medical care 219–20, 222–7
medical professionals 216, 218, 220; compromised by 'sports ethics' 217; in elite gymnastics 216–21, 223–7; and socio-cultural dynamics in elite sports 218; subject to the socio-cultural dynamics of risk-taking in sports 217
medications 211, 222, 224
Meinke, Emily 90–1, 93, 95
Melbourne Olympics 1956 13–14
mental health 88, 94
mental illnesses 91
meso (local organisational) level of clubs 193–4, 196, 198–200
#MeToo movement 83, 93, 95
Mexico Olympics 1968 14–15
Michigan State University 84
mirroring bodies 104, 106, 108, 110–12; *see also* disciplined bodies
model 51, 79, 102, 122, 129, 132–5, 143, 145, 147, 149–52, 154, 194, 232; Dutch WAG multilevel 192, 194; long-term athlete development 159; multilevel 190, 192, 194; pixie-style 58, 61; power-social influence 129; of Sophia Jowett 121, 123–5, 136–7, 143–5, 147–51, 154, 160; Soviet 41, 182
Montreal Olympics 1976 28, 81
moral duties of coaches 165–6
Moscow Olympics 1980 19, 25, 30, 39
Munich Olympics 1972 16

narratives 71, 81, 85–6, 89, 91–4, 108–9, 180; body 100, 102–4, 108, 110, 113; cultural 104; gymnast 83; media 81, 83, 85, 87, 89, 91, 93, 95
Nassar, Larry 3, 47–8, 84, 86, 92–5, 151; and the 'dome of silence' 86; and the embodying of female athlete empowerment 3; exemplary reputation of 86; and the USAG's employment of 47
national average income of gymnasts 40
National Center for Catastrophic Sports Injury Research 159, 168
national competitions 119, 173, 179, 192
National Gymnastics Federation 192, 195–6, 199
National Sporting Organisation 179
national team gymnasts 39, 219–20, 224
national teams 39–41, 44, 177, 184–5, 187, 209, 211, 219, 221, 223–5
NCCSIR *see* National Center for Catastrophic Sports Injury Research
New Zealand 44, 46, 177, 179, 181, 187
New Zealand Gymnastics 179–83, 186–7
New Zealand Olympic Committee 186–7
NGF *see* National Gymnastics Federation
non-Communist countries 52, 54, 61–2
NSO *see* National Sporting Organisation
NZG *see* New Zealand Gymnastics
NZOC *see* New Zealand Olympic Committee

officials 112, 165, 167, 217, 233
Ohashi, Katelyn 88, 232
Olympic Games 1, 3, 11–12, 14, 18, 24, 27, 36–7, 41, 55, 58–60, 81, 145, 179, 219; Athens 2004 40; Atlanta 1996 37–8, 82; Barcelona 1992 48; Beijing 2008 158, 161; Helsinki 1952 13; London 2012 41, 158; Melbourne 1956 13–14; Mexico 1968 14–15; Montreal 1976 28, 81; Moscow 1980 19, 25, 30, 39; Munich 1972 16; Rio de Janeiro 2016 158; Rome 1960 14; Sydney 2000 7, 88; Tokyo 1964 14

pain and injuries 9, 66, 76, 78, 82, 84, 88–90, 92, 101, 162, 197, 210, 212–13, 216–17, 220–4
pain-killers 224
Papendal Training Centre (Netherlands) 57, 60
parallel bars 11, 13, 181
parents 40–1, 84–5, 88–9, 105–7, 146–7, 150, 152, 165, 167–8, 175–7, 183, 187–8, 191–9, 210–12, 231–2; and coaches as surrogate 88, 90, 153–4; complaining about discursive

practices being part of the grooming process 198; complaining about witnessing emotional and psychological abuse at the hands of a coach 88–9, 154; regretful of the toxic culture, suicide attempts and eating disorders in the production of Olympic champions 82
PAT *see* Physical Ability Test
Penny, Steve 47, 181–2
perestroika 38–40
perfection 24, 26–7, 30–2, 81, 217, 231; consistent 26; gymnastic 81; and the methods of coaching child athletes 24; technical 27; as the ultimate goal 24
performances 20–1, 26–8, 31–2, 41–3, 55, 101, 103–4, 119, 121, 123–4, 133, 181–4, 197–8, 208, 222; athlete's 36, 143, 146, 154, 165, 227; ethic 151, 232; faults 99, 118; goals 133, 137; outcomes 147, 149–50; peak elite 159; perfect 27, 31; successes 56, 58, 121–2, 124, 132, 145, 150, 152; superior 26; ultimate 207; women's 13, 17
perspectives 79, 100–1, 126, 135–7, 163–5, 167–8, 212; athlete's 148; coach-centred 163; empirical 122; gendered 233; glocalisation 53; holistic 145; medical 212; psychological 144; socio-narratological 80; therapeutic 225
Physical Ability Test 177, 180–1, 183–4, 187
physical abuse 82, 86, 143, 232
physical contact 162, 164–8; adult-child 163; appropriate 165, 167; desensitising 'victims' for later sexual contact. 161; lucid forms of 161; providing gymnasts with psychological support 160; uses of 165–6
physical education 12, 32, 162, 164
physicians 85, 220, 222
physiotherapists 212, 219, 221–2, 225–6
Pike, Elizabeth 104, 212
Pimenta, Nuno 87, 99, 148, 207, 211–12, 216
Pinheiro, Claudia 87, 203–4, 206, 208, 210–11, 213
Piper, Heather 162–4, 191
'pixie gymnasts' 51
pleasure 2, 73, 190, 194, 196–7, 199–200; discourse of 196; and enjoyment 190;

prioritising 197; on winning medals 117
Podkopayeva, Lilia 40, 81
policies 37, 163, 167, 200; Cold War 24, 26, 32–3, 51; government sporting 179; implementing state-managed sport 57; national sport 57
Potrac, Paul. 127, 160
power 29–30, 92–3, 95, 121, 124–30, 132–7, 144, 151–2, 154, 193, 197, 199, 205, 223, 233; balance of 135, 204–5, 211; bases 134–6, 154; decision-making 128; differentials in the coach-athlete relationship 121–37, 205; disciplinary 12, 101, 193, 199; dynamics 125, 127, 136; imbalance of 2, 151, 153, 212; and influence 124, 126, 129, 132, 135, 205; and the male-female imbalance of 2; positions of 93, 147, 151–2, 210; relationships 125, 206, 212, 231, 233; sources of 127, 132–6, 151; study of 128–9
Pozsár, Géza 45–6
practices 41–2, 44, 47–8, 51, 53, 88–9, 99–100, 109–11, 124–6, 162, 164–8, 190–200, 207–10, 216–18, 232–3; abusive 190–1, 193–5, 197–9; disciplinary 208, 210, 213; emotional 190–1, 193–5, 197–9; sporting 177, 185
pre-pubescent girls 31
pressures 8, 28, 36, 81–2, 117, 119, 173–4, 190, 204, 206, 208, 210–11, 223, 226; explicit 217; external 28, 208; intense 3, 32, 158; moral 161; public relations 28; social 204
problems 24, 28, 33, 40, 47, 82, 99, 103, 112, 118, 125, 198, 221–7, 232; ankle 220; of eating disorders 221; financial 60; gymnasts 39, 112, 222; gymnasts experiencing 104; and the medical profession 223; pain and injury 220; social 112; tail bone 220
processes 70–1, 78, 101, 124, 126–7, 133, 147, 177, 179–80, 182–5, 187, 191, 199–200, 205–6, 211; bargaining 211; bodily 111; dehumanisation 184; governmental 54; rehabilitation 211; social 53, 159, 185, 187, 205–6; team selection 177, 179–80, 182, 185; testing 180–1, 183–4
professional practices 193, 216, 221–2, 226

professional training structures 48
professional values, and lay values relating to sport success 217
professionalisation 35–8, 41–2, 48, 52
professionalism 36–8, 40, 163
professionals 38, 42, 216–20, 223
programmes 13, 40, 57, 118, 168, 197, 199; elite training 159; public health insurance 219; systematic training 41; university sports education 164
programs, computer 182
psychological 75, 81–3, 86–91, 93, 95, 99, 101, 126, 136–7, 144, 160, 166, 190–1, 209, 221; harm 83, 89–91, 93, 95; problems 81; safety 136–7
puberty 81, 101, 109, 111–12; and the effect of drug supplements 66; managing 111; stories 113
punishments 65, 110, 129, 131, 136, 174
Purdy, Laura 127–8

qualities 46, 124, 135–6, 143–4, 151, 154, 178, 218, 224, 232; of effective coach-athlete relationships 144; feminine 19; friendship 146; masculine 12; well-documented 144

Raisman, Aly 38, 47–8, 92, 124
Rastorotsky, Vladislav 17–18
Raven, Bertram H. 126–7, 132, 151
rehabilitation processes 211
relations 53, 91, 102–3, 107, 111, 113, 163, 204, 212–13; companion 70; established-outsider 206; market 52; parental 91; social 209
relationship members 129, 134
relationships 1–2, 90–1, 100, 121–4, 126–7, 129, 131–5, 143–6, 148–50, 152–4, 160, 162, 203–4, 208–9, 211; close 122, 145–7, 154, 211; coach-athlete 143–4, 149, 151, 153–4, 193, 211, 213; critical 143–4; dyadic 124; equitable 134; human 205; interdependent 203–4, 208; outcomes 134; parent-child 144; social 205; trusting 85, 168; utility 125, 153
research 3–4, 53, 78–9, 83, 95, 122–3, 126–8, 135–7, 163, 167–8, 199–200, 209, 211–12, 216–17, 232–3; findings 144, 151; glocalisation 53; literature 161; peer-reviewed 164; projects 209, 211; and Rhiannon Lord 105;

sociological 180; sport science 51, 129, 137
resources 45, 71, 105, 131–2, 134, 151, 153, 208, 210; and athletes 132, 134; and coaches 132, 134; financial 45, 226; human 45
retirement 43, 101
rewards 30, 32, 39, 41, 48, 59, 126, 129–33, 135, 144, 150–1; Communist ideologies of state service and 59; financial 36, 41, 46; post-competition state 42; reduced 35; system 30, 41
rhythmic gymnastics 13, 41
Rio de Janeiro Olympics 2016 158
risk 14, 17, 19–20, 31, 59, 99–100, 123, 136, 159, 162–4, 212–13, 217–18, 223, 226; avoidance 162; culture of 211, 213, 217–18; factors 85, 144, 216; health 216–17, 221; injury 224; interpersonal 136
Robertson, Roland 52–3
Roderick, M. 205, 207, 209, 212, 217
Rodionenko, Andrei 40, 44, 55–6
Romanian 25–7, 35, 41–6, 48, 52, 54, 56–8, 61–2, 81; case studies 59; coaches immigrating to the USA, Australia, New Zealand, and other Western countries 45–6; dominance in WAG 25, 41–2, 45, 59; 'golden girls' 41; gymnastics programme 41–4, 48; gymnasts 19, 25, 42, 48, 52; and Soviet systems 52, 54
Romanian Gymnastics Federation 42
Romanian Ministry for Education 42, 45
Romanian Olympic Committee 43
Rome Olympics 1960 14
Royal Dutch Gymnastics Federation 57, 60
Russia 8, 29, 40–1, 43–4, 48, 52, 54, 56, 58, 61; and 364 coaches leaving to work overseas 43; and the 'circus tradition' used in coaching acrobatics 17; and coach Alexander Alexandrov 55; and the first-generation Soviet-trained coaches improve WAG performance 60; gymnasts 40–1, 52; gymnasts performing at international events 52; sports 40–1; and the win-at-all-costs mentality in sport 40
Russian Gymnastics Federation 17, 40–1, 59
Rutgers University 160
Ryan, Joan 29–30, 70, 81–2, 94–5

schools 9, 51, 58, 66, 73, 117–18, 145, 162, 174, 203, 208, 227; *see also* secondary schools
Schubring, Astrid. 100, 109, 217–18
scientists 179, 181–3, 187–8
score fixing 26
scores 24, 26–7, 81, 183–5, 187
secondary schools 9, 66
Seiler, Roland. 121, 123–5, 127
selection 134, 177, 180, 183, 186–7, 192, 217; athlete 183–4; committees 186; criteria 180; national team 185; processes 177, 179–80
self-esteem 91, 144, 150
sexual abuse 83, 85–6, 90–1, 93–4, 125, 143–7, 149–51, 153, 160, 162–3, 167, 190–1
sexual exploitation 86, 144, 151, 161
silence 25, 78, 83–4, 93, 95, 198, 218, 231; code of 198, 200; discursive practices of 198; maintaining of 84; pain of 224
Simpson, Jeffry A. 129, 132, 134–6, 180
skills 2, 7, 19, 30–1, 51, 61, 73, 75, 108, 158–60, 165–6, 198–9, 207–8, 210, 213; acrobatic 20; athletic 210; eponymous 18; executing 79; new 2, 73, 159, 166–7, 232; performing high-risk 158; social 190; technical 151
Smith, Barbara H. 71, 83, 102, 105
social dynamics 128, 206
socio-cultural dynamics 217–18
sociologists 164, 211
sociology 3, 69, 103–4, 203, 205, 216, 233
Soviet Union 14, 17–18, 20, 25–6, 30, 32, 35, 37–40, 43–4, 46, 48, 54, 56–7, 81; coaches 44, 55, 59–60; era 17, 39–41; and full time gymnastics training program in sports schools 31; and the half century domination of WAG 14; and the historic influence in sport 182; and post-Soviet systems 40; and Romania 35, 43, 48; *see also* Russia
Sparkes, Andrew C. 70–1, 83, 100, 102–5, 113, 219
sponsorship 38, 42, 48, 56; commercial 47; contracts 18, 38, 219; corporate 41; deals 58–9; funding 37, 61; opportunities 38; private 36, 42; revenue 48

sport 1–4, 11–14, 16–19, 29–32, 35–43, 47–8, 51–9, 82–6, 89–95, 123–5, 143–51, 160–8, 206–11, 216–27, 231–3; administrators 35, 89, 165, 203, 208, 210–11; amateur 18, 35–7, 48, 164, 219; careers 148, 196; clubs 162, 191, 193–5, 198–9; competitive 12, 218; elite 18, 52, 57, 59, 183, 196–7, 200, 210, 216–18, 221, 226; elite systems 52, 59, 62, 216; ethic 207–8, 217–18, 222, 226; globalised 41; and health problems 219; high performance 86, 121, 179–80, 187, 197, 210, 219, 221; high risk 146, 158, 216; injuries 7, 9, 76, 78, 82, 84–5, 88–90, 92, 101–2, 158–9, 162, 210, 212–13, 216–17, 220–4; international 35, 37, 48; medicine 217, 227; organisations 52, 59, 62, 132, 161, 164, 166; performance 148, 152, 221; professional 38, 48; psychology 128–9, 135, 137; scientists 2, 35, 178, 180–3, 232; stakeholders 160, 164, 167–8; youth 190, 192–4, 196, 200
Sport New Zealand 179
'sportsnets' (institutionalised networks) 217, 222
state-funded doping 40
state-funding 41–2, 48, 58
Stirling, Ashley 84, 89, 101, 125, 143–9, 151–2, 165, 190–1, 195
strategies 42, 57, 59, 61–2, 129, 132–5, 209–10; adopting development 61; communication 123; negative 129; popularising 52, 61; positive 129, 133; and tactics 133, 135
stress 67, 73, 160, 174–5, 227
success 20–1, 32–3, 35, 39–40, 42, 44–6, 48, 55–6, 58, 60, 121–4, 146, 151–2, 208–10, 217; athletic 48, 149–50; coaching 79, 128, 183; of Communist sport 54; competitive 51–2, 54, 56, 59–61, 191, 207; Dutch WAG 60; gymnastic 16, 24, 32, 38–9, 47–8, 95, 232–3; medal 39; performance 56, 58, 121–2, 124, 132, 145, 150, 152; sporting 16, 126, 128, 217; track record of 151–2
suicide 81–2, 91
Sydney Olympics 2000 7, 88

tactics 129, 131–6, 152
Taylor, Bill 162, 191
teams 2, 25, 30–1, 46, 55, 57, 72, 123, 149, 177, 185–7, 219–20, 225–6; medical 225–7; national 39–41, 44, 177, 184–5, 187, 209, 211, 219, 221, 223–5; selection processes 177, 179–80, 182, 185; training 12, 31–2, 73, 75, 108, 110–11, 117–18, 134–5, 145, 149–50, 158–9, 165–6, 211–12, 221, 223–5; WAG 216, 223, 225
technologies 2, 177–8, 185–6
testing mechanisms 177, 180–4, 187
tests 181–4
Tian, Ju Ping 55, 57–8
Tokyo Olympics 1964 14
touch 158, 160–1, 163–8, 191; adult-child 162; of athletes 162, 164–6; behaviors 165; benefits of 160, 165; concerns in relation to 164; desensitising children to sexual abuse and exploitation 160; as a form of communication 160; a pastoral and pedagogic tool for sports coaching 160; practices in sport 164–8
training 12, 31–2, 73, 75, 108, 110–11, 117–18, 134–5, 145, 149–50, 158–9, 165–6, 211–12, 221, 223–5; balletic 11; camps 54, 134, 220, 225; centres 38–40, 56–8, 219; facilities 40, 55, 60–1; practices 41–2, 99; regimes 12, 31, 33, 127, 207, 231; schedules 227; sessions 3, 75, 104, 110, 118, 144
trampoline 99–100, 103–4, 107–8, 111, 113; careers 104; clubs 105; coaching 105; gymnasts 99–100, 103–8, 111, 113; subculture 105
traumatic injuries 158, 220
trust 16, 83, 85–6, 94–5, 123, 126–7, 143–9, 158–9, 162, 195, 210; of athletes 147; establishing 86; and friendship 86; levels of 147; mutual 145; relationships 85, 168

Ukraine 40, 81; coaches 55; Soviet and post-Soviet systems 40
uneven bars 1, 20, 81
universities 71–3, 79, 232; gymnastics 74–5; teams 75
University of California 88
Unsworth, Chris 161
US Center for SafeSport 94
US Department of Health 147

US Gymnastics Association 232
US National Gymnastics Team 3, 92, 151
USSR *see* Soviet Union

values 43, 75, 79, 124, 126, 136–7, 145, 150, 190, 193, 204, 206–7, 217–18, 233
van Manen, Max 71, 73–4, 76–7, 79
Van Veldhoven, Schipper 190–1
Varney, Wendy 20, 24, 58
vault 1, 13, 16, 27, 76, 82, 89, 118, 160, 166
verbal abuse 87
victims 85, 91–2, 147, 150, 161, 167–8
violence 91, 93, 95, 100, 148, 161
vulnerability 85, 143–4, 147, 151, 153; athlete's 150; of coaches 163; to maltreatment 144; to sexual abuse of female gymnasts 143, 145, 149

Wachsmuth, Svenja. 123–4
Waddington, Ian 209, 212, 217–18, 221–2
WAG 1–4, 8–21, 24–33, 35–48, 51–62, 66–77, 82–96, 100–13, 118–38, 158–69, 174–88, 190–201, 203–13, 216–28, 231–4; acrobatic style of 11, 21, 24, 29; athletes 24, 158–9; clubs and national/international federations 167; and the Communist influence 57; cultures 3, 218, 226, 232–3; development prior to and since 1989 **55**; developments 55, 58–60; and distancing from the Communist system of 61, 216, 227; elite gymnasts 17, 42, 219; examining sport medical practice in 217–21, 223, 225, 227; and health care 226; new style developed by Nadia Comaneci 11, 30; one of the Olympic Games' most popular spectator sports 24; pixie-style model of 51, 61systems 51–2, 54, 57–62; systems afforded international role model status by the Communist gymnasts 51; training facilities 32, 60
WC *see* World Championships
weight 37, 66, 75, 88–9, 101, 117, 173–4, 198–9, 220; control 199, 213, 220–1; management 198–9; problems 223
Western Australian Institute 55
Western countries 18, 43, 46; and the accusation of state funding for

Eastern bloc sports 42; athletes 36; coaches 46; gymnasts 38
women 1–2, 11–14, 17–19, 24–5, 29, 31–2, 35, 51, 92–3, 95, 158, 177, 203, 209–10, 231–2; and amateurism 36; femininity 13–14; and girls 7, 93; and gymnastics 11, 17, 32, 53; gymnasts 14, 18, 31, 200; lean 31; 'pixie-style' 11; and sport 11–14, 18, 32, 36; and WAG 11, 14, 31–2, 39; young 82
work 40–1, 44, 78, 82, 86–7, 100–4, 111–12, 117, 133–4, 136–7, 163–4, 175–7, 217–18, 221, 225–6; creative 60; empirical 137, 167; interactionist 104; interdisciplinary 233; laboratory 182; scientific 181; technical 185
working practices 44, 216
World Championships 3, 18, 37, 44, 47, 55, 179, 185, 219, 231

young athletes 27–8, 82, 85, 94, 150, 190, 200
young gymnasts 18, 28–30, 43, 81, 92, 105, 159, 193, 207, 209, 213
youth sport 190, 192–4, 196, 200